THE HISS FROM HELL ONLY WOMEN HEAR

Is It Truth or Is It Tradition?

© 2000 Virginia Hull Welch

*For laying aside the commandment of God, ye
hold the tradition of men.*

Mark 7:8

Other Books by Virginia Hull Welch

The Lesson, inspirational romantic comedy based
on a true story

Crazy Woman Creek, historical western romance

What to Do When the Blessings Stop: When God
Sends Famine, nonfiction

To my sisters who follow: God loves you.

ISBN - 978-0-9888739-6-4
E-Book ISBN - 978-0-9888739-7-1
The Hiss from Hell Only Women Hear: Is It Truth or Is
It Tradition?

Published by Virginia Hull Welch, 2000
www.virginiahullwelch.com

All Bible quotes are from the King James Version
(KJV) unless otherwise noted.

Cover design by Lidiya Combes

Contents

PROLOGUE V

HISS #1: SOMETHING IS WRONG WITH YOU 1

HISS #2: NICE GIRLS AREN'T VIOLENT 12

HISS #3: NICE GIRLS GET DIAMONDS, NOT
DOMINION 21

HISS #4: YOU DON'T HAVE WHAT IT TAKES......... 49

HISS #5: GOD JUDGES YOU MORE HARSHLY 71

HISS #6: GOD WILL ALWAYS CHOOSE A MAN
FIRST 93

HISS #7: YOU WON'T FIND A WOMAN MINISTER
IN THE BIBLE 110

HISS #8: JESUS DID NOT SET US FREE TO
MINISTER 119

HISS #9: YOU ARE UNDER AUTHORITY IN A WAY
MEN AREN'T.. 136

HISS #10: ONLY HALF THE CHURCH CAN
TEACH—NOT YOUR HALF 152

HISS #11: REAL WOMEN ARE IN THE KITCHEN. 181

=..203

HISS #12: GOD DIDN'T REALLY MEAN PAIN 203

HISS #13: GOD DIDN'T REALLY MEAN
CONCEPTION 235

HISS # 14: EVE'S DECEPTION: YOUR LEGACY 280

SOURCES 297

ABOUT THE AUTHOR 302

Prologue

Every book has a story behind it.

The majority of what you read here I wrote a long time ago, late 1993 and early 1994. I was a young mother in those days, toiling away at free-lance writing jobs at my little desk in Leesburg, Va. while my three kids were in elementary and preschool. I was also expecting my fourth child, Greg.

But despite my busy schedule and increasing physical awkwardness from pregnancy, I felt compelled to take the morning train from northern Virginia into Washington, D.C. to research old bibles at the Library of Congress. I was obsessed with finding the truth about women's place in the Church.

My obsession, this book, was borne from the fire of personal pain. I was suffering. It had begun when I got saved in 1975. The day I accepted Christ as my Savior should have been the beginning of great days of joy. But instead, being a woman in the Church— enduring all the associated ministerial restrictions and silly traditions—became my great crucible.

Then late in 1993 I decided to devote a month to prayer, seeking God like never before. That singular month changed my whole life. Much of the material here resulted from those intense 30 days, particularly the revelation about female submission in Chapter 9.

I could have published this book all those years ago. I'm glad I didn't. Because I know now that I, and the book, were not ready. I've had to lay down much anger at the altar over the years, which led to many manuscript revisions.

And life got in the way. Right about the time I finished the first rough draft, Greg was born, mid-1994.

Thereafter my writing career slowly but consistently took off, while my family moved around the country to follow my husband's job transfers. I was busy rearing four children, running a home, and writing part-time while the kids were little and full-time as they grew up and left home. The manuscript sat in a box in my office for two decades. It was always in the back of my mind, but I never seemed to find time to address its problems.

Then Greg, 18, died in a car accident in 2013, the very day I released my first book, *The Lesson*, a romance based on a true story. Before Greg left us, the plan had been to release all four manuscripts in quick succession: *The Lesson; Crazy Woman Creek*, a historical romance; *What to Do When the Blessings Stop: When God Sends Famine*, a nonfiction title; and *The Hiss*. I had contracted with a Texas public relations agency and was scheduled to speak on radio stations across the United States. I had planned a big kickoff indeed.

But after that dreadful day, publishing seemed meaningless. I was too shaken to write a word, though I had a second historical romance, book five, in the works when Greg flew away to Heaven.

Once again, *The Hiss* sat in a box in my office. I fulfilled my radio speaking engagements and then dropped out of the publishing world entirely. I didn't write another word of *The Hiss* or any manuscript for another five years. I gave in to grief. I just didn't care.

I retired from my full-time writing and editing job in 2017.

By early 2018, when grief finally released the worst of its strangulating hold on me, I felt a stirring in my spirit. God was speaking to me to return to writing, and at last, I felt ready. Then, when I was praying one morning about the historical romance, I distinctly heard Him tell me to put it aside and finish editing *The Hiss*.

But I hesitated. Was *The Hiss* even relevant anymore? A quarter of a century had passed since I had written the first word. A new generation of women had been born. They seem to have everything: education, careers, families, ministries, their own blogs. Do modern young Christian women still wonder at the inequities in the Church? Do they even recognize them for what they are? Maybe today's Christian woman believes she has arrived to be and have all that she is called to, maybe she is unaware of man-imposed limits. Is my frustrating experience as a member of the Jesus Movement generation so outdated that no one can relate now?

But then I realized something. As I prove in the following pages, spurious, silly traditions about women's roles are deeply entrenched in Christian writings (ergo, thinking) dating back *centuries. Of course* their musty influence still abounds. *Of course* they haven't disappeared in the mere 25 years since I wrote this book. From the Bible Belt to the Vatican, modern Christians are still confused about women's role in the Church. We just don't talk about it much anymore because we're not conscientiously trying to smack down feminism as we were in the 1970s.

We shouldn't let culture take the lead. The Word is our guide. I persevere.

And why did I write this book in the first place all those years ago, sitting in our little house on Ayrlee Avenue, waiting for our second son to arrive? I recorded these painful memories, paired with glorious revelations, because I don't want another woman to suffer the confusion about her place in God's plan and resulting dejection based on the lies that I believed.

Christ died on the cross to set you free from the works of the devil. My prayer is that something, *even one thing*, contained in these pages exposes a lie you've

believed as the truth so that you can become the person
God designed you to be—with joy!

Virginia Hull Welch
November, 2018

Hiss #1: Something Is Wrong with You

This book is about you. Though I will talk about God and your relationship with Him, ultimately I write about you. I want you to understand who you are as a Christian woman and why God has called you into his Kingdom.

To discover the real you and your true calling, we start at the beginning. The Word of God, the Bible, is the beginning and end of all truth. It is God's love letter to you. In it He declares his eternal, unshakable, immeasurable love for you. The premise that God loves you is the bedrock of your relationship to Jesus Christ. *You are worthy of love because He loves you.*

This is the truth about you.

But you may not feel loved. Some days you may fear that God is out to get you. You may doubt his love for various reasons. After all, He is invisible, so he seems far away, perhaps unconcerned. On particularly bad days you are aware of your sin and shortcomings. You fail to pray on Monday, screech at the kids on Tuesday, your car breaks down on Wednesday. By

Thursday you conclude that God isn't feeling as loving toward you as He was while you sang in church on Sunday.

You feel unworthy. Why would a holy God bother with repetitively sinful, overweight, out of control you?

Awareness of your sin combined with difficult circumstances create the perfect garden bed for seeds of doubt to grow about God's love. But doubts don't change the truth. Doubts mean only that someone is messing with you. Someone is planting suspicion in your mind about God's love for you.

You know the planter's name, but do you recognize his tactics? You may think you are well defended from Satan's deceptions because you know the Word. But knowing the Word isn't enough. That's a head thing. You must know the One who breathed the Word. You must know *Him*. That's a heart thing.

Eve had this problem. Satan lied to her, we all know it. But do you know why she believed the lie?

Here you are in the Garden of Eden. The sun is shining on a perfectly clear, 70-degree day (like every day), a shimmering stream (never too cold) flows by the lounge chair where Eve is sunbathing in her birthday suit (no strap marks to worry about here). A fruity drink leaves icy rings on the beverage table where sits the latest edition of *Genesis Times*. Eve is pondering what she'll pluck for dinner when she hears a voice.

Serpent (Satan): Did God really say that you can't eat of every tree around the garden?

Eve: We can eat the fruit from all the trees of the garden except one. We can't eat the fruit of that one, or even touch it, because God said if we do, we will die.

Serpent: You won't die. God doesn't want you to touch or eat it because He knows that if you do, your eyes will open and you'll be like gods. You'll know the difference between good and evil (Gen. 3:1–4

2

paraphrased).

Eve and Adam ate, died spiritually, and were bounced out of the garden. But do you know *why* Eve believed Satan's claim over God's? The Bible says that the fruit "was good for food, and pleasant to the eyes, and a tree to be desired to make one wise" (Gen. 3:6). But the fruit had always been good for food, pleasant to the eyes, and desirable to make one wise. Until now Eve had not been tempted.

And here's an interesting thing about Eve: She knew what God had said about the forbidden fruit. She quoted God's instructions to Satan.

But Satan attacked God's character. When Eve heard the lie that God had more good things than his original offer to her and Adam (the entire garden minus one tree) but was withholding them, she began to doubt God's love. That doubt sucked the power out of God's Word. It made it of no effect in her life.

Exposed here are Satan's two slimy messages, the primary ones he uses to attack believers, but particularly in this context, female believers. These lies have slithered in and out of Christian thinking through the ages. They are the outrageous, insidious ideas behind his words in Gen. 3:6 that he used to dupe Eve (but not Adam—the Bible says he was not deceived. He knew that partaking of the fruit was wrong but partook of it anyway. He sinned knowingly and deliberately).

Hiss #1: God doesn't love you as his Word says He does. God is a liar. *His character can't be trusted.*

Hiss #2: God is withholding good things from you because *He doesn't really love you.* See Hiss #1.

Eve interpreted the combined messages like this: God has more but refuses to share. Why trust a God who doesn't love 100 percent? Eve heard God's claim and she heard Satan's. Her problem was not that she didn't know the Word. She didn't know the Author.

How well do you know Him? Would you recognize an attack on God's character if it were presented as a religious tradition—as truth? A religious tradition is the transmission of a custom or belief about God. We should be learning of Him primarily from his Word, but even in the reading of it, our interpretation is influenced by our tightly held religious tradition. Our core beliefs just might be a mingling of truth (God's Word) and religious traditions. I venture that some of us, at times, don't realize which is which.

> *Would you recognize an attack on God's character if it were presented as a religious tradition—as truth?*

The more hopeful news is that all of us walk in different degrees of spiritual light when it comes to knowing God. Some of us glow 25 watts, others 60 watts, and the rest light a room like a blazing chandelier. But none of us sees God perfectly. We all believe something about God that is untrue or is partially true.

But if it isn't 100 percent true, it's 100 percent wrong. We don't know this, however, because the error we believe about God is not always a blatant lie. More often it's a wrong assumption or seemingly innocuous misinterpretation of his character. Often well-meaning Christians impose flawed human characteristics onto God. In a way, we can't help it; we know humans better than we know God, and it's hard for us to fathom just how good God really is.

> *If what you believe about God isn't 100 percent true, then it's 100 percent wrong.*

For some, wrong assumptions about God's nature are easily displaced when presented with truth. For others, they are religious strongholds that require spiritual dynamite to blast them away.

Over time, as we get to know Him by his Word and prayer, and as we experience his dealings, the Holy Spirit exposes our false concepts. We see Him more clearly or, more simply, we come to know his character as it really is, not as we have learned of Him from tradition and religious stereotype.

But we must submit to the religious disciplines of the Word and prayer and yield to the Holy Spirit's dealings for our concept of God to grow clearer. Spiritual growth is a choice.

Meanwhile Satan's method and message never change. Why fix what ain't broke? Thousands of years have passed since the tragedy in the garden, yet Satan is still telling you that God can't be trusted and doesn't love you. Satan uses dark spots in your spiritual understanding to provoke you to move away from God. *Darkness.* If not exposed, Satan will use it to snuff out your love for God. If he fails to get you to walk away from your faith, at minimum he'll try to make your Christian walk impotent and joyless. Satan's target is always your relationship to God.

> *Satan's target is always your relationship to God.*

If you aren't intimate with God, you don't know his character and can't interpret his love letter purely. Instead, like Eve, you project onto God negative human traits, because imperfect human love is the only kind you know. If you suffer from low self-esteem, weak faith, or an untested relationship, you may doubt where you stand with God and his perfect goodness toward you. If the soil of your heart is poor, you may misinterpret his love message or not get it at all. Poor soil, poor harvest. The Bible is full of agricultural allegory, but you get the idea. Like I said, it's a heart thing.

In the spiritual twist of the ages, Satan plows this same lousy dirt to sow weeds that thrive. How does Satan reap weeds where God can't get simple truths to take root? Satan sows different seeds than God sows because he's looking for different fruit. Satan's design for your life directly opposes God's. Satan's goal is to destroy your intimacy with God, to sever you from the life that is available only from your Creator.

> *Satan's goal is to destroy your intimacy with God, to sever you from the life that is available only from your Creator.*

God calls you into relationship to give you fullness of life: abundant and overflowing, meaningful, satisfying, joyful life. And He labors to make you like his Son, because you can't be intimate with God and cling to your sin.

Satan labors 24/7 to draw you away from God because he knows that apart from Him you have no life. Satan seeks bad soil—a hurting, insecure, or offended heart—to plant weed seeds: half-truths, spurious traditions, fallacious man-made doctrine. These sprout into thinking that causes you to do things that lead you away from God. Such thoughts and actions lead to spiritual death, which is the opposite of what God has for you.

> *Satan uses only one method to separate you from God: He entices you to walk away voluntarily.*

God will never leave you (Matt. 28:20), and no one can pluck you out of his hand (John 10:28). Therefore Satan uses only one method to separate you from God: He entices you to walk away voluntarily. He uses deception because he can't force you to abandon your faith.

That didn't stop him from trying awfully hard to entice me to abandon mine.

A Little Background

From the day I made Jesus Christ my Lord, I knew that God loves me. Trusting in his love and forgiveness of my sins was never a problem for me, unlike others who struggle to accept absolute grace. Thanks to my parents who faithfully brought me to weekly Catholic confession and Mass, I came to Christ with a good foundation. I knew that God forgives sins freely by the work of Jesus Christ on the cross.

> *I realized God is love and that He died to prove it. But from unscriptural teachings and insidious traditions, I had absorbed the soul-brutalizing message that women are inferior creations in relation to men, traditions that cast doubt on women's importance to the Kingdom.*

But I suffered another, less understood problem with his love that is just as devastating. I felt that God loves men more than women, or at least, He loves women differently, in some inexplicably limited way.

Unquestionably, part of this faulty thinking is rooted in the Catholic Church's exaltation of male priests above lay people and its intransigent refusal to allow women to minister the Word.

I realized God is love and that He died to prove it. But from unscriptural teachings and insidious traditions, I had absorbed the soul-brutalizing message that women are inferior creations in relation to men, traditions that cast doubt on women's importance to the Kingdom. Although I knew He loved me, and I strove to love him in return, I hurt. If God had favorites, I wasn't one, and as a result I could expect to receive limited spiritual inheritance in this life. Like a spiritual stepchild, I did not feel loved by my heavenly Father. I felt tolerated.

How did I arrive at this soul-destroying, faith-strangling conclusion? It can be explained partly by timing. I became a Christian about the same time I came of age (19) in the mid-1970s. I was just a child during the bra-burning, marching-in-the-street kind of feminism that exploded in the 1960s. But by the mid-70s the notion that women could fill roles in society that had been closed to them for decades—a notion ushered into mainstream thinking by those loud, braless women—was beginning to sound not so radical to most Americans, including me.

So just about the time I was leaving my teenage years and entering womanhood, I found Christ. There I was, simultaneously forming a sense of adult female identity, absorbing the preaching of revolutionaries like Gloria Steinem and Betty Friedan, while learning what it means to be a disciple of Christ.

The Church, of course, flat out rejected all teaching that had even a whiff of feminism. I can hear the doors slam as I type this. Ministers were determined that their female flock did not drink from the polluted well. From the 1960s right through the 1990s male ministers were still preaching that God designed women primarily to serve their husband's needs, minister in the church nursery and fellowship kitchen, and be good homemakers (emphasis *at home*). Regardless that many women of faith back then had to work outside the home, the mantra was repeated ad nauseum in the pulpit, but particularly in Christian publications: Women's God-assigned role was in the home. Period.

I was so confused. I loved God, Church, and my pastors. I loved the Word. How I wanted to serve Jesus

Christ to the best of my abilities in whatever way He chose for me! But the messages I heard in the Church clashed with the dreams I had for my life. In my ignorance of the Word combined with my unwavering loyalty to my pastor(s), I concluded that one of two scenarios was playing out: 1) I was deceived about what I thought was God's plan for my life (college then publishing and other business ventures) or—and this was my biggest fear—2) I had never really repented of my worldly ways since finding Christ, and even the Holy Spirit couldn't scrub the "evil" feminist leanings out of my heart.

I was not redeemable.

> I thought that serving God as a Christian businesswoman was very hard; I wondered if it were even possible for women like me to be happy in the Church.

Lies, lies. The lies I fell prey to about God's limited love and plans for women rubbed against my heart like a tight shoe on a tender foot, creating daily anguish. I thought that serving God as a Christian businesswoman was very hard; I wondered if it were even possible for women like me to be happy in the Church. *There must be something wrong with me*, I would think. I aspired to do so many big things in the business world, but when I shared these ideas with Christians I was discouraged, rebuked, and criticized as being hopelessly brainwashed by the feminist left, which, in evangelical circles, is akin to being a pedophile.

It came to a point where I resolved that, even if I never found joy or acceptance in the Church, I would continue to serve God, miserable and unfulfilled, because surely this burden was a test of my love and loyalty.

Mostly I kept these ideas to myself, not just

because I knew what Christians would say, but because I couldn't well articulate what I felt. For 18 years I carried this hurt, which made me a prime target for Satan's slanders about God's character and intent. Worse, my ignorance of the Scriptures reinforced the hurt. These lies created a stronghold of spiritual darkness in my mind, and in the darkness a lying spirit grabbed a foothold. He began to attack God's loving nature to draw me away from the Father.

I had no idea that Satan was browbeating me with lies, and I was naïve. I believed everything, the

> *Lying spirits use the darkness of well-meaning but deceived, ignorant, and/or traditionalist Christians to perform the evil strategies of the enemy.*

good and the wrong-headed, that ministers said about women's role in the Church. I didn't know that lying spirits use the darkness of well-meaning but deceived, ignorant, and/or traditionalist Christians to perform the evil strategies of the enemy.

After a while I shut up altogether and withdrew into months then years of depression, despair, and aloneness. My overwhelming impression of those days is marked by intense isolation.

But that was on the bad days. On the good days I was resolute to serve Him, to force myself to be content as an inferior creation performing limited tasks in the Church because of one thought: God is love. I concluded, therefore, that He must have good reason for making women second-class citizens in his Kingdom. Surely there had to be some explanation as to why He would give women gifts and abilities He wouldn't allow them to use, why everything women are called to do in the Church and the world has some spiritual limit on it that doesn't apply to men, and why He takes pleasure in our pain.

But what was it?

Hiss #2: Nice Girls Aren't Violent

A man was walking across a bridge when he saw another man standing on the edge about to jump to his death.

"Stop! Don't jump!" he cried.
"Why?" said the jumper.
"We have so much to live for!"
"Like what?"
"Well ..." The would-be rescuer thought for a second. "Are you a church-going man or an atheist?"
"A church-goer," said the jumper.
"Me too! Are you Christian or Jewish?"
"Christian."
"Me too! Are you Catholic or Protestant?"
"Protestant."
"Me too! Are you pro-tongues or anti-tongues?"
"Pro-tongues."
"Wonderful! Me too! Are you for divine healing or against it?"
"For it."
"Me too! Are you for infant baptism or

against it?"

"Against it."

"Me too! Are you pre-Tribulation or post-Tribulation?"

"Post-Tribulation."

To which the first man said, "Have a nice day!" and shoved him over the edge.

The Power of Tradition

Jesus stated in Mark 7:13 and in seven other places in the Bible that tradition robs his Word of power. What is a tradition, and how can it be so powerful that it nullifies God's Word?

According to *American Heritage*, a tradition is the passing down of cultural elements, especially by oral communication, or a mode of thought or behavior followed continuously from generation to generation, or a body of unwritten religious precepts. The Greek root emphasizes oral law. Jesus speaks of the unwritten stuff of religion we inherit from our ancestors.

We own our religious traditions; they become who we are. They are familiar, they are comfortable. They make us feel safe. They give our lives structure. They validate our faith, and we are proud of that heritage. We don't always know their origin, only that they emanated from those who came before us, and that is enough— good or bad, we glory in the connection to our ancestors.

For Christians, the temptation is that we'd rather jettison a believer who disagrees with us than abandon our religious legacy. Worse, we accept religious traditions without curiosity. We smugly accept their validity. These facts about religious traditions give them great power over us.

Traditions are powerful, but God's Word is also

powerful: "My word ... shall not return unto me void, but it shall accomplish that which I please, and it shall prosper in the thing whereto I sent it" (Isa. 55:11). As I said earlier, God's Word bears fruit because it is spiritual seed. That's why his spoken Word created a universe and raises the dead. When we plant it in our hearts, the life in it produces spiritual fruit.

"Prosper" means to push forward, to be profitable. God's Word will push forward his plans, make profitable his will, and bear fruit where you apply it to your life.

So traditions and God's Word are both powerful, but here's the thing: Jesus said tradition can be more powerful than his Word. When we put our faith in a tradition instead of God's Word, we stop the germination process. We rob

> *When we put our faith in a tradition instead of God's Word, we stop the germination process. We rob the seed of its power.*

the seed of its power. That's why the absence of fruit in a Christian's life is evidence that the person believes something other than truth.

Our friend on the bridge received instant revelation of this—on the way down.

You must be able to recognize tradition from truth. Bear with me while I explain why it's critical that you understand the power of tradition and the influence it has over your spiritual victory. If you don't grasp how seriously damaging it is to walk in tradition instead of God's truth in an area of your life, you expose yourself to being taken captive by a lie like I did. Spiritual death in that area of your life will result.

Tradition v. Truth

You are what you believe (Prov. 23:7). Is what you

believe tradition or truth? We often confuse traditions with truth because traditions usually surround God's Word, or sound like his Word, or contain a portion of his Word. Remember: Satan (and his message) appears as an angel of light—truth—precisely so that we will swallow his lie (2 Cor. 11:14).

Therefore, *the surest way to sift tradition from truth is to know what God's Word says about a subject.* I offer you no shortcut—you must regularly study the Word. You must renew your mind with God's Word daily so that your thinking lines

> *The surest way to sift tradition from truth is to know what God's Word says about a subject.*

up with his so that you can differentiate lies from truth. God commands us to do this. We must be "… casting down imaginations, and every high thing that exalteth itself against the knowledge of God, and bringing into captivity every thought to the obedience of Christ" (II Cor. 10:5).

The Greek word from which we get "casting down" means to lower by violence, to demolish, or to destroy. That's tough language. But any thought that contradicts God's Word is a lie; you must expose it. This requires spiritual violence. By this I don't mean an action that requires a big stick. I mean you must 1) commit to know what the Word says about an issue, 2) live by what it says even if it costs you, and 3) be ready to teach others to do the same. It takes time and effort, but it's worth it because his Word is the most powerful weapon God has given you to silence the hiss. It's the weapon Jesus used to silence it when He was tempted by the devil in the wilderness.

Jesus also used the Word to silence the scribes and Pharisees. Here they come again in Matt. 15:1–14, questioning Jesus regarding their revered traditions.

15

'Why do your disciples disobey the ancient Jewish traditions?' they demanded. 'For they ignore our ritual of ceremonial handwashing before they eat.'

He replied, 'And why do your traditions violate the direct commandments of God? For instance, God's law is "Honor your father and mother; anyone who reviles his parents must die." 'But you say, "Even if your parents are in need, you may give their support money to the church instead." 'And so, by your man-made rule, you nullify the direct command of God to honor and care for your parents." You hypocrites! Well did Isaiah prophesy of you, "These people say they honor me, but their hearts are far away. Their worship is worthless, for they teach their man-made laws instead of those from God."'

(Matt. 15:1–9, Living Bible)

Let's examine what the Pharisees did wrong.

Error #1: Religion was their god, an idol. They sacrificed the well-being of the elderly (their own parents) who needed their financial support to temple maintenance—a temporal structure of inert stone they exalted above the physical needs of eternal beings. But God's religion is people, not buildings (I Cor. 3:9, 16). The Pharisees' hypocrisy made it difficult for others to enter the Kingdom (Matt. 23:1–13).

How kindly would you feel toward the synagogue if you were the frail elderly parent who starved because your adult rabbi son supported it but neglected your daily needs?

16

Error #2: They chose man-made doctrine to the neglect of God's Word, rendering the Word powerless. Jesus told them that by stubbornly clinging to religious tradition they were setting aside his Word. "For laying aside the commandment of God, ye hold the tradition of men ..." (Mark 7:8).

Error #3: They added to God's Word. This error is like that made by Christians who use their tithe to pay for Christian school for their children or some other good work instead of bringing it to the "storehouse" as God commanded in Mal. 3:10. It sounds like a reasonable alternative, but it's disobedience, a man-made doctrine they wrap around the Word to give their rebellion a sense of legitimacy.

Error #4: The Pharisee's hearts were far from God's (Matt. 15:8). This is the most damning of accusations. God's tender heart beat for the welfare of his people, but the Pharisees' hearts were hardened by sin and shriveled by greed. They didn't care about anyone's welfare but their own, and they didn't want to submit to God's authority. They craved only the praise of men.

How could the scribes and Pharisees, who knew the law so well, apply it to life so poorly, misinterpreting its intent? The answer is in—

Error #5: Like Eve, they were acquainted with the letter of the law but not its Author. They knew nothing of what made God's heart beat for mankind. If they had known the Father, they would have recognized the Son and that his words reflected the Father's. And speaking of the heart, Jesus said there was no room in theirs for his Word, "My word hath no place in you" (John 8:37). They couldn't follow Christ because his Word had to remain in them for them to conform to his image. The Word couldn't remain (take root) in their hearts because the soil was bad. They heard the Word and immediately rejected it. They were carnal men parading in religious robes, standing in positions of authority, proclaiming to the masses the supposed way to God. The blind leading the blind.

> *A little Pharisee lives in all of us. To various degrees we all accept tradition over truth.*

Yet ... a little Pharisee lives in all of us. To various degrees we all accept tradition over truth. We do so for three reasons: 1) We don't know what the Bible says about a subject, so when we hear religious sounding teaching we don't recognize how it contradicts God's Word (at one time I held the world record in this sport); 2) We're familiar enough with the law to recognize the letter of it, but too unfamiliar with the Holy Spirit to realize that our twisted interpretation contradicts his nature (I won a blue ribbon in this); and 3) Traditions contain a little truth, which makes them acceptable to people who think they know God's Word.

As an example of the last, let's examine the two claims Satan made to Eve. He said if she touched or ate of the tree she would not die (lie). But he also said that touching or eating would cause her eyes to be open and she would become like a god, knowing good and evil (true). This latter claim was true because God said so in Gen. 3:22, "And the Lord God said, Behold, the man is become as one of us, to know good and evil...."

Absorbing Tradition

Satan's proposition to Eve was a lie packaged in truth, which is how Satan often spoon feeds lies to Christians. Carefully examine Christian teachings now and from the past and you'll find a startling mix of spiritual revelation and questionable opinions flavored by the culture of the period in which the authors lived.

18

Teachings of men such as Augustine, Luther, Calvin, and Wesley profoundly impacted Christian thought, and they had much to say about what Scripture says about women. Especially during Augustine's and Luther's times when the common person didn't own a Bible, and when church leadership was the sole source of spiritual light, their treatises on women were tantamount to a telegram from Heaven. Later I will discuss their writings in our search for the origin of spurious Christian traditions about the nature and role of women.

No matter the source, worldly philosophy or Christian traditions, bad seed will sprout. Weed seeds bring forth weeds just as surely as grape seeds bring forth grapes.

> *Tradition's harvest is undesirable because it bears nothing to increase the Kingdom and chokes the seed that does.*

Tradition's harvest is undesirable because it bears nothing to increase the Kingdom and chokes the seed that does. God's Word is clear: "To be carnally minded is death; but to be spiritually minded is life and peace" (Rom. 8:6). He's talking about your thought life, that stuff you put into your heart, the truth and everything else. Plant God's Word in your heart, make it your thought life, and you'll enjoy good fruit: spiritual growth, peace, righteousness, and prosperity in every area. Truly, this is the abundant life that Jesus came to bring us.

I have more good news. Immediately after Jesus castigated the scribes and Pharisees for teaching traditions instead of God's Word, his disciples asked him if he realized that the Pharisees were offended by his Words (Matt. 15:12). Jesus' response was the key I sought for 18 years. He explained how to deal with them and what their end would be. "Every plant not planted by my Father shall be rooted up, so ignore them" (Matt. 15:13–14, Living Bible).

The Master Gardener won't tolerate weeds forever. He'll pluck them when the time is right. They're God's problem, not ours. Don't concern yourself with them.

One more thing: Like Jesus, if you're committed to living the truth, you're going to offend traditionalists from time to time. The faster you get over it, the faster you'll find peace. *Ignore them.* I do.

Hiss #3: Nice Girls Get Diamonds, Not Dominion

> Any law that uplifts human
> personality is just. Any law that
> degrades human personality is unjust.
> All segregation statutes are unjust
> because segregation distorts the soul
> and damages the personality. It gives
> the segregator a false sense of
> superiority and the segregated a false
> sense of inferiority.
>
> Martin Luther King
> Letter from a Birmingham Jail
> April 16, 1963

What is God's purpose for woman?

After God created the man, He made a revealing statement. "And the Lord God said, It is not good that the man should be alone; I will make him a help meet for him" (Gen. 2:18).

I have listened to many ministers expound on this verse. God's purpose for creating woman was a HUGE topic in church sermons in the 1970s and into the early 1980s—a counterpoint to the rabid and rapidly spreading feminism that flowed over the land. Ministers

21

would say much about how unnatural it is for a man to live alone, that Adam was lonely, etc. They usually added a few words about how grateful they were for their God-given "helpmeet" and what a great help their wives have been in "the" ministry or "my" ministry.

Traditional treatment of the story of creation follows this line, that Eve was created for companionship and to help Adam get his work done.

> *God gave Adam and Eve the same command:*
> *Dominion.*

Traditional treatment is true but incomplete. It's true that the woman was created for the man, not the man for the woman (I Cor. 11:9). But they were both created to fulfill God's, not Adam's plan. Nor did God command Adam to do one task and Eve another. He told them both to subdue and have dominion. Look:

And God blessed them, and God said unto them, Be fruitful, and multiply, and replenish the Earth, and subdue it; and have dominion over the fish of the sea, and over the fowl of the air, and over every living thing that moveth upon the Earth" (Gen. 1:28)

Eve had work to do, too. When God said it wasn't good for Adam to be alone, in the same breath He said He would make him a companion fitting to the task. *What task?* He said He would make Adam a helper "meet" for him. *Meet to do what?* If Eve was placed on the scene solely to fulfill Adam's need for companionship and to serve his needs, then God wastefully gave her way more talent than she required.

God Said unto Them

Key to understanding what God has to say about his male and female creation is the meaning of the word "man" in vv. 26 and 27, which comes from Hebrew *adam*. It means human creation or mankind, man and woman, not just males. Man, or male, comes from another word, *iysh*. So these verses can be understood as, "Let us make humans in our own image," or, "So God created man and woman in his own image."

Even without a Hebrew translation, it's plain in v. 27 that man means both man and woman, because the Holy Spirit explained himself at the end of the verse, "male and female created he them."

> *God uttered his plan for man and woman right there in the garden, and his will has never changed: **dominion**.*

God uttered his plan for man and woman right there in the garden, and his will has never changed: dominion. God's edict is not his suggestion. It's his command, and even sin has not changed his mind. In v. 28 God commanded them both to have dominion over creation, and in Gen. 2:15 He commanded them to maintain it, "And the Lord God took the man (*adam*), and put him into the garden of Eden to dress it and to keep it."

The Hebrew word for dominion means to tread down, subjugate, reign, or rule over. Subdue means to conquer or to bring into subjection. God said that both men and women should rule over the earth and its resources, to dominate other creatures (but not each other) equally together. *Dominion isn't a coveted position to be wrested from anyone. It is a gift from God.* Not long after God spoke these words, sin entered and

> *Dominion isn't a coveted position to be wrested from anyone. It is a gift from God.*

changed the balance of authority between husband and wife. But it didn't cause God to rescind his gift, nor did it alter his command that they both walk in it.

In God's usual efficient way, He used few words to command them to exercise dominion. He didn't dictate to them exactly how they should do it. He gave them no instructions that we know of. If He did, it's merely speculation on our part, because nothing of this was recorded in the Bible. Evidently God had faith in the intelligence and judgment He'd deposited in them. He knew they would figure it out on their own.

They did, too. Although sin soon entered, by the second generation, Cain was a successful farmer and Abel was a prosperous rancher. Genesis 4 records the rapid development of the earth. Cain fled from the Lord's presence (v. 16) yet he still had innate ability to build a city. And within one or two generations Adam and Eve's descendants were raising cattle, forging brass and iron, and composing music.

Humans began to subdue the earth and take dominion over it despite obstacles ushered in by sin. We know this because dominion is always associated with fruitfulness. God told Adam and Eve to be fruitful, multiply, replenish, subdue, and have dominion. These actions are interdependent.

> *Dominion is always associated with fruitfulness.*

Dominion required them to be fruitful in the field, to develop natural resources, and to multiply their numbers. They did so by divine ability and desire to walk in dominion over creation.

Denial of Dominion

We have failed to acknowledge the innate drive for dominion God has planted in everyone, specifically in this context, women. Traditionalists believe God designed women to play mostly supporting roles in the pursuit of dominion, to assist Adam with *his* plans. The Church treats exercise of dominion as a masculine pursuit.

As a result, to maintain our idea of femininity, women are cast in a rigid, limited role. We portray women as primarily followers without significant, legitimate goals of their own, whose chief role in marriage is to see that God's plans for a husband's ministry or career come to success—getting her husband's work done. If she sacrifices her own dreams to meet this goal, she's considered all the more spiritual. As of this writing, the "feminine mystique" has been exposed in all areas of society except the Church (more on this later).

> *The feminine mystique has been exposed in all areas of society except the Church.*

Women's efforts at spiritual and material dominion are rarely encouraged except in minimal ways, and sometimes, as you shall see, are outright discouraged. Fueled by a desire to surround ourselves with the comfortable, familiar, and predictable, Christians have created a feminine culture that wonderfully complements our notion of chivalry but dangerously flirts with the rudeness of reality. The result is less fruit for the Kingdom.

Because we don't acknowledge dominion as women's spiritual property, we don't train them to walk in it. After all, why would you bother training someone to use an ability you weren't convinced she possesses? If we do train them, we usually limit our focus to the spiritual realm, content to leave them ignorant of how to achieve victory in the material realm. We think that part will take care of itself, again, usually by association with another. As a result, the Church is full of women who are doomed to be dominated in one or both areas by spiritual and natural forces determined to keep them under the curses of the law.

Denial of a woman's call to dominion is tragic. We deny God's image when we don't acknowledge women's ability and desire to fulfill his command. And women deny it when they are convinced that their inner urgings and heartfelt longings emanate from the soul and not the spirit. Because in most cases, persistent dreams are leadings of the Spirit that, if pursued, would lead us to dominion in every realm, not just the spiritual.

> *We deny God's image when we don't acknowledge women's ability and desire to fulfill his command to walk in dominion.*

How Dominion Operates

We can't talk about dominion without first explaining how it operates. Scripture says these forces (dreams, visions, plans) come from deep within the human heart, or spirit: "Keep thy heart with all diligence; for out of it are the issues of life" (Prov. 4:23). (For brevity, hereafter I refer to the issues of the heart as dreams.)

"Issues" comes from Hebrew *totsa'ah*, an enigmatic word of many meanings: issues, but also exit, boundary, deliverance, source, or goings forth. *Totsa'ah* is an offshoot of another word, *yatsa'*. It means to go or cause to bring out, begotten, bring forth, carry out, issue out, grow, proceed, shoot forth, spread out, and spring out. The point is this: These actions reside in and burst forth from the garden of the human heart. The heart is the place where dreams begin, because dominion is a spiritual seed God plants there before you are born. If the seed is nurtured, in time it bursts forth from the spiritual to the natural realm. The dream becomes reality, or fruit, in your life.

The heart is the place where dreams begin, because dominion is a spiritual seed God plants there before you are born.

Have you heard people say that God has a plan for your life? They're right. Search your heart and you'll find it.

A dream grows in four stages.

1. You recognize a dream. You see yourself doing something or procuring something. This is the seed. It manifests as early as preschool. We've all known firefighters, teachers, or others who wanted to be in their chosen field since they were small children. Their dream seed was big inside of them early on.

2. Confidence grows as the dream becomes more real, more detailed. The dream grows in importance in your heart. The confidence-building stage is the most critical, when your parents, peers, and culture wield the most influence. At this stage you begin to nurture the dream on our own or abandon it.

3. Once you are convinced that your dream can become reality, you begin to look for ways to make it happen. You don't try to do something until you think they can, and you don't come to that point until you have sized up your ability against your provision or counted the cost. ("I know I can be a success at college, but can I afford it?")

4. The Bible calls this stage "due season." From your faith and work combined with God's guidance and provision, the dream springs forth into the natural

realm.

Because the heart is the womb of yet unborn
realities, God instructs us to keep it with diligence.
There's nothing deep about the use of the word "keep"
here. It means primarily to guard, but also to protect,
preserve, maintain, or be a watcher(man) over. If you
must protect your heart because it's the source of good
things, then likewise you must also protect it from bad
things (weeds) that inhibit good things from springing
forth. For the believer, that means doubt, unbelief,
deception, worldly philosophies, and fruitless traditions.

Sometimes we miss the Holy Spirit's leading when
He tries to bring us into dominion because we don't
recognize the divine source of our dreams. We don't
understand how He operates. When He drops a dream
into our hearts we think it's "only me." Or we don't set
aside time to receive dreams from Him in the first
place. I have been guilty of both.

But I remember one time when I didn't miss my
divine appointment. Years before we had children, my
husband and I lived in a small, two-bedroom apartment
in Mt. View, Calif. One afternoon I was kneeling in
prayer. As I waited before Him, the idea for a
congregation-wide, weekly classified ad page dropped
into my mind. I heard nothing, but saw everything:
format, title, dimensions, and distribution method. It
would be an inexpensive vehicle for members to buy,
sell, swap, exchange babysitting services, look for work
or potential employees, and request prayer.

In a flash I could see that the ad page would be far
more effective to reach the membership than the
inadequate, out-of-the-way bulletin board we were
using. The long and short of it is, I presented my idea to
my pastor, he liked it, I got busy, and it became reality.
The ad page was a blessing to my church family and a
satisfying way for me to minister. When I saw it fall

together exactly as I had envisioned while on my knees, then I knew the dream had come from God. I'd had no teaching about the issues of life until that time, and afterward I still didn't receive any teaching about it for many years. But I was convinced then and still am now that the dream emanated from Him.

That was my first lesson in dreams. It was a small lesson. But I discovered that small or big, every dream the Holy Spirit plants is marked by this fact: It takes more energy to deny it than to fulfill it. Push it down. Try to ignore it. Tell yourself it's just you. Tell yourself you're eccentric and out of step. Indulge in self-pity. Browbeat yourself that no one understands your dream but God. Set your heart to sacrifice your dream. Resign yourself to being unhappy and unfulfilled your whole life if that's what it takes to please people. I have done all these things.

> *Small or big, every dream the Holy Spirit plants in your heart is marked by this fact: It takes more energy to deny it than to fulfill it.*

But the dream does not go away. MAJOR CLUE HERE.

On the other hand, if you believe the dream is from God, you'll pursue it. As you exercise faith, believing God is with you, He begins to give you more details, provision to make it happen, and guidance for each step. And every detail, provision, and bit of guidance energizes you. It's easier to pursue the dream than deny it.

So why, then, do we deny our dreams? We do so because we are conditioned by tradition to deny our unique selves to fit into a one-size-fits-all Christian womanhood uniform. We do it because we have more faith in the rightness of tradition than we do in that still small voice within that tries to direct us into dominion.

The result: We are discouraged from pursuing the Holy Spirit-inspired dreams in a manner that goes dangerously beyond our Lord's admonition that we must deny ourselves to follow Him. What Jesus instructed us to do is to deny our selfish, carnal desires.

If your heart is upright and sincere when you bring your dreams to Him in prayer, He will show you which ones are of Him. God said He wants you to learn how to prove what is his good, acceptable, and perfect will for your life. He is happy, He is waiting to show you the way.

Dominion v. Feminism

Pursuit and attainment of dominion is God's will for all his children. From Scripture we know that God has placed in the hearts of women and men a pure desire to dominate our circumstances, our finances, our physical condition, our world. Even those without Christ recognize this universal desire to be on top of life and not crushed beneath it. The modern word for this phenomenon is empowerment. The New Testament calls it victory in Christ.

Empowerment, dominion, or victory—many Christians are uncomfortable with women having it. They are conflicted because of a lie. They fear that pursuit of dominion is a masculine trait. The Church has failed to teach that the liberating truth of Gen. 1:28 is for women too.

> *Feminism has redefined godly dominion to mean a stereotypically loud, hard-nosed, in-your-face Amazon who charges all over everyone demanding her slice of the pie, and after she consumes hers, gobbles the man's.*

Feminists have stepped in where the Church has failed, but their solution is an unscriptural, fleshly one borne from carnal understanding. Feminism has redefined godly dominion to mean a stereotypically loud, hard-nosed, in-your-face Amazon who charges all over everyone demanding her slice of the pie, and after she consumes hers, gobbles the man's. This is a distortion of godly dominion conceived by the enemy, whose plan is always to divide.

So what *does* godly dominion mean for women? It means exercising control over your life by acting as directed by the Holy Spirit, with God's provision, to obtain your dreams. In an endless variety of ways God will direct you into a life that reflects this kind of dominion. The alternative is to be dominated, to settle for whatever life dishes out.

When a woman seeks dominion by the Holy Spirit, the only violence is in the spirit realm. She seizes it from Satan's kingdom, not from another person. Violence occurs in the kingdom of darkness when you reclaim territory by faith. A woman who knows God's Word knows she already has dominion. The fight in the natural is over. All she must do is use the same gender-neutral spiritual weapons that a man uses. The woman who gives Satan a good swift kick in the pants isn't masculine—she's smart.

And because God granted dominion to women, it's error to think that when a woman walks in it she does so only by seizing it from a man, the pie scenario just mentioned. She can't steal what's already hers. Such thinking implies that God gave dominion only to men and there's not enough of it to go around. Satan would like men to get their eyes fastened on spiritually and materially successful women, to blame them for their own failure to walk in dominion in either area. Thinking like this engenders envy and resentment on both sides. Again, Satan's plan is to divide, a goal he accomplishes by deception.

31

My first lesson in dominion is embarrassing. In the winter of 1987–88 I was living in a small, furnished house in northern Virginia with my two preschool children, near the federal government training camp where my husband lived while he prepared for his new job. The old stone house had been remodeled into two apartments. The kids and I lived on the ground floor; an unmarried man occupied the basement. The landlady told us when we signed the lease that the tenant below us was quiet and no trouble. "You'll never know he's around," she said.

The landlady had never lived upstairs from Robert.

Robert was a heavy marijuana user. The stench and smoke of his habit hung thickly in my children's bedroom seven nights a week, forming a bluish haze that encircled the ceiling. Between his television, which droned all night after he fell asleep in a weed-induced stupor, and the smell and the smoke, the man drove me crazy. And to top it off, as soon as Robert found out that my husband was away at school, he started coming around, wanting to know if I wanted a little "company." *Yuck!* The guy gave me the creeps.

All I wanted was a peaceful, quiet, smoke-free home for me and my children. I wanted dominion over my circumstances, but as usual I wanted someone else to get it for me. I'd been taught from the pulpit and in marriage seminars that, as my spiritual head, it was my husband's place to fight my battles. God had made me somewhat emotionally delicate, I was told. My feminine frame wasn't meant to handle confrontation. I didn't really believe that, but right then it sure made a handy excuse! I called the police, but they, incredibly, said they couldn't do anything. I called my husband, who sympathized with me but wasn't free to leave campus to assist me. I called the landlady, but she wasn't interested in kicking out her long-time basement tenant.

That left only one person to do the job, Mrs. Wimpy Welch. The thought of confronting Robert paralyzed me, so I did what I always did to avoid confrontation—I ran! I started looking for another furnished place, all the while knowing in my heart that running was not God's will. I had no peace about searching for another rental, but I was desperate. Robert so vexed me I could think of nothing else. I prayed, but I still didn't know what to do.

After following multiple ads for a new place, I couldn't find another rental except for one. It was located way outside of town, far from neighbors, set back into dark, spooky woods. The thought of going home at night to a haunted house surrounded by forest blackness was scarier than dealing with Robert.

I was stuck. I realized my only choice was to rely on God, but I still didn't know what to do about Robert.

Then during a morning worship service, our music leader led us in a chorus I'd never heard before. I remember only one line: "Every place whereon the soles of your feet shall tread shall be yours" (Deut. 11:24). As I sang the

> Dominion is yours NOW because you are Abraham's descendant.

words, revelation exploded in my spirit. The Holy Spirit showed me that now, in this century, wherever I am, in every situation I must exercise dominion over my circumstances. I don't have to secure it myself, because He has already delivered it to me. It's a gift. It's not something I have to work up, build up, or "psyche" up. Dominion is mine because I am Abraham's descendent. The dominion that God granted to Adam and Eve, lost to Satan, promised to the Israelites, and purchased by Christ is mine *now*. My part is only to believe it, listen for the Holy Spirit to show me how to get it, and act on

33

what He tells me. No one can take dominion from me. I can only forfeit it through ignorance, fear, or unbelief.

Immediately afterward, God showed me what to do to get the goods on my smoky thorn in the flesh. Within a few days I confronted him with unusual boldness. He backed down. My house was smoke free and quiet from that day forward until the day we moved out.

Friend, I would have gladly let my husband handle the problem if he'd been around. But the Lord allowed it to come about when it did precisely because my husband was not around. If Ken had been there, he would have charged downstairs to slay the smoking dragon and I wouldn't have learned about dominion in such a life-changing way. I wouldn't have learned that God means for me to walk in it myself. Experiencing it firsthand is what made the lesson stick.

> *Walking in dominion is not a feminine or masculine religious exercise but a covenant right of all believers.*

Though I told you earlier that dominion means, among other things, having power over creatures and not each other, there was nothing feminist or unscriptural about how I handled my problem. Walking in dominion is not a feminine or masculine religious exercise but a covenant right of all believers. All I did was get informed about my right to dominion and exercise it.

The problem is that often when Satan tries to regain territory, he does so through human vessels yielded to his will. In this instance, it was my neighbor, who just happened to be a man.

God doesn't restrict women who seize spiritual territory when Satan uses a man to deny them covenant rights. We don't war against flesh and blood but spiritual wickedness in high places (Eph. 6:12). We must get our eyes off the weapon (the human who oppresses) and take a good look at the hand that's holding it (Satan). In our sensitivity and revulsion to the modern loss of gender boundaries and in our zeal to counteract the excesses of radical feminism, we forget that we are first spirit beings dealing with spirit enemies and second fleshly men and women.

Dominion transcends gender.

Dominion transcends gender.

Compared to the big picture of how God wants us to walk in dominion, these examples are hardly worth mentioning because of their small impact. However, they show how God had me cutting my spiritual teeth so that I could eventually take a bigger bite out of Satan's kingdom. Other women have traveled farther and faster than I have, because they were convinced earlier that God Himself planted the dreams in their hearts. They've gone into politics to fight the cultural war. They've stayed home to minister to children—with peace of mind. They've entered the medical field to combat suffering. They've entered the world of education to combat ignorance. They've started their own businesses to earn more for their families or to get control of their schedules. God calls women to exercise dominion in many ways.

Women's aspirations for dominion are identical to men's: to contribute, to influence, to make a difference, to develop a strong family life, to relieve human suffering. Women's drive for dominion mirrors men's because God created them as counterparts to men for that purpose. Women may have different interests than men and may go about pursuing dominion in different ways, but ultimately, the drive for dominion is a shared one.

What is God's plan for men and women? "Let

them have dominion." So let them have it!

Woman as Counterpart

In Hebrew, "meet" is amplified to mean a part opposite or counterpart. "Counterpart" means one that closely or exactly resembles another, as in function or relation (*American Heritage*). God designed Eve to reign and work opposite Adam, to be his *counterpart*ner. Eve had the same standing with God as Adam and was made in God's image like Adam. All that Adam was in spiritual preeminence over creation, Eve was. Creation verses do not suggest that Eve was an inferior being or less qualified than Adam to dominate the earth. For these reasons, Eve (and Adam too) had three things granted to her from the beginning: ability, authority, and supply.

Ability

Women don't lack any ability necessary to subdue the earth. If they did, then God was unjust when He commanded Eve to do the impossible.

As a creature with a task to accomplish, God endowed Eve with more than adequate governing capability, intellectual ability, natural and supernatural powers, and the same access to God as Adam, notwithstanding very different packaging. Women don't lack any ability necessary to subdue the earth. If they did, then God was unjust when He commanded Eve to do the impossible. Such an act on God's part would have been a crime. God cannot commit crime.

For centuries, however, the Church has scorned a woman's ability to exercise dominion in the Church or society because of a perceived mental, emotional, or spiritual weakness that God has supposedly built into her nature. I will discuss this perceived weakness in the next chapter.

Authority

God gave Eve and all women authority to dominate the earth. All authority comes from God: "For there is no power but of God: the powers that be are ordained of God" (Rom. 13:1). God charged Eve and you and me to dominate and subdue. God's spoken Word conferred all the authority you need to reign over creation. Eve received her authority the same way Adam received it—directly from God's mouth.

Yet the Church has suffered and still suffers great confusion in the areas of women and authority, and there are several reasons for it. I will discuss them in Chapters 8 and 10.

Supply

It was the day of my high school graduation. A male cousin was graduating from high school also, so our families decided to have one big party. My family home was filled with other cousins and aunts and uncles and, being that we are Sicilian, food, food, food. When the time came to open gifts, my cousin and I took turns as everyone looked on.

As I watched my cousin open card after card full of gift cash, I couldn't help but notice the difference in the choice of gifts my relatives had made. I received not one cash gift. But when that party ended, I owned seven new necklaces.

Why did my relatives think my cousin needed or preferred money and that I didn't? My cousin was one of two children born to working-class parents. He had no college plans. He had worked in high school and was going to continue in his job after graduation. I, on the other hand, had been accepted into an expensive private university and everyone knew it. My working-class parents could only contribute a fraction of my education costs, as there were four of us kids. I had worked and saved all through high school and had won a scholarship, but it wasn't enough.

The necklaces were beautiful, and I was grateful for the love they expressed. But I guarantee you, all that gold hanging around my neck didn't make me seven times more appealing to some wealthy suitor. I ended up working long, tiring hours and taking out loans to pay for my college and graduate degrees.

> *In subtle ways we discourage women's initiative to build significant wealth, because we still assume that a woman will at least partially be taken care of by someone else.*

My relatives meant well. But actions speak. We think women don't need money as badly as men. So prevalent is this notion that we are blind to it and its detrimental effect on women. In subtle ways we discourage women's initiative to build significant wealth. We still assume that a woman will at least partially be taken care of by someone else. We don't encourage girls to stand on their own two feet financially, to become money smart and self-supporting. Even educated career women, craving respect above all else, are more likely to be concerned with a self-affirming, professional title than the big money it can bring.

But Luke 8:1–3 describes women who traveled with Jesus and ministered to his physical needs from their wealth. If they hadn't had it, they couldn't have given it.

Helen Andelin (*Fascinating Womanhood, 1992*)—

a book that exemplifies the culture in which I grew up—quotes Scripture to support her theses on women and money. She believed that what makes a woman feminine and attractive is dependency. Except for liberal arts, she opposed higher education and job training for women. Education for daughters, she advised parents, will cause them to be independent people (why is this sinful for women but not men?) and "provides an easy escape from marriage."[1] (Sounds a bit like a prison, doesn't it?)

I wonder, however, why Andelin thought an educated, well-paid man can be trusted with the same temptation. It's incomprehensible to me how anyone can disapprove of women's education, or of them having their own money, and plenty of it.

We have other weird, unbiblical traditions about women and money. I remember a respected California minister, speaking from a Mt. View pulpit, say that in virtually every case, a married woman works outside the home only to satisfy her lust for luxuries. Men work for honorable reasons but women for dishonorable. I have read many variations of this theme in Christian publications.

Thinking like this is a no-winner for Christian women who want dominion in their finances. If they stay home, they're frustrated, unfulfilled, and often broke. If they work, those whose respect they crave the most condemn them as greedy Christians or neglectful mothers or both. Teaching like this contradicts God's command that men and women go forth and take dominion over their finances *in the way they see fit*. It also denies women's God-given desire to do so.

Women who face this dilemma are forced to

---

[1]Andelin, p. 290.

wonder if, again, something is spiritually or morally wrong with them. If they hear preaching like this often, they will come to believe that there is.

Christian women need to be well off enough to comfortably take care of themselves, their dependents, the work of the Gospel, and the poor. So why aren't they?

The main reason is the influence of Old Testament laws of inheritance, nearly always through the male, the assumption being that the woman will be taken care of by her husband or son. And pre-20th century civil property laws have their basis in, what else? Old Testament law. Our laws have changed but our assumptions have not. We still tend to think that vicarious ownership should satisfy a woman's desire for financial dominion. For some women this is true. For others, it's continual frustration. For elderly widows, it can be tragedy.

Questionable translations of Scripture concerning women and money obscure our understanding. Consider how Prov. 11:16 has been twisted, rewritten to diminish its power to teach women about God's opinion of their personal wealth:

KJV:

"A gracious woman retaineth honour: and strong *men* retain riches."

New KJV:

"A gracious woman retains honor, but ruthless *men* retain riches."

Amplified Version:

"A gracious *and* good woman wins honor [for her husband], and violent men win riches ..."

"Men" did not appear in the original text. The translators added it. But it's unlikely that the Holy Spirit meant men because the conjunction "and" is meant to link the first phrase (about women and honor)

40

to the second phrase (about riches). Without the translators' insertion, both phrases share the one and same subject just introduced, "a woman." According to *Strong's Concordance*, the word woman was translated from Hebrew *ishshah*, a word "often unexpressed in English." So the line should be understood: "A gracious woman retains honor and a strong woman retains riches," a testimony to the profitability of both her honor *and* her strength. Also, the substitution of "but" for "and" further deceives the reader by making it appear that the business of women (honor) opposes the business of men (riches). Is it logical to juxtapose two disconnected ideas, that of honorable women to ruthless men?

And strangely, this translation implies that men who hang on to their wealth are ruthless.

But worst of all is the Amplified's sexist conclusion that if a woman gains honor by her conduct, it isn't hers to enjoy—it becomes the intellectual property of her husband.

So we see women going from gaining honor and riches, to gaining honor and foregoing riches, to giving away the honor. What does that leave them with?

The final, most illustrative examples I can give you of this type of small thinking are my favorites, because they get at the heart of the double standard regarding women and money. More than any example

---

THE ORANGE JUICE CAN PENCIL HOLDER
SECRET TO WEALTH

---

thus far, what I'm about to tell you exemplifies the pervasive, subtle, insulting treatment Christian women receive from poorly informed believers who are ignorant of God's plan for women to exercise dominion in their finances.

I remember reading a Christian marriage manual

41

published in the early 1980s (remember, I was saved in 1975 and reading everything I could about what God expected of me as a Christian woman). Written by a male author whose name I no longer recall, in it the writer set out to discourage married women from working outside the home. And what was his solution to a woman's financial troubles? He went into elaborate detail to describe a little pencil holder made from a 5-oz. metal juice can, miniature craft tiles, and plaster of Paris. The holders, he said, could be sold from the home, eliminating the need for the wife to seek outside employment.

The silly, worthless craft item he described was the identical work of art I'd made in grade school. What a howl. Even a particularly industrious woman would have been fortunate to earn a dime off her creation.

Would you like fries with that?

My husband and I still chuckle over the story, but at first reading, I was deeply troubled by things I read in that book. The author also described the damage a woman would inflict on her marriage if she earned more than her husband. This situation, he explained, would humiliate the man, making him unable to feel like a leader in his home, a heresy that kept a lot of Christian writers up at night during that decade. He went on to say that the husband would be too ashamed to admit his humiliation, so it was her responsibility to see that things never deteriorated that much. Her only choice was to turn down high paying work. Or, if she currently earned more than her husband, she should do the honorable thing: look for a lower-paying job. (Would you like fries with that?)

This last wisdom distressed me greatly, because at the time my husband and I, both students, were working but I earned more than he did. (Not that it mattered. We

42

were equally broke.) Guilt nagged at me for several days. Was I really humiliating my husband? Was he secretly unhappy at my bigger paycheck? Were my earnings threatening the peace of our home? Ken seemed like a normal macho guy, the kind the writer described, yet he never gave me any inkling that he was annoyed at my bigger paycheck. Perhaps he was hiding his humiliation from me? Maybe I should quit my job and find one that pays less?

I decided to confront Ken with the allegations in the book, share my fears, and assure him of my willingness to quit my higher paying job to secure his leadership.

His response: "Ginny, you bring home *a-l-l-l-l* the money you want!"

I never read another Christian marriage manual.

Instead of encouraging business-minded women in serious ventures, like the Prov. 31 wife and mother who invested in real estate, people like that writer would have us competing with second graders in nickel-and-dime operations that frustrate and discourage. We think it's nice if a woman has serious wealth, especially if she doesn't leave home to get it. But we're not convinced that it's necessary.

What pitifully small thinking. Why did God give dominion over the earth to Adam and Eve in Gen. 1:26 and then command them both to go and get it in v. 28? Because He knew that women need victory in this area as much as men. Whether you wear a dress and heels or coat and tie when you shop, a loaf of bread costs the same.

Every church I've worshipped in had its share of single mothers. They all had the same problems, but when it came to money, only the educated were not on welfare or working two jobs. I'm thinking of Melinda[2], who works all day in an office then stands on her feet, waiting on tables through the best part of the evening, weekends too, to support herself and her teenage son. I'm thinking of Allison and her son, Kaylee and her son, Rebecca and her three, and many others, who live on inadequate incomes, most in cramped apartments, all struggling.

But when Lisa's husband left, money wasn't one of her problems. The eldest of three daughters of an evangelist-pastor, Lisa was a practicing attorney. She's the only Christian single mother I've ever known who lives comfortably.

The Sin Factor

Sin changed many things. It was sin, not divine design that upset the balance of authority between husband and wife. And we are continually tested by confrontations with sickness, disease, lack, disappointment, contrary people, and other forces that threaten to steal our victory. But God assures us that sin did not change his plan for men and women to rule and reign in life. Rom. 5:17 guarantees it. In Christ we are restored to spiritual and material dominion. When Adam and Eve sinned, they sold to Satan their right and their descendants' right to dominate the earth. Christ redeemed us from Satan's kingdom (Col. 1:13) and bought back our right. Because He was the one who paid the price, dominion legally belongs to Him ("All power is given unto me in heaven and in earth," Matt. 28:18), but He has graciously returned it to us (Luke 10:19). When God made us into new creatures, He brought back women just as much as men full circle to

---

[2] Not their real names

44

the position of dominion. In God's eyes men and women are equals when it comes to exercising dominion in the earth. We are truly one in Christ Jesus.

Denial and Feminism

> *Denial of God's command to women to exercise dominion is not a backlash to feminism. It's what caused it.*

Whether it's the Church or society, denial of a woman's dominion and her desire for it violate the command God gave her in Gen.1:26 and 28. Denial is not a backlash to feminism. It's what caused it. Denial of dominion, continuing for decades and committed on a wide scale, was at the heart of the confounding rage behind the women's movement that exploded in the mid-1960s. It's self-evident that the movement has gone off the deep end. But denial of dominion that provoked justifiable outrage is what sparked the rebellion in the first place.

It's tempting for the Church to put the blame on society, to distance itself and point the finger at our culture, making it the villain when we look for someone to blame for the explosion of feminine anger. But if we, the Church, say society is to blame, then we condemn ourselves, because to convict society is to admit that our influence hasn't been as salty as it should be. After all, we *are* society; it's not as though the Church has been living on the moon the last 2,000 years. Only as recently as the 20th century have we seen a significant decline in the Church's influence. In all prior centuries, Christianity defined culture wherever God's Word was preached and took root. Our laws, schools, and major institutions were founded on the divine rightness of Bible truth. Until now, at least in the West, Christianity *was* culture.

But with the late 20th-century/early 21st century shift away from Christianity and toward secular humanism, modern Christians are keenly aware of our them-us relationship with the world. The world reminds us daily of our minority status and that our beliefs and values no longer dominate. As a result, we don't appreciate how modern culture, specifically our ideas about women and dominion, are still shaped predominantly by Christianity. We think feminism is an intellectual product of *this* generation, unrelated to the primarily Christian teachings of earlier ones. We blame all that we don't like about feminism on feminine outrage that exploded in the 1960s, when in fact what we saw in the '60s was the harvest of yesterday's seed of denial.

If we do acknowledge our pre-20th century influence, we tend to focus on the positive results we made, which were many. But because there was no clear-cut separation between the Church and society from colonial days until the early '60s, we can't fairly give the Church all the praise for uplifting society but none of the blame for denying dominion to women.

We can't fairly give the Church all the praise for uplifting society but none of the blame for denying dominion to women.

Radical feminism, like Black anger, did not spring up overnight. Its seeds were planted long ago. It's the fruit of an unholy union between the worst of Christian and cultural traditions about women, both of which substituted carnal thinking for God's Word. And as with natural offspring whose behavior causes grief, the parents point fingers at one another, blaming each other's ancestry for bad genes that show up in the child. That's why feminist book after feminist book begins its history of male dominance by focusing on the influence of Christianity on western culture. Feminists like to blame their troubles on patriarchal church dogma. And that's why Christian publications that denounce feminism begin their arguments by focusing on the effects of the undeniable sins of a rebellious, humanistic generation. The Church likes to blame society's troubles on those godless secularists. Neither is willing to admit that what they see in the child reflects the worst in the parents.

But blame isn't the issue. Does it matter who's at fault? I said earlier that the whole point is to compare traditional ideas of a woman's nature and role to Scripture. To do so is, I hope, to positively shape the future. Don't be angry or disillusioned with the Church. It has enough problems. Take it from one who's trudged down that angry path: Nothing good comes from it. It's a waste of energy.

What I want is to provoke you to study God's Word, to see Christian women in a new and freer way. Once you're convinced of the truth, for your sake and your Christian sisters, concentrate on it alone and be courageous to speak it.

> *Women who pursue spiritual and material dominion fulfill a divine command, righteous and pure, which neither defeminizes women nor emasculates men.*

We must teach that women who pursue spiritual and material dominion fulfill a divine command, righteous and pure, and that doing so neither defeminizes women nor emasculates men. To teach this truth is to violently cast down tradition.

Because if we don't, we leave women no choice but to embrace feminism, which for too many former church-going women has become a vent for their anger and a sympathetic embrace they've not felt from the bosom of Christianity.

Hiss #4: You Don't Have What It Takes

> Likewise, ye husbands, dwell with
> them according to knowledge, giving
> honor unto the wife, as unto the weaker
> vessel.   I Pet. 3:7

True story. Years ago, before cell phones were in everyone's pocket, a friend of mine and her sister, both single, were traveling to a ministry event. On a deserted California highway their recreational vehicle broke down, leaving them stranded and too far from civilization to get help. Seeing there was no hope but to trust the kindness of a stranger, the first sister hitched a ride to the nearest town while the other stayed behind to guard the RV.

While the second sister waited in the cab by the side of the road, a man stopped to ask if he could help. But instead of helping, he suddenly thrust a gun in her face and forced her into the passenger's seat. As she leaned protectively against the passenger door, trying to calm herself, the man ranted and raged about all the evil things he was going to do to her. He was going to kill her.

I promise to tell you what happened to my

stranded friend. But before I do, I want to talk to you about the ultimate urban legend, one that has survived centuries in the annals of Christian orthodoxy. We're going to go back in time and learn all we can about that deadly spiritual pox, the virus of the Church age: the "weaker vessel."

Mental Weakness

Before the KJV was printed in 1611, Peter's description of the woman as the weaker vessel wielded a profound impact on society, literature, and the Church. And before the disciple Peter was born, Greek philosopher Aristotle (384–322 B.C.) concluded that woman was the "weaker animal,"[1] and when speaking of males said, "The fact is, the nature of man is the most rounded off and complete."[2]

Plainly, these men never accompanied a woman to the mall the day after Thanksgiving.

Aristotle blamed a woman's weakness on her inferior mind. He believed that by divine design women are subordinate to men from birth because of men's superior rationality and women's tendency to "pettiness" and "capriciousness" that resulted from mental deficiency. Her weaker state was the natural order of things, he said, because it was an act of God. It couldn't be traced to original sin.

Later (Saint) Augustine (354–430) claimed that Satan targeted Eve because she was the "weaker part of

---

[1] Quoted in Rosemary Agonito, *History of Ideas on Woman.* G.P. Putnam's Sons, New York, 1977, p. 43.

[2] Agonito, p. 49.

50

that human alliance."[3] (Saint) Thomas Aquinas (1225–1274) concurred. He said that it's evident throughout nature that women are subject to men because men's "discretion of reason predominates."[4]

Samples of similar sentiment in secular literature abound. English poet Geoffrey Chaucer's (c. 1340–1400) Wife of Bath called herself the weaker vessel,[5] and that was 200 years before the KJV was printed (but consider who put the words in her mouth).

> *The notion of women's weakness was woven into the social fabric and survived with vigor for at least two centuries before the two most quoted words to describe women wormed their way into religious vernacular.*

William Shakespeare (1564–1616) loved the term and made space for it in *Love's Labour's Lost*, *As You Like It*, and others.[6] More samples exist, but these alone prove that the notion of women's weakness had already woven itself into the social fabric and survived with vigor for at least two centuries before the two most quoted words to describe women wormed their way into religious vernacular.

---

[3] Augustine, Saint. *The City of God.* Trans. Marcus Dods. The Modern Library, New York, N.Y., 1950, Book XIV, p. 458.

[4] Agonito, p. 85.

[5] Jeffrey, David Lyle, Gen. Ed. *A Dictionary of Biblical Tradition in English Literature.* Wm. B. Eerdmans Publishing Co., Grand Rapids, 1991, p. 820.

[6] Shakespeare, William. *The Complete Works of Shakespeare.* Xerox College Publishing, Lexington, 1971. "Love's Labour's Lost," Act, I, Scene I, lines 257–258, p. 185; "As you Like It," Act II, Scene IV, lines 3–5, p. 367.

Father of Protestantism Martin Luther (1483–1546), though ahead of his time spiritually, was a product of his times culturally. He may have been convinced that his ideas were influenced by *sola scriptura*, but his commentary on Genesis smells curiously of the 16th century. Speaking of the creation of Adam and Eve:

> Moses here places the man and the woman together in order that no one might think that the woman was to be excluded from the glory of the future life. The woman certainly differs from the man, for she is weaker in body *and intellect*. Nevertheless, Eve was an excellent creature and equal to Adam so far as the divine image, that is, righteousness, wisdom and eternal salvation, is concerned. Still, she was only a woman.
>
> As the sun is much more glorious than the moon (though also the moon is glorious), so the woman was inferior to the man both in honor and dignity, though she, too, was a very excellent work of God. So also today the woman is the partaker of eternal life, as the apostle writes (I Pet. 3:7) that she is a coheir of grace. Therefore the woman should not be excluded from any honor which human beings enjoy, even though she is the weaker vessel.[7]

---

[7]Luther, Martin. *Luther's Commentary on Genesis*. Zondervan Publishing House, Grand Rapids, Mich., 1958, p. 34.

(emphasis mine)

Luther's insight on the nature of women is familiar: equal before God but inferior to men (which sounds a bit like separate but equal: racially segregated but ostensibly ensuring equal opportunities to all races). Despite the laudatory things he said about women, his closing "even though" said more.

Luther also believed that women are condemned to lag behind men in spiritual gifts because of Eve's sin. It was divine justice. "Therefore Eve was not as women are today. She was far more excellent so that she was behind Adam in no bodily or spiritual gift."[8]

> *"The natural imbecility of the female sex." Natural? Does this mean God designed us as imbeciles? And who can argue with God?*

The Puritans did more to elevate the position of women than other reformers because of their commitment to walk in the light of Bible truth. Yet in their geographical flight from religious tradition they couldn't escape without dragging along some cultural baggage from the society they left behind. Richard Baxter wrote that ministers who marry are handicapped by their close association with "the natural imbecility of the female sex."[9]

Natural? Does he mean that God *designed* us as imbeciles? And who can argue with God?

John Winthrop (1587/88–1649), an English Puritan

---

[8]Luther, p. 55.

[9]Quoted in Leland Ryken, *Worldly Saints, The Puritans As They Really Were*. Academie Books, Zondervan Publishing House, Grand Rapids, Mich., 1986, p. 196.

lawyer and one of the leaders of the Massachusetts Bay Colony, was happy to explain why the wife of Governor Edward Hopkins of Connecticut had succumbed to insanity. Sadly, reading too much and taking an interest in matters of the mind—strenuous business designed for a man's larger intellect—would make a woman crazy (Maybe he was on to something. While researching this chapter, many things I read made me want to howl at the moon.):

> For if she had attended her
> household affairs, and such things as
> belong to women, and not gone out of
> her way ... to meddle in such things as
> are proper for men, whose minds are
> stronger, etc., she had kept her wits and
> might have improved them usefully and
> honorably in the place God had set
> her.[10]

British founder of Methodism John Wesley (1703–1791) wrote in his Genesis commentary that God created Eve equal to Adam, but because of pride God condemned her to subjection (to men). Her new state, he said, means women are inferior to men,[11] though he didn't say in what way. Nevertheless, he tempered his observation with an admonition that, considering women's weakness, they ought "to be used with all tenderness."[12]

---

[10]Quoted in Ryken, p. 196.

[11]Wesley, John. *Explanatory Notes Upon the Old Testament*. Schmul Publishers, Salem, Mass. 1975, Vol. I, p. 18.

[12]Wesley, John. *Explanatory Notes Upon the New Testament*. Baker Book House, Grand Rapids, Mich.

British naturalist Charles Darwin's (1809–1882) "scientific" conclusions about women are spiced with sexual and racial bias—close cultural bedfellows—as he explains differences between the sexes:

> It's generally admitted that with woman the powers of intuition, of rapid perception, and perhaps of imitation, are more strongly marked than in man; but some, at least, of these faculties are characteristic of the lower races, and therefore of a past and lower state of civilisation.
>
> The chief distinction in the intellectual powers of the two sexes is shewn by man's attaining to a higher eminence, in whatever he takes up, than can woman—whether requiring deep thought, reason, or imagination, or merely the use of senses and hands. If two lists were made of the most eminent men and women in poetry, painting, sculpture, music (inclusive both of composition and performance), history, science, and philosophy with half-a-dozen names under each subject, the two lists would not bear comparison. You may also infer, from the law of the deviation from averages, so well illustrated by Mr. Galton, in his work on 'Hereditary Genius,' that if men are capable of a decided pre-eminence over women in many subjects, the average of mental power

---

1981, Vol. II., I Peter 3:7, no page given.

in man must be above that of woman.[13]

No one influenced 20th century scientific thought about women's mental weakness as did Austrian physician and neurologist Sigmund Freud (1856–1939). Colleges and universities still devote a sizable portion of their psychology curriculum to his teachings. I studied them while attending a private religious university in the mid-1970s. So immersed was Freud in his theory of male superiority that he asserted that, as a class, even women acknowledge their inferiority. From childhood they secretly wish for penises, "penis envy" he called it, and only by becoming inured to their unfortunate state of physical castration can they attain normal femininity. (Anyone who believes this must also believe that a woman's physical design and psyche, being flawed and incomplete, logically couldn't have originated from the mind of an all-wise Divine Being. Also from this theory springs the idea that man alone is physically complete, a contradiction of God's own assessment that it was not good that Adam abide on the earth alone. God did not rest from his creation labors, implying creation was complete, until after He had created Eve.) Women who don't accept their inferior state, declared Freud, are doomed to neurosis (I feel that howling coming on again).

All of this would be more laughable were it not that this balderdash has been taught as serious science since the late 19th century, and where it's taught Freud is regarded as legitimate. Just before I delivered my fourth child, I picked up a Christian magazine for guidance on mothering. I blinked when I saw Freud quoted in *Focus on the Family's,* "The Most Important Job in the World," (April 1994, p. 3). I guess the writer

---

[13] Agonito, pp. 260–261.

thought it would bolster the article's scientific appeal.

Writers referred to women's inborn weakness until about the beginning of the 20th century. John Lyly (c. 1554–1606) in *Euphues,* "Men are always laying baytes (baits) for women, which are the weaker vessels;"[14] English poet Thomas Hardy (1840–1928) in *Far from the Madding Crowd,* "(She) in spite of her mettle, began to feel unmistakable signs that she was inherently the weaker vessel;"[15] Oscar Wilde (1854–1900) in *The Importance of Being Earnest,* "Men should be more careful; this very celibacy leads weaker vessels astray."[16]

Finally, from *Fascinating Womanhood,* a huge bestseller from the 1960s, comes Andelin's definition of the feminine nature and its inherent weakness:

> The feminine nature is *weak, soft,*
> and *delicate,* compared to the man's
> strong and firm nature. This does not
> imply weakness in a negative way,
> such as weakness of character, or lack
> of moral courage.[17] (emphasis Andelin)

This is like saying a person is fearful, but not the negative kind of fearful. Other than the fear of the Lord, what kind of fear is positive? And speaking of fear,

---

[14]*A Dictionary of Biblical Tradition in English Literature*, p. 820.

[15]Hardy, Thomas. *Far From the Madding Crowd.* Viking Penguin Inc., New York, 1978, Chap. 31, p. 260.

[16]Wilde, Oscar. *The Importance of Being Earnest.* Penguin Books, New York, 1985, p. 148.

[17]Andelin, Helen. *Fascinating Womanhood.* Bantam Press, New York, 1992, p. 273.

Andelin maintains that feminine women have a natural fear of danger, while men are disinclined to be fearful of the same threats.[18]

Yet God says He has given no one a spirit of fear (II Tim. 1:7). Note that Andelin did not say that a woman's *body* is weak; she said her *nature* is weak.

Her book sold more than two million copies.

Moral Weakness

Traditional treatment emphasizes not only woman's weak mind but her divinely designed moral weakness, an obvious reference to the temptation of Eve. God created Eve more likely to sin than Adam, so the thinking goes.

Luther agreed. "The subtlety of Satan showed itself also when he attacked human nature where it was weakest, namely, in Eve."[19] He believed that, given the chance, Adam would not have succumbed to the same temptation. He didn't explain, however, why Adam's superior nature failed him when he caved in so quickly to his wife's suggestion to partake of the forbidden tree. After all, the Bible says it was the serpent that was the "subtil" or crafty character, not Eve.

English poet John Milton (1608–1674), when describing in his famous play, *Paradise Lost*,[20] how easily Satan tempted Eve, painted a picture of her in a spiritually weak state *before* the fall. His thesis was not unique. Lesser known writer Guillaume du Barta, in *La*

---

[18]Andelin, p. 273.

[19]Luther, Martin. *Luther's Commentary on Genesis*. Zondervan Publishing House, Grand Rapids, Mich., 1958, p. 68.

[20]Milton, John. *Paradise Lost*. New American Library, New York, 1968, Book IX, p. 255.

Sepmaine, asserted that Satan tempted Eve and not Adam because she was naturally "wavering, weake and unwise."[21] English writer Sir Walter Raleigh (c. 1552–1618) argued in his *History of the World* that Satan targeted her because of her "unquiet vanity."[22] English writer Thomas Peyton (1595–1626) claimed Satan targeted her because of her tendency to "much idle pratter."[23]

All these writers portrayed Eve as mentally and spiritually weak *by design*; therefore, it's easy to see how paternalism, already established in the culture, was nearly impossible to eradicate from church dogma. They figured her weaknesses were God's ideas. How can you argue with God? **It follows then, that women's activities had to be strictly regulated to keep them from causing more trouble than Eve had already caused.**

> *All these writers portrayed Eve as mentally and spiritually weak **by design**; therefore, it's easy to see how paternalism, already established in the culture, was nearly impossible to eradicate from church dogma. They figured her weaknesses were God's ideas.*

It's foolish to think that the Church has survived, isolated, from such powerful traditional conclusions about women's mental and spiritual ability. Misinterpretation of this one verse more than any other has distorted our perception of women's call to serve. If women are mentally weak, they have no business aspiring to dominion in the secular or spiritual world. If they are spiritually weak, they can't be trusted with

---

[21]Agonito, p. 253.
[22]Agonito, p. 253.
[23]Agonito, p. 253.

spiritual gifts. If they are emotionally weak, they can't handle responsibility and shouldn't lead.

> *If women's psyches or spirits are defective by divine design, or as a result of original sin, it's easy to justify limiting their influence.*

If women's psyches or spirits are defective by divine design, or as a result of original sin, it's easy to justify limiting their influence.

And if women hear only about their mental, spiritual, and emotional limitations, their achievements will reflect the reduced expectations that have come to be reality in their self-assessment of who they are in God.

"As a man thinketh in his heart, so is he" (Prov. 23:7).

You really are the sum of your thought life.

The Contradiction of Bible Testimony

> *Bible heroines are systematically strong in spirit, faith, and intelligence.*

Notwithstanding the Talmud's[24] bald statement that "Women are light-minded,"[25] Old Testament accounts of women whose actions the Holy Spirit thought significant enough to record do not reflect weakness in mental acuity or spiritual dynamism. The reverse is true. Bible heroines are systematically strong in spirit, faith, and intelligence.

— One of the first Bible matriarchs, **Sarah's**

---

[24] A collection of ancient rabbinical writings containing instructions for living.

[25] Cohen, A. *Everyman's Talmud.* Schocken Books, New York, 1975, p. 161, (Shab. 33*b*).

respectful behavior toward her husband is lauded in I Pet. 3:6 as an example for women. Her faith is lauded in Heb. 11:11.

- **Ruth** was hailed as virtuous—spiritually strong—for not chasing young or rich men, though she might have been tempted considering her widowed state during famine.
- **Hannah** was rewarded for her faith with a spiritually above-average son who became a great prophet.
- **Abigail** (I Sam. 25) was called a woman of good understanding and lived up to her name by using her brains and humility to employ the goods of her household to save it from destruction at the hands of David.
- Jesus commended the **Gentile widow of Zarephath** in Luke 4:25–26 for her uncommon faith; God chose her over Israelite widows to feed Elijah during famine.
- **Esther** proved her courage and worthiness of a royal title by risking her life to save her people.
- The **Prov. 31 woman**, traditionally known for her virtue, should be lauded for her strength. The Hebrew word from which we get "virtue" means a force, as in the force of an army or the power of wealth. The word is used repeatedly to describe her (more on this later).

In the New Testament, Jesus commended the woman who anointed his feet for burial and said her act of repentance and humility would be remembered wherever the Gospel was preached because she loved much (Mark 14; Luke 7). He marveled at the faith of the Gentile woman in Matt. 15:28, then granted her request. Finally, though this is not an exhaustive list, Heb. 11 includes women in the Hall of Faith. Paul said that he had dragged Christian men *and* women to prison and martyrdom for their profession of faith.

Do you think those martyrs were *weak* Christians?

Where are the weak women of the Bible of whom our forefathers wrote so voluminously? Eve who was deceived by the serpent? Adam yielded to the same temptation, but did so knowingly. The Bible says he was not deceived. Delilah who tempted Sampson? She was a heathen outside the covenant and untrained in the law. Sampson enjoyed the privileges of both yet sinned because of lust. Sapphira who lied to the Holy Ghost? Her husband lied too.

The Dilemma of Experience

For years after I got saved I scratched my head over I Pet. 3:7, wondering why women had been handicapped with the "weaker vessel" moniker. I grew up without any brothers, so my overburdened parents assigned chores to myself and my three sisters that in other homes fell to male siblings. As a result, it never occurred to me that girls couldn't do practical things like mow grass, change a flat tire, strip and refinish furniture, prune and graft fruit trees, garden, and preserve food. My father taught me to do all these things.

My mother taught me how to type, cook, run a home, serve as hostess, and a great many domestic fine points that still serve me today. She also worked outside the home (though sometimes she brought work to her home office) her entire married life because she had to, and, I think she liked to.

I grew up thinking of women as capable, productive, and strong.

But until I got saved, I never thought about my parents' examples in religious terms. All that changed when I became a Christian. The Church's message was clear. I knew where it stood. Christian marriage experts told me about a woman's frail nature, emotional and indecisive, and her domestic obligation (I'm tempted to say imprisonment) to eschew outside employment.

My confusion stemmed from the intersection of the Christian message from the pulpit and in religious publications, with the other one, the one I received by rubbing shoulders with real flesh-and-blood Christian women and by reading Bible accounts of Jewish ones.

I have known women and men of weak faith. Alcoholics, adulterers, men who have taken advantage of their wives' faithfulness, women who have slid back into a sinful lifestyle, those who fail to grow and must be pulled from the pit of their sin again and again. From what I've seen, moral weakness is an equal opportunity trait. Which reminds me …

Locked in a commandeered RV with a killer on a desolate California highway with a loaded gun pointed at her head, she tells herself she will not panic. She will stand on God's Word. She will live!

This story has a happy ending for the one and only reason that my friend knew the authority of the Word and the power of the name of Jesus. She used them to defy the evil spirit who influenced her attacker. To every foul design that spewed from his mouth, she looked him in the eyes and boldly stated, not under her breath but aloud: "IN THE NAME OF JESUS YOU WILL NOT HARM ME."

Finally, miraculously, the attacker lost steam. He climbed out of the RV and drove away. My friend was unharmed, just as she prophesied.

My friend is not unique. I've known women who have fasted days, others weeks to see God's hand move in their families. If you've tried fasting even one day you know this takes commitment and inner strength.

Fasting is not for wimps. Other women have remained faithful through years of waiting to see God answer prayer when others would have given up.

I've recounted, briefly, just a few personal observations of strong Christian women. Many stories remain to be told. My point is that, from observation alone, as a young Christian I knew there were weak and strong men and women. But personal experience is not the deciding factor to determine spiritual truth. We don't trust experience to reveal truth to us. We trust God's Word. My experiences with strong women did, however, pique my curiosity as to what God's Word says about strength.

Definition of the Vessel

The Greek from which we translate weaker is *asthenes*. It means weaker, more feeble, or lacking strength. The Greek for vessel is *skene*. It means a tent or cloth hut, habitation, or tabernacle. The Israelites' first worship tabernacle was a campsite tent they pitched as they trekked through the desert on their journey to Canaan. There in the tent God's presence dwelled between the cherubim, and there Moses worshipped and conferred with Him.

The Israelites also dwelled in tents. The tent way of living symbolized the temporal nature of their journey. Paul referred to it in Heb. 11:9 when he said that Abraham, his son, and grandson dwelled in tabernacles or *skene*.

Our bodies are the New Testament equivalent of a tent (plenty of room for jokes here, but I'll spare you), a temporal dwelling for the Holy Spirit. "Know ye not that ye are the temple of God, and that the Spirit of God dwelleth in you?" (I Cor. 3:16). Paul confirmed this in two verses of II Cor. 5 when He said, "For you know that if our *earthly house of this tabernacle* were dissolved, you have a building of God, an house not made with hands, eternal in the heavens" (v.1), and "For you that are in this *tabernacle* do groan, being burdened: not for that you would be unclothed, but clothed upon, that mortality might be swallowed up of life" (v.4). Also, "Therefore you are always confident, knowing that, whilst you are at home in the *body*, you are absent from the Lord" (v.6).

"Tabernacle" in vv. 1 and 4 share the Greek root *skenos* derived from *skene,* but additionally *skenos* means the human body in a figurative sense.

Finally, "... You have this treasure in earthen vessels, that the excellency of the power may be of God, and not of us" (II Cor. 4:7). Here's proof that our bodies are vessels for the Holy Spirit to dwell in while He accomplishes his purposes in the earth.

Yet there is more. The Bible tells us that our bodies are earthly containers, like pitchers, that God wants to fill with Himself. Adam (and Eve, too, because she was made from Adam) were formed from the dust or *aphar*, meaning clay, earth, or dust. Adam was not called a living soul until God breathed life into his nostrils (Gen. 2:7). Prior to that moment he was only an empty, useless container (or vessel) waiting to be filled. We are all vessels:

> For this is the will of God, even your sanctification, that ye should abstain from fornication:
> That every one of you should know how to possess his vessel in sanctification and honor. I Thess. 4:3–4

A note in my KJV Bible says that "vessel" here means wife. This is incorrect. Verse 3 warns against fornication. Verse 4 is an amplification of v. 3, so a person's vessel can't be his wife because a man can't commit fornication with his wife. It also says that "every one of you" should know how to possess his vessel in sanctification, and every one of you means all people, women too.

Your vessel is your body.

Therefore, to understand Peter's admonition about the weaker vessel, you must acknowledge that man or woman, your "vessel" is your body. According to I Pet. 3:7, men and women have weak bodies (relative to the Spirit), but women's are weaker than men's. It's undeniable, it's universal: men are genetically programmed to be physically stronger than women. That's why, in this verse, God tells men to care for their wives' physical well-being. The verse speaks only of a woman's physical body and can't be misconstrued to mean that women are weaker than men mentally or spiritually. A woman can be as mentally and spiritually strong as she is willing to study and pray, converting her soul (mind) by the washing of the water of God's Word. Anyone willing to pay the price to seek God can grow in grace unlimited. In this arena men have no advantage.

That's why, years ago, my friend survived a wicked man's sinister plan to blow her brains out on a dusty California highway.

The Solution for Weakness

Church tradition portrays women as spiritually and emotionally weak, delicate creatures subject to tearful episodes of hysteria in the face of life's daily pressures and disappointments. Weaker from birth, women must be protected from circumstances that tax their lesser capacity, weaknesses that left unchecked endanger themselves and those they influence.

> *Traditional treatment of a woman as a weaker vessel denies resurrection power and the Holy Spirit's work in a woman's soul.*

This tradition is built on the romance of swooning damsels and shining white knights, not God's Word. It denies resurrection power and the Holy Spirit's work in a woman's soul. God's Word is clear about how all believers obtain inner strength. "That he would grant you, according to the riches of his glory, to be *strengthened with might by his Spirit* in the inner man" (Eph. 3:16); and "Finally, my brethren, *be strong in the Lord*, and in the power of his might" (Eph. 6:10). Also,

> That ye might walk worthy of the Lord unto all pleasing, being fruitful in every good work, and increasing in the knowledge of God; *strengthened with all might*, according to his glorious power ... Col. 1:10–11

Strong men and women of God live by prescribed disciplines. They enjoy a consistent, intimate relationship with the Lord and are filled with the Holy Spirit and God's Word. They are living demonstrations of his love, bold in faith, and prone to good works. The seed of God's Word does not produce shrinking violets but mighty oak trees.

Who is strong? Who is mighty? From the Old to New Testament, the message is the same: Strength comes from tapping into his Spirit and knowing how to use spiritual weapons. "Not by might, nor by power, but by my spirit, saith the Lord of hosts" (Zech. 4:6); "For the weapons of our warfare are not carnal, but mighty through God to the pulling down of strong holds" (II Cor. 10:4). God's spiritual weapons are available to everyone, and Eph. 6:10–18 is the weapons checklist you can use to win life's daily battles. This GI (God-issued) arsenal is fail-proof, guaranteed to equip anyone to defeat every attack of the enemy.

> *Your strength comes from tapping into his Spirit and knowing how to use spiritual weapons.*

When it comes to the spiritual warfare that is a fact of our earthly experience, have you ever considered that Satan is no gentleman? Gender blind, he doesn't care whose faith he destroys. He attacks women as viciously and mercilessly as men. So what kind of unjust Creator do we preach if we say that God made women less capable of overcoming than men?

The Church has no excuse for continuing to forward this unscriptural picture of women. It was this maddening stereotype that finally drove me to cease attending church-sponsored marriage seminars. I can't bear to hear one more hackneyed vignette about a weeping woman (or pregnant woman or menopausal woman or nagging woman—ad nauseam) or one more tired scenario about a confused man who can't understand his weepy wife. This kind of teaching doesn't encourage faith. It encourages more stereotyping.

Why not go to God's Word? There you read that men *and* women are made in his image; that you can do all things through Jesus Christ; that He is able to make all grace abound toward you that you might be all sufficient in everything and abound to every good work; that you are a member of a royal priesthood. There you read that God always causes you to triumph in Jesus Christ.

It's universally accepted that women are emotionally different from men, but in no way are their differences inferior, as if the standard to determine the correct response to every situation is, "How would a man respond?" and if a woman responds differently, her response is wrong. God made women the way they are—in his image—for his purposes. Even the softer lines of a woman's body and her tendency to be more nurturing and less aggressive than a man reflect maternal qualities of her Creator, which are mentioned several places in Scripture.

Although a woman's body is, muscle-wise, weaker than a man's, even this difference reflects the consistently paradoxical character of God. He is just, but He is merciful. He is loving, but don't tempt his anger. He is rich, but he made Himself poor. He forever lives, but He died on a cross. How magnificent and wondrous is our God, whose multifaceted image is mysteriously reflected at once in both male and female.

So why do we cling to our tired stereotypes that portray women as defective merchandise? We do it because of ignorance on the part of leadership, who, in nearly every case, means well but is uninformed. We do it because women are afraid to speak up, as I was for years. But mostly, we do it because we give more place in our thinking to our traditions than to God's Word. If we would take the time to study and pray over Scripture, traditional thinking would soon be exposed and just as soon rejected.

Traditional thinking about the weaker vessel has limited women in their God-given privilege to serve to their full capacity, where they could be excelling to the edification of the Church. Let's get rid of it.

Hiss #5: God Judges You More Harshly

> When Jesus had lifted up himself, and
> saw none but the woman, he said unto her,
> Woman, where are those thine accusers?
> hath no man condemned thee?
> She said, No man, Lord. And Jesus said
> unto her, Neither do I condemn thee: go,
> and sin no more.
> John 8:10–11

We use this passage often to illustrate Jesus'
compassion. And it's a good lesson on grace for sin.

But the story teaches another lesson that by and
large the Church has missed. Today when so many
women decry a double standard in the Church and our
laws regarding sexual sin, there's no better time to study
and publish the liberating message of this Bible story.

But first you need a short history of the Old
Testament's treatment of female sexuality and how it
affects the modern movement for sexual equality.

The Old Testament Standard

Old Testament law demanded sexual purity of everyone. Adultery, fornication, homosexuality, incest, bestiality, necrophilia, prostitution, and rape were forbidden, and there were clear-cut penalties for each, death in most circumstances.

But the law required a more stringent level of chastity for women than men. For example, Deut. 22 laid the burden of proof for a bride's virginity on her and her family. If a husband accused his wife of not being a virgin at the time of their wedding, her family had to show the "token" of her virginity, namely, a blood-stained cloth remaining from the wedding night. If they couldn't provide one, the woman was stoned.

It's unlikely, however, that a bride's family ever forced a groom to submit to a chastity test. The law did not demand one, and if it had, it would have been highly unworkable.

Similarly, Num. 5:15–31 laid out steps for priests to follow when a man was overcome with the "spirit of jealousy." When a man suspected his wife was guilty of adultery but had no witness, the priest made a water and dust concoction called "bitter water," and caused the accused to drink it in his presence. If the woman was guilty, she was cursed with illness ("to make thy belly to swell, and thy thigh to rot," v. 22). If she was innocent the mixture did her no harm. Again, the law made no similar provision for women who suspected their husbands of hanky-panky.

If an unmarried woman had sexual relations with a man in the city and no one heard her cry out, people assumed the relations were consensual. The man could not be accused of rape, so the thinking went, because if the relations had been forced, people nearby (theoretically people are always nearby in the city) would have heard the woman's cries. The woman was stoned, and as usual, the burden of proof of innocence was upon her.

This last requirement is hard to comprehend, since rape is a crime of violence and secrecy, and fear of physical harm would quiet almost anyone.

If an unmarried man had sex with a virgin, he had to pay 50 shekels of silver to her father to reimburse him the loss of her bride price. The offender was also required to marry the woman because he had defiled her; it was unlikely anyone else would have her. No such payment was made to the woman for her loss and humiliation, and the parents of the young man involved didn't expect payment for their son's loss of virginity.

Not even sexually innocent widows were spared. Levite priests could marry only virgins.

These laws underscore how highly the Israelites esteemed virginity in women and how closely they associated nonvirginity with defilement.

In addition to the troubling double standard I saw in the law, the Old Testament story of Lot's horrible treatment of his daughters pained me deeply as a young Christian. Abraham's nephew Lot was living in the wicked city of Sodom when he offered his home for the night to two angels who appeared at his door as men. Upon hearing that Lot had male house guests, homosexuals of the town began beating on Lot's door, demanding that he release his visitors so that they might have sex with them. Lot refused. Instead he sought to pacify them another way. Lot went out to them—

> And said, I pray you, brethren, do not so wickedly.
> Behold now, I have two daughters which have not known man; let me, I pray you, bring them out unto you, and

do ye to them as is good in your eyes:
only unto these men do nothing; for
therefore came they under the shadow
of my roof. Gen. 19:7–8

Observe: 1) Lot said that the homosexuals' desire
was wicked (v. 7), yet he saw nothing wicked about
giving over his daughters to their perverted appetites. 2)
Lot said that the angels had come under the "shadow"
of his roof (Hebrew *tsel* meaning shade, protection, or
defense); he felt obligated to protect them. But he felt
no obligation to protect his daughters. 3) Lot lied. He
told the intruders that his daughters, both married, were
virgins.

But here's the truly amazing part. Paul called Lot
just and righteous (II Pet. 2:7–8) and said Lot was
"vexed in his soul" at the evil deeds he witnessed in
Sodom. Paul's account is silent, however, about Lot's
own evil deeds, implying that they did not vex him.
How can this be?

For years I gave mental assent to Lot's
righteousness. In my mind I agreed to agree with what
God's Word said about him. But I must admit that, in
my heart, I thought Lot was despicable. I saw him as a
lousy father who cowardly sold his children to pacify
his wicked neighbors, then had to be physically dragged
by angels out of Sodom after he dawdled at God's
command to flee, and then got drunk and committed
incest with both his daughters (Gen. 19:30–38). How in
the world could anyone call this man righteous? How
could God? Every time I read that God called Lot
righteous I concluded that God had overlooked Lot's
heinous treatment of his daughters, that such treatment
did not offend Him. It certainly offended me! After all,
nowhere in the Bible do you read that God rebuked Lot
for his sins against his daughters.

Then there is the disturbing story of another righteous man's shabby sexual treatment of a woman, the Gen. 16 account of Abram and Hagar. Traditional teaching emphasizes that Abram should have ignored Sarai's request that he have intercourse with Hagar to raise up a son for Sarai, and that Abram operated in the flesh and not the spirit, and so forth.

All that is true, of course. But being a woman myself, I felt sorry for Hagar, not Abram.

Here is an Egyptian slave, sold as a young woman or even as a child to wait hand and foot on a wealthy woman of another language in another country. Hagar has no money, no rights, no hope of freedom.

Now she is instructed to have sex with a crusty old man, another woman's husband, and the child she conceives will belong to her mistress. She has no say in the matter. How can you not feel sorry for this pitiful young woman?

Further, after Hagar conceives, Sarai treats her harshly and no one comes to her aid. Hagar, however, brings some of the wrath upon herself because of her big mouth about being the first in the household to conceive.

You can imagine how Sarai treated her. Beaten her maybe? Possibly.

Hagar is desperate over her situation and flees into the desert. An angel of the Lord appears to her and encourages her to return and submit herself to her mistress. She returns to Sarai's tent.

Ishmael is born to Hagar. All seems well, but then Sarah (formerly called Sarai) bears Isaac. Now the strife begins, and Abraham (formerly called Abram) has no choice but to turn Hagar and Ishmael out of the house, even though in those days the custom was for masters to provide for children of slaves until adulthood. And what does Abraham provide for them as they leave?

Gen. 21:14 says Abraham, an extremely wealthy man (Gen. 13:2), sent his natural born son and the child's mother away with only a bottle of water and a loaf of bread!

> *Abraham—an extremely wealthy man—abandoned his firstborn and the child's mother in the desert with only a cruse of water and a loaf of bread.*

Once again in Gen. 21 we find Hagar and Ishmael wandering in the wilderness, desolate. How could God allow this "righteous" man to so shamefully treat Hagar and *his* son?

With so much evidence in the law of the demeaning, exploitive sexual treatment of women (there's more than this; for one amazing example see Judges 19, the story of the Levite who cut his dead concubine into 12 pieces and sent them to the tribes of Israel), it's obvious that a double standard existed in those times. A married woman had no recourse if she suspected her husband of adultery, so what incentive did he have to be faithful? She couldn't divorce him, and even if she did, she faced penury and hunger, as his family certainly wouldn't have taken her in and it's unlikely her family would have. The law was so rigorous regarding virginity that only a foolish or daring unmarried woman would spend time alone with a man. In every way, women were at risk of ostracism or even death because of harsh laws that regulated their sexual conduct more scrupulously than men's. They may not have called it the double standard in those days, but woman knew what it was and towed the line to avoid being victims of it.

Romans 15:4 says the accounts of people who came before us are for our learning and comfort. But reading how shamefully these women were treated by men whom God called righteous gave me anything but comfort. How can a woman feel like his beloved child when it appears that God looks the other way when men, especially *his* men, sexually abuse her?

For many years I doubted the depth of God's love for women partly due to stories like these. No matter how hard I tried to agree with God's Word in my head, it was impossible for me to ignore the nagging feeling in my heart that women were nearly worthless in God's eyes, because it appeared that He didn't punish those who harmed us.

> *No matter how hard I tried to agree with God's Word in my head, it was impossible for me to ignore the nagging feeling in my heart that women were nearly worthless in God's eyes, because it appeared that He didn't punish those who harmed us.*

My only consolation was the better treatment we receive in the New Testament. But regardless, in my early years, lack of assurance about my worth to God as a woman inhibited my faith. Your estimation of who you are to and in Jesus Christ, your self-esteem, is tightly interwoven with your faith. Jesus said in Mark 11:23 and Paul said in Rom. 10:10 that to get results believing must be from the heart. But for reasons I've already explained, my heart was not filled with faith borne of confidence in God's love.

Fortunately, we don't live in Old Testament times, so let's turn to the New Testament to see what our salvation package holds for women.

The Effect of Christianity

Jesus' coming fulfilled the law and did away with its rigorous exercises in letter if not always in spirit. This meant that a lot of double standard sexual practices should have been abolished, but that wasn't always the case. Strict Victorian codes of sexual conduct rooted in Old Testament law were so rigorously applied to women in the 19th century that it was the moral code itself that led many into the waiting arms of the feminist movement.

The code affected every level of society. As Sheila Rowbotham details in her book, *Hidden From History* (New York: Pantheon Books, 1973), in England especially, upper- and middle-class women castigated working class men who were preoccupied with maintaining their daughters' virginity yet disinterested in stamping out prostitution among working class women.[1]

Women involved in rescue work, the mission of getting streetwalkers and their children out of prostitution and into morally acceptable work, saw firsthand the results of a moral code written by and for men. Even when the rescuers managed to get them into homes and new occupations, the women were still considered moral failures. But the men who had consorted with them and contributed to the growing pool of poor and fatherless were not similarly ostracized.

Before 1873 military men couldn't be sued for paternity and civilian men were required to pay only a paltry sum for the maintenance of their offspring.[2]

These hypocrisies outraged the first feminists. As a result, reconstruction of the prevailing double standard was a persistent theme of feminists through the late 1800s and was repeated in the rhetoric of the American women's movement early in the 20th century.

---

[1] Rowbotham, Sheila. *Hidden From History*. Pantheon Books, New York, 1973, p. 53.
[2] Rowbotham, p. 53.

More than a century later we're still influenced by Old Testament-inspired traditions about women and sexual purity. Consider how we teach the lessons of Prov. 31, the "virtuous woman" chapter. So revered is this woman that entire books have been written devoted solely to the twenty-one verses of the Bible that speak of her. Traditionally our emphasis has been on her virtue, or, as we define it, her moral excellence and freedom from vices (*American Heritage*). You meet her in v. 10 as the virtuous woman and the chapter closes (v. 29) describing her conduct as "virtuous."

> *Not a single verse of Proverbs 31 deals with the heroine's sexual faithfulness.*

Yet 18 of the verses say nothing about her morals. Instead they applaud her industry inside and outside her home. The other four verses, namely 10, 11, 25, and 28, deal with her strength, honor, and value to her family. Not one verse deals with sexual faithfulness. Her sexual faithfulness is assumed.

Despite the Bible's emphasis on her many good works, we continue to emphasize sexual purity as the trait that makes her an asset to her husband. We are mired in the 17th century translation (virtue) of the Hebrew word *chayil*, which the original writers used to mean something entirely different. Mentioned earlier, *chayil* means force, whether of men or other resources, but specifically the force wielded by an army or the force of power via wealth.

> *"Virtue" means force, whether of men or other resources, but specifically **the force wielded by an army or the force of power via wealth**.*

For example, look at verse 11, "The heart of her husband doth safely trust in her, so that he shall have no need of spoil." It doesn't mean he trusts her to be sexually faithful. It means he doesn't worry that she'll plunder his bank account. Spoil is translated from *shalal*, which means the booty of war that goes to the victor. The word appears many times in the Old Testament, and in every citation refers to material items such as food, clothing, cattle, houses, and lands, usually in context of the wealth that the Israelites swooped in and grabbed after God had delivered another Gentile nation into their hands. The verse means that her husband trusts her not to waste his money or goods, that he doesn't need to risk his life by going to war for the sake of the spoils to be gained thereafter because of her poor financial decisions and spendthrift ways. She can be trusted with money.

This interpretation complements everything the author had to say about her. Watch how her industrious ways cause her whole household, and especially her husband, to prosper:

v. 12 She does her husband only good.

v. 13 She works willingly with her hands to procure wealth.

v. 14 She provides food for her household.

v. 15 She gets up early to look after her employees – she puts in a long day.

v. 16 She buys real estate and develops it, increasing its value.

v. 17 She strengthens her body and mind.

v. 18 She is confident that her work is good and puts in long hours.

v. 19 See v. 13.

v. 20 She distributes goods to the needy, guaranteeing that multiplied blessings of wealth come back to her family for her diligence to fulfill God's Word.

v. 21 She provides everyone in her house warm clothing.

v. 22 She adorns herself beautifully.

v. 23 She brings honor to her husband.

v. 24 She improves raw materials and sells them for profit.

v. 26 She fills herself with God's Word so that out of her mouth come wisdom and kindness.

v. 27 She runs an orderly home.

v. 29 She excels all others in conducting herself as a force (of wealth) – "doing virtuously."

v. 30 She fears God.

v. 31 She knows that fruit (reward) is coming to her, and that her works (not her sexual purity) will bring her praise.

So other than the 17th century translation of *chayil* to mean moral chastity, where in these verses do you see this woman being praised for living a sexually pure life? How have we missed the central point of this lengthy, detailed account of the prosperous activities of this woman? She sounds like a working mother to me.

We haven't renewed our minds to come out from under the Old Testament sexual double standard. Remember the law that said a father was to be paid for the loss of his daughter's virginity? We have interpreted Prov. 31 in like vein to mean that her sexual purity makes her "price far above rubies." But then, that idea was still strong when KJV translators were at work. This overly sexual interpretation has clung like moss on the north side of a rock. Modern translations still render some words to describe a man's character in a manner free of sexual overtones yet render the same word in a sexual manner to describe a woman (more on this later).

Witness the triumph of tradition over truth. We emphasize moral purity as the building women should build, but purity is just one brick in its foundation. The Prov. 31 woman built her holy life, a praiseworthy record of a sound relationship to God and a long list of good works, on such a foundation. The epitaph in the last verse confirms it: "Let her own *works* praise her in the gates."

But what does any of this have to do with the woman taken in adultery?

* * *

The story begins in the temple. Because Jews didn't mix with Gentiles in public or private, we know that the woman dragged in by the Pharisees and scribes was Jewish. She was familiar with the law and had no excuse. How is it that these men came upon her in a compromising circumstance? I don't know, although I have heard preaching to the effect that they may have set her up; they were, after all, intent on tempting Jesus (John 8:6). The man she was caught with might have been one of their own. But it doesn't matter. The woman was guilty.

The most important thing to understand here is that the Pharisees' own words condemned them. In v. 5 they quoted a portion of the law regarding adulterers: "Such," they said, "should be stoned." Pharisees and scribes were teachers, experts of the law, and they were correct about the punishment for adultery.

If you look up the verse they cited, however, you'll see that they quoted only half of it, the part about the woman. They were silent regarding punishment for the man:

> And the man that committeth adultery with another man's wife, even he that committeth adultery with his neighbour's wife, *the adulterer and the adulteress* shall surely be put to death.

82

Lev. 20:10 (emphasis mine)

Jesus noticed their omission. He too was trained in the law and quoted it regularly. He was aware of their intent to twist the law to suit their purpose, as this wasn't the first time they had tried to trap Him into saying or doing something to violate it. Pharisees, scribes, and lawyers referred to the law when debating with Jesus because the law was the highest authority in Jewry. If they could get Him to say or do something to violate it, then they would have the evidence they wanted to accuse him of heresy.

But what a mistake they made when they tried to trick Jesus by misquoting the law. In the presence of the Lawgiver himself, they not only failed to execute the guilty man, they failed to accuse him as well. Verse 4 says the woman was taken in the very act, so these hypocrites had good opportunity to seize him when they seized her. But they chose to punish one and let the other go free. Does this sound like our laws in some states that go after the prostitute but fail to prosecute her customers? Fortunately, our laws are improving.

When Jesus stooped to the ground (v. 6) and wrote words of mystery in the dirt with his finger, the men ignored his message, for in v. 7 we read, "they continued asking him," (what ought to be done to the woman). Either they were so occupied making their case against her that they didn't bother reading what He wrote, or what He wrote wasn't convincing enough to make them change their plans. In either case, they continued to press for an answer.

Then Jesus said these famous words, "He that is without sin among you, let him first cast a stone at her" (v. 7). Again He stooped and wrote a message on the ground. After this the Bible records that "they which *heard* it" (not saw it) were convicted by their

83

consciences and one by one abandoned the stoning party, turned, and walked away. "Heard" is a literal translation of the Greek word used here. It was what these men heard Jesus say combined with what they saw Him write that moved them to shame.

What did He write? We like to speculate, but I don't claim any private revelation. We do know that whatever He wrote, together with his words, were convicting enough to deflate the self-righteous energy that drove them to the temple at the first.

Personally, I'm convinced that Jesus wrote the lines from the law that were sure to convict, "The adulterer and the adulteress shall surely be put to death," and perhaps his follow-up message was another Scripture attesting to God's ability to look upon the heart. Possibly He wrote the names, followed by a question mark, of those in the crowd. Or maybe He quoted the thunderous words of Nathan, "Thou art the man," (II Sam. 12:7) that sent David into spasms of remorse over his own sins of adultery and murder.

I think He wrote God's Word because it's his Word that pierces to divide soul from spirit, discerning the thoughts and intents of the heart. And like I said, it was Jesus' practice to refer to the law when dealing with the Jews. He did so consistently throughout all four Gospels. Nothing could have been more effective to provoke guilt and shame in these men than the authority of the law they so revered.

His message worked. Every man changed his mind about stoning the woman, and that's what's important here. There's no story in the New Testament like this one that illustrates how Jesus freed women from religious tradition. It's encouraging to see how He refused to go along with their hypocritical plans. These religious men would have gladly stoned her to death and walked away with a lying conscience, one that cleared them of their own adultery, fornication, and who knows what else. Jesus exposed their sin with the truth then pointed them down the path of mercy, and they took it. Then He offered the woman the same.

The other message of this story goes beyond compassion. It's an attack on moral hypocrisy in the Church, a direct hit at the double standard that existed for centuries. God will not tolerate the sexist tradition of using a harsh moral standard for women and a lenient one for men. Jesus Christ abolished the double standard.

> *God will not tolerate the sexist tradition of using a harsh moral standard for women and a lenient one for men. Jesus Christ abolished the double standard.*

Equally encouraging is the example set by the early Church. Nowhere in the New Testament is there a hint that early Christians imposed a stricter standard of sexual conduct for women than men. New Testament treatment of sexual sin and the need for self-control is applied equally to both sexes, confirming that in Christ there is no male or female. Paul wrote in his first letter to the Thessalonian Christians that God expects sexual purity of everyone:

> For this is the will of God, even your sanctification, that ye should abstain from fornication:
> That *every one of you* should know how to possess his vessel in sanctification and honor. I Thess. 4:3–4 (emphasis mine)

Other Scriptures that deal with sexual purity, such as Acts 15:20, I Cor. 6:13, and Eph. 5:3, are likewise written to admonish both sexes alike and contain no special references to either one.

And if that isn't enough good news, Jesus Himself spoke to the Old Testament custom of a husband's right to present his wife with a "bill of divorcement" and send her away for any reason. In Matt. 5:32 Jesus set women free from the tradition that made them penniless outcasts because of their vulnerability to trivial divorce suits. Even though the verse appears to speak directly to men, over centuries Christians have interpreted it to mean that women now also have the right (but not a mandate in either case) to divorce unfaithful husbands.

In I Cor. 7:15 Paul repeated this theme when he addressed the problem of marital strife generated by a nonbeliever who dwells with a believer. "A brother or a sister is not under bondage in such cases; but God hath called us to peace." Though the verse does not deal with adultery, even so, just as Matt. 5:32 freed women from unfaithful husbands, I Cor. 7:15 freed them by giving them the choice to remarry should their nonbelieving husbands divorce them. No longer under bondage to the first marriage and no longer considered defiled, a woman abandoned by her nonbelieving husband stood a better chance of remarrying and was free to do so. In light of Old Testament law that denied women authority to divorce, this was a radical idea indeed.

A last example that underscores the abolition of the double standard is the story of Ananias and Sapphira in Acts 5. Though their sin was not sexual, their mutual punishment was severe enough to demand attention. Both allowed Satan to fill their hearts with a lie (v. 3), and both dropped dead for repeating it to the Holy Spirit. This fear-inspiring account of conspiracy assures us that, in New Testament times, God has one standard for men and women. He offers mercy to both, and He applies judgment to both, and that indiscriminately. Our standards should reflect his.

The Case for the Righteousness of Lot and Abraham

What do we conclude about Lot's treatment of his daughters? By God's failure to rebuke Lot did He condone Lot's giving his daughters over to be ravaged by a band of homosexuals? It's unthinkable that God would condone it.

It's true that God did not rebuke Lot for his despicable breach of familial trust (at least it is not recorded in the Bible). But it's also true that God prevented the homosexuals from harming the women. God ordered the angels to interrupt Lot's nefarious negotiations by reaching outside the door and pulling him into the house.

> *God valued Lot's daughters more highly than Lot.*

Further, God sent the angels to Lot's house to bring not only him but his wife and daughters (and sons-in-law, though they refused) out of Sodom before it was destroyed by fire and brimstone. Psalm 103:20 says that angels act when they hear the Lord's instruction, "the voice of his Word." From these facts, we know that God valued Lot's daughters more highly than Lot.

When Paul called Lot righteous, he was referring to Lot's earlier conduct, in Sodom, when God

> ... delivered just Lot, vexed with the filthy conversation of the wicked:
> (For that righteous man dwelling among them, in seeing and hearing, vexed his righteous soul from day to day with their unlawful deeds).
> II Pet. 2:7–8

The conduct Paul termed righteous was the lifestyle Lot had kept, in Sodom, before the angels arrived at his doorstep. Lot's determination to live a holy life was one of the reasons God sent the angels to rescue him and his family. Despite his imperfections—he was a sinner just like you and I—he did try to live righteously.

But that still doesn't explain why Lot's offer of his daughters was not specifically condemned. Old Testament law was plain that Israelite parents were not to give their daughters over to prostitution, and rape was never condoned.

> *Lot's honor was more important to him than his daughters' welfare. Lot was a sinner. Don't misconstrue his actions as the work of God.*

When threatened with violence by a homosexual mob, Lot had a choice: He could defer to the law and believe God to provide a solution to his dilemma or break the law to save his skin. But his faith was weak. So instead of risking possible humiliation by endangering his house guests, cowardly Lot chose to sacrifice his daughters to save his reputation instead of letting God save it for him.

Lot's honor was more important to him than his daughters' welfare—like I said, he was a sinner. And though I can't make a case that in those days all or nearly all men who might have found themselves in the sticky situation Lot found himself in would have responded the same, it's true that Lot's action reflected his times. Eastern men then (and some now) honored men as a class and devalued women. For the day in which he lived, Lot's action may have been extreme, but it was socially acceptable in accordance with his culture and tradition. Fathers so often sold their daughters into prostitution that God spoke against the practice in the law.

Remember the bride price paid to parents for the loss of their daughters' virginity? Old Testament law reflects the culturally entrenched notion of daughters as economic assets, property subject to liquidation at a father's discretion. It was acceptable to expend with property—livestock, houses, land, crops, slaves—if it meant greater good and spared the honor or life of a man. In this case, Lot's daughters were the property and the greater good was the safety of his angelic "male" house guests, whom he may or may not have recognized as divine. It was Lot's prerogative to swap his daughters for the angels' safety. He reacted to his tight situation in the traditional manner of men (not *faith* men) of his period, which was a reasonable response according to his conscience. I suspect that is why God did not rebuke him for his decision.

> *Lot reacted to his tight situation in the traditional manner of men (not faith men) of his period, which was a reasonable response according to his conscience.*

Lot's sin of not trusting God is not much different than the sin of bible patriarchs—great men of faith—who had many wives and concubines, though God's plan was for a man to have only one wife (Matt. 19:8). We are fortunate that God is patient and gracious, because in every era, including this one, God's people have shown a tendency to prefer the ways of their culture over the clear commands of God.

Although the Bible does not record an express condemnation on God's part for Lot's sins of unbelief and incest, don't think for a minute that he escaped the spiritual consequences of either. Sin reaps a harvest, even when God forgives. Both actions were indisputably evil and only bad fruit resulted.

Lot set a lousy example for his daughters when his lack of trust in God's provision moved him to devalue their sexual purity. His action inspired them to devalue it, for it was they and not him who plotted to commit incest when they realized they were cut off from potential husbands to continue the family line. It's no coincidence that Lot's daughters turned to a fleshly solution to meet their need instead of trusting God to provide. They picked up the habit from their father. All three compromised themselves due to unbelief and all three suffered. From these two incestuous unions sprang the Ammonites and Moabites, two tribes that caused Israel centuries of anguish.

> *It's no coincidence that Lot's daughters turned to a fleshly solution to meet their need instead of trusting God to provide. They picked up the habit from their father.*

As for Abraham's inadvisable sexual relations with Hagar, it wasn't God's idea, because He hadn't planned to build a spiritual nation by fleshly means, and it was never his design for a man to have sexual relations with any other than his wife. Whatever is done outside of faith is sin (Rom. 14:23).

Did Abraham act in faith when he had relations with Hagar? No. God had given him no instruction in this regard on which to fasten his faith. But Abraham didn't act in unbelief, either, because by custom (tradition) it was lawful for a man to father children by a slave or servant, and bible accounts exist of other godly men who did so.

So even though Abraham should not have tried to help God by having relations with Hagar, he did so with an untroubled conscience because he acted on the cultural rightness, the privilege of masters to raise up children by slaves.

Further, it wasn't until *after* Ishmael was born that God told Abraham that his seed would be called through Isaac (Gen. 17:19–21).

God was faithful to watch over Ishmael; Abraham sent him away only with God's permission (Gen. 21:10–12). God couldn't work in Isaac's life with Ishmael in the way, so He removed him. But God planned all along to make a great nation of him, because Ishmael, though not the spiritual seed, was the natural seed of Abraham, and God had promised to bless *all* Abraham's seed.

And despite Hagar's Gentile birth, unfortunate slave state, and imperfect treatment suffered at the hands of Abraham and Sarah, God showed inordinate kindness to her not once but twice, intervening when she and her son were perishing in the desert.

Did Abraham suffer for acting in the flesh? Very much. His heart broke when he had to send Ishmael away (Gen. 21:11). But Abraham was not the only one to suffer. God blessed the Ishmaelites and they grew in number exponentially just as He said they would. But their descendants, the Arabs, have always been and still are a thorn in the flesh to the descendants of Isaac, the Jewish nation.

> *Despite Lot's poor treatment of his daughters and Abraham's poor treatment of Hagar, God was not the author of their actions, and He didn't approve. God is for women.*

The bottom line is that, despite Lot's poor treatment of his daughters and Abraham's poor treatment of Hagar, God was not the author of their actions, and He didn't approve. God is *for* women. He loves them as much as He loves men. God Himself stepped in and saved these unfortunate women from destruction at the hands of righteous men who unwittingly exalted tradition over truth.

God is still rescuing women from the hurt that results when religious men operate from darkness.

I know, because He stepped in and rescued me.

Hiss #6: God Will Always Choose a Man First

> And the princes of Issachar were
> with Deborah; even Issachar, and also
> Barak ...   Judg. 4:15

It happened many years ago, the epiphany of
epiphanies. I was sitting in a worship service one
evening, listening to my beloved pastor expound on the
story of Deborah. I've forgotten every word of his
sermon, even the main point. But I keenly remember
one thing he said:

"What a shame it was to the Israelites," my pastor
declared, "that God had to use a woman to save Israel
because he couldn't find a suitable man."

Deborah a *shame* to the Israelites?

Is God only looking for a few good *men*?

It's an old idea. "Whenever God wishes to brand
man with a mark of ignominy," John Calvin wrote in
the 16th century, "he chooses a woman to do his
prophesying. The only reason God exalted women to
the place of prophetess," he said, was "to shame the

93

men."[1] Calvin's opinion of women must have been very low indeed if he thought that their exaltation made men look bad. Worse, Calvin thought God agreed with him.

Yet Acts 2:18 declares that centuries before Christ, God planned to pour out his Spirit on women during these times: "… On my handmaidens I will pour out in those days of my Spirit; and they shall prophesy."

Well. At least Calvin acknowledged that God lets us prophesy!

Kathryn Kuhlmann, world famous evangelist, faith healer, and preacher, said that God first chose a man to do her job, but when he refused God gave it to her. Five hundred years of revelation has been poured into the Church, yet some people still think God uses a woman only when He can't find a man or that He exalts a woman when He wants to shame men.

Would you feel good about yourself if you believed that God was stuck with you and your inferior ability to fulfill his plans?

How can a woman feel good about her role in the Kingdom after hearing such slander? Would you feel good about yourself if you believed that God was stuck with you and your inferior ability to fulfill his plans? Would it make you feel secure in your ministry? Does *anyone* like being second choice?

More than a decade after that jarring experience in church service, I sat through a formal meal in my own dining room and listened to my guest, a male minister, expound on how men are God's specially anointed vessels. God always chooses a man first for important ministry, he said.

---

[1]Quoted in Tucker, pp. 68–69.

This brother really believed his own words.
Was he right?

*   *   *

Judges 4 and 5 tells the story of Deborah, the prophetess God chose to judge the Israelites. Judg. 4:4 says that Deborah "judged" Israel. Judged is translated from *shaphat*, which means a person who pronounces sentence, or to vindicate, punish, govern, litigate, avenge, condemn, defend, execute judgment, be a judge, reason, or rule. The Israelites acknowledged her anointing for they came to have her judge different matters (Judg. 4:5). But the account gives us little personal background about Deborah, wife of Lapidoth.

The story opens in 4:6–7 when Deborah reminds Barak, leader of Israel's armed forces, that God has promised him victory in battle. God had commanded Barak to assemble 10,000 men, for He planned to deliver Sisera, the captain of Canaanite King Jabin of Hazor's army, into Barak's hand.

God had made an unconditional promise to Barak. But Barak's faith was weak, moving him to put a condition on his obedience. Verse 8: "And Barak said unto her [Deborah], If thou wilt go with me, then I will go: but if thou wilt not go with me, then I will not go."

Conditional obedience is disobedience.

Although she was under no obligation, Deborah overlooked his weak faith and agreed to accompany him into battle, but she prophesied a different outcome. "Notwithstanding the journey that thou takest shall not be for thine honour; for the Lord shall sell Sisera into the hand of a woman" (v. 9). The result was that Barak's armies routed the Canaanites, but Sisera escaped on foot and found refuge in the tent of a Gentile woman named Jael. Exhausted from battle and from flight,

Sisera fell into a deep sleep. He died when Jael drove a tent peg into his head.

From this story you learn several things about Deborah: 1) She was a true prophetess and judge, for her words came to pass (Deut. 18:21–22; Judg. 4:9, 21). 2) Her married state did not restrict her ministry. Nothing in Scripture intimates that she served against the wishes of her husband. She didn't serve as a partner with him, nor was she ordained as a stand-in upon his death, as many women pastors are, because Scripture does not say she was the widow of Lapidoth but his wife. 3) She was a woman of courage. She accompanied Barak to the battlefield. 4) She was a woman of faith. She believed God would deliver Barak and his army.

It's true that at this time in Israel's history the Jews were not serving God as they should have been. Judges 4:1 says Israel was practicing evil. But it's also true that when God used the prophetess Huldah (a married woman, II Kings 22:14) to prophecy ruin to Israel, King Josiah sought her counsel, and he was a righteous king. In fact, II Kings 23:25 says that there never was another king like Josiah, whose heart, soul, and might were devoted to God and his law.

How can anyone think that God raised up Huldah strictly to humiliate this great man of God? If prophetesses are only God's tools to shame men, as Calvin believed, then why didn't He raise up an anointed *man* for Josiah's sake, to save him the appearance of God-ordained humiliation?

And what about Barak? Why did Deborah prophesy that the honor of the "journey" (battle) would be taken from him and given to a woman? Did God set out to shame Barak for his disobedience? At first glance, it does seem that Barak deserved it.

But this logic fails based on the testimony of Barak

in Heb. 11. There he is listed with the prophets, including David, in the Hall of Faith, a roster of those who obtained a good report because of their faith, not a bad report because of their disobedience.

Rahab is there, too. Remember the Gentile prostitute that housed the two Israelite spies? If God

> *If God uses women only when He wants to shame men, whom does He use to shame women?*

only uses women as a last-ditch effort to get his work done, then it makes no sense that Rahab's name is there. Surely God could have found an honorable man to aid the spies instead of a streetwalker who, according to the law, was worthy of death. God was blessing the Jews for their obedience at the time they overran Jericho. He had no reason to shame them.

If God uses women when his back is against the wall, if women's participation is God's Plan B, his back-up plan, then what was God's Plan A when it came to the birth of Jesus Christ? Only three chapters into the Bible, God foretold his plan to honor a woman as the earthly mother of our Lord. Who was God trying to shame in this instance?

And if God uses women only when He wants to shame men, whom does He use to shame women?

Or, is it that, in the estimation of people who think such things, only the affairs of men are weighty enough to merit God's intervention?

Traditional Treatment of Barak and Others

The problem with traditional treatment of Barak and others is that tradition zeroes in on their sin to the exclusion of the feats God accomplishes by them by faith.

Scripture does the opposite. It records the sin but

97

doesn't dwell on it, then gives a good report of their faith exploits. Faith, not sin, is the Holy Spirit's focus, even if the sin is egregious. God looks for faith. He responds to and rewards faith. His focus is always on the pure heart, filled with faith.

Barak's faith was imperfect but God honored him anyway. The same is true of everyone on the list. Noah had a problem with drink. God told Abraham, the Father of Faith, to leave his relatives behind in Haran because He would make a great nation from him. But Abraham dragged his troublesome nephew along, most likely to provide his childless self with an heir. Yet 22 verses of Rom. 4 are devoted to Abraham's extraordinary faith. Sarah laughed then lied about it when God said she would bear a son. Moses killed a man; he also disobeyed God and struck the rock twice instead of once. Sampson had a terrible problem with lust; he married a heathen because she was pretty. David committed adultery then murder to cover up his sin.

God knew all about the sin of his saints and made sure it was recorded for our sakes. None escaped the consequences, and He demanded their repentance. But once they repented, He extended his grace and mercy and went on with his program. He didn't focus on their failures. He focused on their faith. He wants us to do the same.

The Truth About Deborah

The truth about Deborah is that God looked at her heart, saw that it was pure and full of faith, and for this reason chose her to do his work. God always chooses using the factor of the heart, the part that He alone can see. We choose using our carnal understanding, so our sight is limited. And even if we could see as fully as

God sees, we'd still choose differently because our priorities are not as pure as his.

A biblical example of our limited sight is the experience of the prophet Samuel. Like my former pastor who looked at the vessel—not the contents—and rejected it, on his own Samuel sized up a king for Israel and picked the wrong one (I Sam. 16:6–7). He looked at Jesse's tall, attractive son Eliab and felt certain he was gazing upon Israel's next king. But in v. 7 God said,

> Look not on his countenance, or
> on the height of his stature; because I
> have refused him: for the Lord seeth
> not as man seeth; for man looketh on
> the outward appearance, but the Lord
> looketh on the heart.

God, "... whose eyes run to and fro throughout the whole earth, to shew himself strong in the behalf of them whose heart is perfect toward him" (II Chron. 16:9), does not look for a big, strong man. He'd rather use an unimpressive, weak vessel, because He wants to show *Himself* strong.

The battle is his, not ours (I Sam. 17:47). God performs the work through us, so it doesn't matter if the vessel is male or female. God can save (heal, bless, speak, raise the dead) by many or by few, by big or by small, by male or by female. But to do it He needs a pure heart, full of faith, and most of all, yielded—a spiritual condition that transcends gender.

God does not look for a big, strong man. He'd rather use an unimpressive, weak vessel, because He wants to show Himself strong.

The Truth About Barak

God said He would deliver Sisera into Barak's "hand." The Hebrew root means "the open one." God could only deliver Sisera into Barak's hand if it was open to receive. But Barak shut up his hand, so to speak, by his unbelief; He questioned God's Word.

Barak also focused on the wrong thing. Because of her anointing, he focused his faith on Deborah instead of God's promise to deliver him. His error is similar to the one made by Christians who put their faith for healing in the prayer of an anointed evangelist. We should focus our faith on the settled Word of God, not the man or woman who prays. Just as you can receive healing any time you stand on God's Word without an evangelist's prayer, Barak could have received victory on the strength of God's promise. He didn't need Deborah.

Barak's faith confession determined what he would receive from God.

So why did the Holy Spirit speak by Deborah that a woman would receive the victory? He did so because Barak's words had already determined the outcome of the battle. Barak, not God, intervened and altered the outcome of the prophecy. Barak had put his faith in a woman, so he received victory by a woman. Barak's faith confession determined what he would receive from God. Jael's hand was open to take Sisera's life, but Barak closed his by his words. Barak himself gave away his victory when he insisted Deborah accompany him. God had given him victory, but it was his to give to anyone else. In this case, he gave it to a woman. Just as Jesus told others many times in the Gospels, Barak received according to his faith. In the gospel accounts people demonstrated their faith by confessing what they believed Jesus would do for them ("I

believed, and therefore have I spoken," II Cor. 4:13).
Barak did the same. He opened his mouth and spoke
what he believed: he couldn't be victorious in battle
unless he had help from another. Therefore, the honor
of delivering the death stroke went to another, namely
Jael.

The honor God granted Barak in Heb. 11:32
confirms that God isn't in the business of shaming
anyone. To the contrary, God elevated Barak by giving
him victory despite his unbelief, then praised his
military prowess in Judg. 5, then honored him again by
recording his faith example in Heb. 11.

No, God never set out to shame Barak. Instead,
true to his nature, He forgave his servant and piled on
more honor. The last Old Testament mention of
Deborah and Barak is in Judg. 5:1, 12, 15, and
wherever Deborah's name is listed in connection with
their rejoicing, Barak's name follows immediately
afterward. Verse 15 says that the princes of Issachar
were with Deborah as much as they were with Barak.

You really have to strain to see these passages as
anything less than a testimony of honor heaped upon
two of God's chosen vessels.

Other Biblical Examples

If ever God had opportunity to use a woman to
shame one of his men, it was in Saul's case. Saul's
disobedience certainly merited him a good dose of
shame. In his fear and impatience, he failed to wait for
Samuel to make burned offerings and made them
himself, acting as priest (I Sam. 13). And he disobeyed
God by sparing the lives of King Agag and the
Amalekites' livestock whom he was commanded to kill
(I Sam. 15:9, 15).

But God didn't look for a woman to shame Saul.

The Bible says the Lord took Saul's kingdom from him and then "sought him a man after his own heart" (I Sam. 13:14). God specifically went looking for a "man"—the Hebrew word in this verse means male—because the Israelites had demanded that Samuel anoint them a king (I Sam. 8:5), not a queen.

God said He was looking for a perfect heart, which agrees with II Chron. 16:9. That God searched for a perfect heart and not a woman, which some think would have fittingly shamed Saul, proves that God is more interested in forwarding his redemptive plans for his people than shaming one of his servants for sin. God doesn't have to go out of his way to shame his people. We do a fine job of it all by ourselves.

> *God is more interested in forwarding his redemptive plans for his people than shaming one of his servants for sin.*

Consider the worldly insignificance of other biblical characters and their faith examples. Nothing about these winners suggests the attributes you normally associate with greatness:

- Sarah was a physically dried up woman, a little old lady, when she used her faith to receive the promise that she would be the mother of nations.
- Moses was adopted and nurtured by an idolatrous Egyptian mother, committed murder, fled to avoid the consequences, and yet is admired for his faith, humility, and obedience.
- The widow of Zarephath was near starvation when she obeyed God and gave the prophet her last meal. As a result, she, her son, and Elijah were fed supernaturally during three years of famine.

102

- When Syria besieged Samaria, the aggressive action of four lepers, society's outcasts, ushered an end to the siege and hunger.
- A willing little boy with his simple lunch provided the seed for the harvest of loaves and fishes that Jesus used to feed thousands.

God tells us not to trust in the arm of flesh (II Chron. 32:8). To trust a man to do God's work *because he is a man* is to trust in the arm of flesh. God said it's not by might, nor by power, but by his Spirit (Zech. 4:6) that He accomplishes his will, and He said He would pour out his Spirit upon *all* people (Acts 2:17).

> *To trust a man to do God's work because he is a man is to trust in the arm of flesh.*

You are limited in God's work only by your faith and the amount of the Holy Spirit you receive.

> *You are limited in God's work only by your faith and the amount of the Spirit you receive.*

God's Method of Chastisement

God has always carefully forewarned his people exactly what awful things would happen to them if they sinned. He warned Adam that to eat of a particular tree meant death. He used Moses to warn the Israelites of the curses they would suffer if they disobeyed the law. He sent prophets to warn their descendants that idolatry would bring bondage and destruction. And the New Testament is full of warnings for Christians if they turn from holiness and faith. Warnings and punishment prevail from Genesis to Revelation.

> *Using a woman, solely because she is a woman, to humble his people never has and never will be God's way of doing things.*

In all cases, never, ever from the beginning of the Bible to the end is there any verse that can be used to claim that God elevates women only to shame disobedient men. Using a woman, solely because she is a woman, to humble his people never has and never will be God's way of doing things. To teach such heresy is to shamefully twist Scripture.

When God humbles his people for their disobedience, He does so by one of three scripturally mandated ways: 1) affliction by their enemies (II Chron. 33:9–19; Lev. 26:41); 2) sickness or disease; and 3) poverty (Deut. 8:2–3 and the curses of the law, chapter 28).

God does have a way to correct his people that involves elevating others above them, but it has nothing to do with gender. One of the curses that Moses listed for disobedience reads:

> The stranger that is within thee shall get up above thee very high; and thou shalt come down very low.
> He shall lend to thee, and thou shalt not lend to him: he shall be the head, and thou shalt be the tail.
> Deut. 28:43–44

Gentiles (strangers, foreigners) living within the Israelite's borders would grow more in number and wealth, overtaking the power and material goods that were promised to the Israelites (women too). This would be the antithesis of God's plan for his people outlined in Deut. 28:12–13, wherein God said they would be the head and not the tail and they would lend and not borrow. Nothing in these verses points to the elevation of women as a method of shaming God's people.

> *The notion that God elevates a woman only to shame a man is merely the arrogance of sexism dressed up in religious robes.*

The notion that God elevates a woman only to shame a man is merely the arrogance of sexism dressed up in religious robes. If a man walked in the spirit and not in the fleshly superiority of his mind, he wouldn't interpret God's anointing on women as a slight. Instead, he would desire even more anointing to come upon them to greater advance the Kingdom.

This sexist interpretation of Scripture follows the errant thinking of the man who believes that when a woman gets a good job, it's one less job available for a man. But you rarely find men clamoring for the low paying, low status grunt jobs historically filled by women. It's when women occupy desirable, high paying jobs that you hear murmurs from the male quarter.

Likewise, it's **when women seek respected ministries of authority, especially responsible ones that involve ministering God's Word, that you begin to hear Scripture interpreted in such a way as to restrict them.** No one cares if only women wash the dusty feet of the saints and wipe runny little noses— important but unglamorous

> *Only when women seek respected ministries of authority, especially responsible ones that involve ministering God's Word, do you begin to hear Scripture interpreted in such a way as to restrict them. We don't debate bible verses and their real meaning when women want to stuff envelopes or pick up trash in the church parking lot.*

jobs. We don't debate bible verses and their *real* meaning when women want to stuff envelopes or pick up trash in the church parking lot.

The assumption in the first scenario is that secular jobs are first and foremost meant for men. Women should be satisfied with the leftovers. But isn't God able to supply enough employment for everyone? And isn't He able to supply enough anointing for everyone? Do you worry that the river will run dry? God said it's his will that *all* flesh walks in the anointing. How can God's anointing on *anyone* be anything but positive? And *Who* sends anointing anyway?

The notion that an anointed woman reflects badly on a man erodes a woman's confidence. How can a woman be full of faith if she suspects her ministry is something she's not really meant to have? That God never really wanted to use her? That she is shaming her Christian brothers? That they resent her labors? A woman can't soar to spiritual heights when she is dragging around a heavy chain of doubt about her call. When tradition triumphs over truth, fruitlessness results.

The Deborah Syndrome

The elevate-a-woman-put-down-a-man thinking of my former pastor, Calvin, and others is an example of what I call the Deborah Syndrome. It's religious tradition, thinking not rooted in Scripture. It exalts the flesh over the spirit, infers that women are inferior to men, and fails to give honor to whom it's due. It's insulting to women. We should reject it.

The Deborah Syndrome exposes our lack of respect for women as creatures meet to the task of ruling and reigning.

The Deborah Syndrome exposes our lack of respect for women as creatures meet to the task of ruling and reigning. Women feel it, and it fuels their sense of inferiority.

Respect. R-E-S-P-E-C-T. "All I'm asking for is a little respect when I come home." I'm sorry if you hear Tina Turner belting this out in your head the rest of the day—it seemed appropriate here, because it wasn't in the Church where I learned what respect feels like. It was in the secular world, specifically a publishing house in Birmingham, where I was hired as associate editor in the crafts (quilting) division.

I was young, just 35, when I started at Oxmoor House, and associate editor was the lowest rung of the editorial career ladder. Despite my youth and first-time title, I knew I was respected by my peers, particularly the editors above me in the department. No one told me they respected me or my work. I discerned it by the way I was treated, the increasing responsibility given to me, the discretion in judgment they trusted me with, and the good paycheck I received.

That job gave me a satisfying, complete feeling inside; I knew the respect I enjoyed was genuine. And by experiencing it for the first time, I also knew that I had never received anything like it from the Church. This awareness was a turning point for me. It caused the Church's lack of respect for women as creatures called to have dominion equal to men to come into sharp, painful focus.

A man can't say that he is shamed when a woman is exalted in ministry and then at the same time claim that women have no reason to feel like inferior vessels in the Church. If a man says that God uses a woman only when He has no other choice, or only to shame a man, then that man exposes his carnal opinion that women are inferior, because God, as he sees it, had to find someone lower than (inferior to) himself (the man) for the job.

The preaching of one, that God only uses a woman when He's forced to or only when He wants to shame men, is the antithesis of the other, that men have a genuine respect for women and that women enjoy an equal position in the Kingdom with men.

We are not shamed when someone superior to us is exalted. We expect a superior person to be exalted over us. In fact, a superior person (in skill, ability, or anointing) needn't be exalted for us to feel inferior; their inherent superiority alone makes us feel inferior. We are not shamed when someone equal to us is exalted; we rejoice with or envy them. We are only shamed when someone is exalted who is, in our estimation, lower or inferior than us. The preaching of one, that God only uses a woman when He's forced to or only when He wants to shame men, is the antithesis of the other, that men have a genuine respect for women and that women enjoy an equal position in the Kingdom with men.

If a woman truly is worthy, her exaltation in ministry is lauded as the most reasonable reward for her work.

The confounding part of all this is that women are told that this unscriptural thinking shouldn't affect their estimation of their position in the Kingdom. But how can we think otherwise? How many times have I sat in worship service and listened to some preacher go on and on about how much he respects women, how important our contribution is? (We usually hear this sermon around Mother's Day.) Male ministers perceive that we feel inferior in the Body and need to be reminded of how much respect they *really* have for us.

I contend that if they *really* believe women are equal laborers in the Gospel, then just like my experience at the publishing house, it wouldn't be an issue. But it's always an issue. Every time you read a list of supposedly biblical restrictions on women's ministry, from Phoebe to present day women, right after all the restrictions on what women can and cannot do when it comes to teaching and preaching, there follows a disclaimer listing all the reasons why their limited role is actually *so* important, *so* deserving of honor, *so* worthy of respect.

If women's restricted, collective contribution in the Church is really so important in the big picture, and if we really are so respected by male leadership and others, then why do they keep telling us, over and over again, how much this is so? Why aren't they yet convinced that we feel respected? Do they think we have some doubts?

I don't see how they can think anything else. Because when ministers preach an interpretation of the record of Deborah and other biblical heroines that enshrouds their service not with glory but with shame, it defies common sense to think that women will be blind and deaf to the obvious.

We know our contribution has been belittled.

Hiss #7: You Won't Find a Woman Minister in the Bible

> I commend unto you Phoebe our sister, which is a servant of the church which is at Cenchrea:
>
> That ye receive her in the Lord, as becometh saints, and that ye assist her in whatsoever business she hath need of we:
>
> for she hath been a succourer of many, and of myself also.
>
> Rom. 16:1–2 (KJV)

Phoebe

Why did translators render *diakonos* to mean "servant" to describe Phoebe, a woman, but rendered it "minister" to describe Timothy and other men? Paul used the same, gender-neutral word to describe the gospel labor of them all, but translators made a significant change, and it *does* make a difference to the reader.

Paul called Phoebe a succourer, or *prostatis*, the feminine form of *proistemi*, meaning to stand before, to preside over by rank, to maintain, be over, or rule. Any of these definitions is consistent with the work of a gospel minister, especially because *diakonos* means a Christian teacher and pastor.

Paul told the Hebrews to assist Phoebe in whatever she needed. Her work was important to Paul or he wouldn't have admonished the saints to cooperate with her goals. Still, many today refuse to acknowledge any biblical examples of women ministers.

Dr. C.I. Scofield (Scofield Bible) was one of the refusers. He called the ordination of women an abomination.[1] Dr. Scofield erred along the usual traditional lines. He confused the brother-sister relationship between Christian men and women with female submission to male authority, a relationship found only in marriage. Immediately after Scofield blasted the ordination of women, he reminded us of the "prohibition" of Gen. 3:16, "and he shall rule over thee," and I Tim. 2:13, "For Adam was first formed, then Eve."

Some of Scofield's and others' confusion can be blamed on KJV translators, who used "man" and "brother" to mean, at different times, husband or all Christian people, but some is due to translator bias. A look at several versions illustrates this:

1) From 1380 until 1901, only a few translations existed. The first English Bible by Wycliffe (1388) was quickly followed by five others, all within 231 years. Ending with the KJV, these nine were the predominant sources of spiritual light for the English-speaking world. Compared to the frequency of new translations that we see now, they enjoyed an enduring impact: 621 years. Not until the American Standard Revised

---

[1]Pohle, Ella E. *Dr. C.I. Scofield's Question Box.*
Moody Press, Chicago, Ill., no date or place given, p. 159.

Version of 1901 did their influence, and especially the KJV, begin to wane.

2) After 1901, new versions were often only paraphrases. The translator's goal was to put the Bible into common vernacular, not to provide a literal understanding of Hebrew and Greek. Though at times paraphrases can be enormously helpful, it's amazing how often they cloud the sense of the original language.

In the table that follows, all KJV verses cited are ones where *diakonos* was applied to a person of explicit gender. In every case this was a man, except for Rom. 16:1, the first verse, that describes Phoebe. *Diakonos* was translated in other places in the Bible, but in those citations no gender is stated or implied, so they can't be used for comparison.

How was diakonos translated when referring to a specific person?

Verse	Man or Woman?	Translation
Rom. 16:1	Phoebe/Woman	Servant
Eph. 3:7	Paul/Man	Minister
Eph. 6:21	Tychicus/Man	Minister
Col. 1:7	Epaphras/Man	Minister
Col. 1:23	Paul/Man	Minister
Col. 1:25	Paul/Man	Minister
Col. 4:7	Tychicus/Man	Minister
1 Thes. 3:2	Timotheus/Man	Minister
1 Tim. 4:6	Timothy/Man	Minister

Every version refers to Paul and Epaphras as ministers. The New American Bible of 1970, a Catholic publication, refers to only Timothy as something other than minister: "brother and co-worker." Ironically, translators faithfully translated all other gender-specific instances of *diakonos* as "minister," including the one describing Phoebe, though the Catholic Church is notorious for its refusal to ordain women to do that very thing.

A scan of the matrix reveals the translators' ambivalence about women ministers. Paul used one word to describe the ministry of these four men and one woman, but translators were uncomfortable with the thought of a woman minister, so they substituted an alternate, less ministry-specific word. Yet 92 percent of the times *diakonos* appears in the KJV New Testament it was translated "minister." This proves three things: 1) They knew what it meant; 2) They translated consistently when it came to men; and, 3) Just how outrageous it was for them to translate the word differently to describe Phoebe.

Gender is the only distinguishing feature to explain their switch from "minister" to "servant," or "almoner," (Thomson translation—a person who distributes food and clothing—not God's Word—to the poor) or "deaconess" to describe Phoebe. It's no coincidence that 78 percent of the renderings of *diakonos* as something other than "minister" apply to the one woman. The switch itself is the issue here, not that *diakonos* was rendered "minister," "deacon," or "servant." How they rendered it wouldn't matter if only they had done so consistently.

Tragically, after the 1568 publication of the Bishops Bible, you never again see Phoebe portrayed as a minister of God's Word. Instead, she is 1) "serving," which can mean who-knows-what; 2) distributing food and clothing to the poor; or, as you shall see, 3) tending the sick. These ministries are good and important. But why was Phoebe, and not the four men named, limited only to these works when Paul used a term that means pastor and teacher to describe her?

Translators stripped the Bible of a faith picture of a woman minister by substituting a variety of vague terms that share a common denominator: none describes Phoebe as a minister of God's Word. Worse, we have translators and others such as Thomson going out of their way to explain how Phoebe specifically did *not* minister the Word. Thomson's rendering of *diakonos* to mean "almoner" is egregious bias. The Greeks had three words that meant charity worker, and none came from *diako,* from which Paul got *diakonos*.

Wesley also strained to add his own peculiar limitation to the office of *diakonos* as it pertained only to Phoebe (and all women). In his *Explanatory Notes on the New Testament*, he qualified the term to mean "deaconess," which it can mean, though he didn't qualify it to mean "deacon" where it described men. Women described by *diakonos*, he said, were limited to one area of ministry and specifically excluded from another:

> In the apostolic age, some grave and pious women were appointed deaconesses in every church. It was their office, *not to teach publicly*, but to visit the sick, the women in particular, and to minister to them both in their temporal and spiritual necessities.[23] (emphasis mine)

It's difficult to comprehend how Wesley came to his narrow conclusion, other than by cultural influence, as Paul himself said that Phoebe had ministered to (succoured) him, and Paul was no woman. Further, Paul admonished the Philippians to help "those women which laboured" (or "wrestled in company" from Greek

---

[2]Wesley's notes on Rom. 16.
[3] Wesley's notes on Rom. 16.

sunathleo) with him in the Gospel (Phil. 4:3).

The Virtuous Woman

Let's return to *chayil*. This is the Word used in Prov. 31 to describe that busy woman. Faith Martin discovered questionable renderings of *chayil* in a modern translation, the Revised Standard Version (RSV). Translators rendered it to mean "brave" ("Jeroboam was a mighty man of *valour*" I Kings 11:28) when speaking of men but "good" or "virtuous" when speaking of women (Prov. 12:4, Ruth 3:11). *Chayil* is translated "valour" 36 times in the KJV Old Testament to describe a man. But the same translators never rendered it "valour" to describe a woman, even though the Holy Spirit used it for both.

The problem is sex. Pre-17th century translators couldn't shake their fixation with women's sexual purity. From the New Testament, Martin notes:

> The Greek word *sophrosune* means 'sane' or 'self-controlled.' The Revised Standard Version translates it 'modest' when women are discussed (I Tim. 2:15) and 'sensible' when men are the subject (I Tim. 3:2). If Paul used the same word for men and women, why didn't the translators do the same? Translators have given us brave and sensible men but kept the women virtuous and modest. The translators have made subtle decisions with enormous implications at a level where the ordinary reader is helpless to

discern their prejudice.[4]

And here's a twist on "valour" (valor). Hebrew writers described God's men *and women* as exhibiting valor, or bravery. But Andelin, who purportedly assesses the feminine nature from Scripture, maintains that it's not the work of the Holy Spirit but a bad career choice that brings about bravery (boldness) in a woman, a trait which she says exclusively belongs to men by design. Aggressiveness, boldness, capability, efficiency, and independence are traits for men, says Andelin, and, if nurtured in a woman, result in the loss of feminine "charm."

Deborah the prophetess may have a bone to pick with Andelin on this one. Had she been more "feminine" and less "masculine," her story of triumph for Israel might have ended in failure. The same is true for Jael. If she had been an Andelin devotee, she might have beaten Sisera to death with a lipstick case instead of braining him with a tent peg, but it wouldn't have convinced me of greater femininity on her part.

If we think the Prov. 31 woman should be lauded primarily for her virtue—moral excellence and chaste behavior—then we don't benefit from the lesson on strength that the Holy Spirit meant to impart. If we knew this and taught it to girls and women, we'd have churches full of females striving for spiritual strength in addition to moral chastity.

Priscilla

Priscilla (Prisca) is an important New Testament figure because she doesn't fit the traditional mold at all. Each of the six times her name is mentioned it's linked

---

[4]Quoted in Tucker, p. 197.

with her husband's, and half the time her name is listed first, a special honor considering the tradition of the day, suggesting that their ministries were tightly bound.

Paul praised her dedication to the Gospel. Of her and her husband, Aquila, he said, "Who have for my life laid down their own necks" (Rom. 16:4). What did Priscilla do for Paul that endangered her life? God's Word is not explicit. But just by traveling with him she put herself at risk. Paul lived under constant threat of persecution and death from the Jews; his account of physical suffering in II Cor. 11:27 would have discouraged the faint hearted. Priscilla's co-laborer status with Paul, his commendation of her work, and her fearlessness suggest she labored publicly and did a lot more than just make safe, private visits to sick women and children.

Chloe

> For it hath been declared unto me
> of you, my brethren, by them *which are*
> *of the house* of Chloe, that there are
> contentions among you.
> I Cor. 1:11

For years I read this verse and interpreted it like this: "Some members of Chloe's family told me that you are having problems getting along." Then one day I read a modern translation that spoke of these unnamed people not as family but Christians who met at her house. Then I thought that Chloe, a woman, must have offered her house for home meetings. How nice.

Friend, this Scripture means neither. The italicized words did not appear in Paul's letter but were added by translators. What Paul wrote was this, "For it hath been declared unto me of you, my brethren, by them of

Chloe, that there are contentions among you."

But what does "of Chloe" mean?

The answer is in the next verse. "Now this I say, that every one of you saith, I am of Paul; and I of Apollos; and I of Cephas; and I of Christ." To be "of" someone is to follow that person's teachings. Nowadays some are "of" Kenneth Copeland or "of" Joyce Meyer, or others. It simply means we're one of their students, and likely our doctrine sounds like theirs.

Adding to God's Word robs it of power.

That's what Paul meant when he wrote about those "of Chloe." They followed her teachings. She was their teacher. But translators couldn't believe what Paul had said about Chloe and added their own spin to the verse. Adding to God's Word robs it of power. Chloe is still there, but a record of her gospel work and spiritual leadership has been stripped from the passage.

Why, you are thinking, *is this woman making such a big deal about Bible women and how translators treat them? Sounds feminist to me.* But it isn't. Not all women are called to the five-fold ministries, just as not all men are called. But women in every age look to the Bible to establish their identity as Christians. They want role models. They want to know what they can and cannot do for the Gospel. They want to know how others did it, what God expects of them, what they can expect of God, and how to prepare. When we translate God's Word in a way that trivializes women's contribution by calling them charity workers instead of ministers of God's Word, or deny their work entirely, women are short-changed. And it's sexism.

Women must see themselves ministering God's Word *in God's Word* before they'll pick up a Bible and go do it.

Hiss #8: Jesus Did Not Set Us Free to Minister

There is neither male nor female.
Gal. 3:28

What did Paul mean when he said there is now
neither male nor female? Aren't we all one or the other?
Know anyone who isn't? Paul surely wasn't preaching
the end of gender boundaries—too many verses
contradict that. Two thousand years after Paul penned
these words, men are still fathering babies and women
are still delivering them. So what was it about being
male or female that disappeared in Christ?

Traditional teaching of this verse sounds
something like this: Now that we are all under the blood
of Jesus Christ, when God looks at us, He sees only the
righteousness of his Son, not us. He no longer sees Jew,
Gentile, slave, free, male or female, only Christ. We are
dead, hidden in Him.

Although these facts about our new nature in
Christ are true, they are not the thrust of this verse.
Traditional interpretation has buried its power to free.
Other Scriptures explain how we are new creatures in

Christ. This verse confirms that and more.

Six Classes of Bible Characters

Paul speaks of six distinct classes, and I do mean classes, of people. The old covenant assigned each a particular status from birth, with different rules for worship. There were also vast cultural differences between them, such as dress, social expectations, and so forth. But in this study, we're only concerned with their individual covenant status.

Jews. These were God's chosen people, Abraham and his blood descendants, who enjoyed every temporal and spiritual blessing, including possession of the Promised Land and the hope of the Messiah. God declared them holy, sealing his covenant into the flesh of Jewish males by circumcision, emphasizing their spiritual separation from the world. He honored them by entrusting them with his law, which enhanced their sense of divinity and prestige.

Greeks. In the KJV this word means a non-Jewish person. Jews of Bible times recognized only two kinds of people, themselves and everyone else. For simplicity, all non-Jews in this study are called Gentiles.

Old Testament law was specific and repetitious regarding the Jews' relationship to Gentiles. They were to have nothing to do with them. They were not to mingle with them, not marry them, and especially not have anything to do with their pagan gods.

Segregation by holy writ continued in the New Testament. The Samaritan woman was surprised when Jesus requested she draw water for Him and said so (John 4) because Jews had nothing to do with Samaritans since they were only part Jewish. Samaritans descended from Jews who had intermarried with Syrians when they overran the northern Israelite kingdom in 722 B.C. As a result, Jews viewed Samaritans as filthy mutts because of their mingled bloodlines. Even Jesus called the woman of Canaan a "dog" when she came begging Him to heal her daughter (Matt. 15).

Whereas God opened his storehouse of blessings to the Jews, Gentiles were outside the covenant and could expect nothing. We read of a few exceptions, however. Besides the Canaanite woman just mentioned, whose daughter Jesus did heal, Rahab the prostitute from Jericho and Ruth the Moabitess were spared destruction because of their faith. God also made provision to save the house guests of the Hebrews as they prepared the first passover in Egypt.

But until Christ came, God extended favor to only a handful of Gentiles, consequently the Jews looked down their noses at them. Their condescending attitude was based on the Gentiles' covenant status. Jews still felt that way about Gentiles when Jesus arrived.

Bond. We don't have a clear picture of bond people (slaves) as did biblical Jews because few, if any, of us have known or lived as slaves. The covenant made a distinction between servants and slaves and how Jews were to treat them (Lev. 25:39–40). Often servants were Jews who served other Jews temporarily to pay off debts. But the law forbade Jews to make slaves out of their own people. That meant all slaves were of Gentile blood, which only served to lower, if it were possible, the status of a slave in the eyes of Jews.

Slaves in Israel had no legal rights. They were outside the covenant and could claim none of its privileges. Levitical law declared enemies captured in battle to be slaves forever. They owned nothing, not their bodies, their lives, their children, their spouses, clothes, or food. They could expect only a life of hard labor from capture until death. Worse, they could expect no better for their children, as slaves were not automatically set free in the year of jubilee as were hired servants.

Female slaves, like Hagar, were often drafted as concubines.

As with their masters, however, slaves refrained from working on the Sabbath, participated in religious ceremonies, and males participated in circumcision. Male slaves and foreigners became as "one that is born in the land" (Exod. 12:48–49) if they were circumcised.

Free. In the Roman world, freedom conferred at birth was the primary distinction between peoples. A free person was unrestrained, says the Greek, to go at pleasure as a citizen and specifically not a slave. Free persons, men and women, Jews and Gentiles, enjoyed privileges denied to slaves, except for free women, who had fewer choices and rights than men.

Birth distinction was important; one could never escape the status of one's birth. Freed slaves carried in their titles the lesser distinction of being former property, "freedman" and "freedwoman," and never enjoyed the full status of freeborns. Children born to them while in bondage remained their masters' property. If they died without heirs their property reverted to their masters, and they could not serve in high military positions or hold public office.[1]

Male. The law treated men with a deference and distinction in spiritual matters that is difficult to comprehend in this day of equal rights. Jewish and Gentile men alone were educated in letters and numbers and only Jewish men were taught Scripture. Only male Levites could minister among the holy things in the temple, and only adult males counted as participating members of the tribes and were accorded privileges

---

[1] *Harper's Bible Dictionary*, p. 322.

thereto. Laws regarding redemption of vows set a higher price for males than females, and only firstborn males were consecrated to the Lord.

Female. Women fared better than slaves but worse than men. Their persons were their fathers' property, and when they married, their husbands'. A woman's father could sell her as a servant but she couldn't expect to be set free automatically in the seventh year as would a male (Exod. 21:7). Jewish women made vows to God only by permission from father or husband.

Contrary to tradition about women having no say in choosing a husband, Num. 36:6 granted women choice if the man was from their own tribe. Even so, the comforts of marriage weren't guaranteed. Though a man could divorce his wife for just about any "uncleanness" in her, a woman had no legal right to make a divorce claim for any reason.

Jewish women inherited their parents' property only if they had no living brother and only if they married within their tribe. When widowed they didn't necessarily regain their freedom. A needy Jewish widow customarily moved in with her deceased husband's family and often married his brother. This normally was a blessing and not a bondage, however, as the stigma of nonvirginity made a widow less marriageable and hence reduced her chances of reestablishing her primary source of income. Even though the law gave widows gleaning rights and a portion of the third-year tithe, from the Old Testament to the New, the problem of neglected and hungry widows is mentioned frequently. As a class, women were unschooled and ignorant.

Although men and women alike were considered unclean under certain condition such as leprosy, sexual sins, and consumption of unclean animals, only women were subject to the stigma of uncleanness by gender.

Women were considered unclean 13 weeks a year due to menstruation and for a time after childbirth, and twice as long after the birth of a daughter than a son. Consequently they couldn't enter the temple or touch holy things as often as men.

Most important to this study, however, is the issue of circumcision. Unlike Jewish men, women did not carry in their bodies this token of covenant relationship, a mark of distinction and honor, a sign of intimacy with and lifelong commitment to God. That God abolished the symbol that honored men and bypassed women is significant to understand the status that women now enjoy under the new covenant. I will discuss this more later.

Relationship to the Covenant

All six classes had one thing in common: Birth alone was the factor that determined their covenant status. From birth Jews could make a claim to covenant blessings. From birth Gentiles were outside the covenant because they didn't descend from Abraham. From birth slaves were locked into the lowest caste in society and excluded from the covenant even if they lived, one generation to the next, among the Jews. From birth free men enjoyed worldly rights and privileges denied women. From birth Jewish women were forbidden from participation in nearly every form of temple worship. Covenant status conferred at birth extended until death.

Understand too that the role of religion deeply affected how these people saw themselves. The Hebrew language of Old Testament times did not even embody the concept of religion. They had no word for it.[2] The covenant defined who and what they were; religion and self were inseparable. Remember this when you read Gal. 3:28.

Scholars date Paul's letter to the Galatians between 48 and 56 A.D., about 20 years after Christ's ascension, barely a generation. If you consider that the oldest writings of the Bible date to approximately 2,000 B.C., it's no wonder the Galatian Jews had a difficult time accepting Gentile converts. Twenty years is but a moment when compared to the influence the covenant had wielded over the Jews for generations.

The Lesson of the Galatian Jews

Into this narrow world came Paul, a Jew trained in the law. Paul's discourse on the law and the six classes was provoked by a disturbing incident. Because Peter, Paul's coworker in the Gospel, knew that the restriction regarding eating with Gentiles had been lifted in Christ, he was happy to take his meals with new Gentile converts. However, when critical Jews (Judaizers, those who had been taught the way of faith v. works but refused to walk in the new way of liberty) were watching, Peter removed himself from the Gentiles' table so as not to offend the Jews. Worse, other Jews followed Peter's lead and refused to eat with them.

With little imagination, you can hear those indignant Jews exclaiming in horror, "But they're Gentiles!"

Paul couldn't overlook Peter's hypocrisy, so from Gal. 2:14 to 3:28 he schooled them on the purpose of

---

[2]Friedman, Richard Elliott. *Who Wrote the Bible?* Summit Books, New York, 1987,
    pp. 37–38.

the law and justification by faith. "O foolish Galatians," he said, as he chastised those who insisted on referring to the former distinctions of the law by treating the Gentiles as though they were still unclean. Paul marveled that they so quickly turned back to the rigorous tenets of the law when, "Know ye therefore that they which are of faith, the same are the children of Abraham" (Gal. 3:7). The law, he said, was only a teacher to point them in the right direction, to help them understand the holiness of God and the enormity of their sin. Now that the way of faith had been revealed, they no longer needed a teacher. And then,

> For ye are all the children of God by faith in Christ Jesus.
> For as many of you as have been baptized into Christ have put on Christ.
> There is neither Jew nor Greek, there is neither bond nor free, there is neither male nor female: for ye are all one in Christ Jesus.
> And if ye be Christ's, then are ye Abraham's seed, and heirs according to the promise.
>
> Gal. 3:26–29

In Christ no spiritual distinctions exist between Jew and Gentile, slave and free, man and woman. Restricting people in the free exercise of their new faith by reference to the law is no longer acceptable, because now we look to the cross, not the law, to fulfill all righteousness.

These verses summarize what Paul said from Gal. 2:14 up to this point. Contrary to traditional teaching, his closing verses do not preach a message only to help us understand our new relationship to God. Paul also tries to make us understand *our new relationship to one another.* In Christ no spiritual distinctions exist between Jew and Gentile, slave and free, man and woman. Restricting people in the free exercise of their new faith by reference to the law is no longer acceptable, because now we look to the cross, not the law, to fulfill all righteousness.

The removal of spiritual distinctions between us is the only interpretation that makes sense to apply to Gal. 3:28, because clearly, *natural* distinctions still exist. Paul said there is now no Jew, Gentile, slave, free, male, or female. But obviously all of them still walk the earth today in the flesh. We

> *The removal of spiritual distinctions between us is the only interpretation that makes sense to apply to Gal. 3:28, because clearly, **natural** distinctions still exist.*

conclude, therefore, that Paul must have been talking about a change that occurred in the spiritual, not natural realm.

And what was the Jews' basis for the former spiritual distinctions? It was the law. Everything the Jews ever believed about the need to restrict women in temple service or to deny covenant privileges to slaves and Gentiles they believed because they read it in the law. But the whole point, Paul said, is that the law has been abolished—it died. And when it died, so died the grounds for making spiritual distinctions. The restrictions on Gentiles, slaves, and women were put aside when the law was put aside.

Had Paul not put a stop to this early spiritual nepotism, today there might be two ministry tiers. "Real" Jews, of blood descent, might be the preachers, teachers, music ministers, and so forth: those who minister God's Word and Spirit. Meanwhile, Gentile

Christians might be limited to handling the nonholy things: the toilet-cleaning, vestibule-sweeping, envelope-stuffing areas of ministry. These are necessary but are not the holy things indicative of the priesthood.

The Bible calls this practice being a "respecter of persons." Now we call it discrimination, and in the Church it's an unthinkable sin but not a new one. In Acts 6:1 Greek converts complained against the Jews because Greek widows were neglected in the daily food distribution. It doesn't say they *thought* they were neglected. It says they *were* neglected. Naturally the Greeks were resentful.

Revival of the Distinctions of the Covenant

When it comes to men and women, the two-tiered system still enjoys support. A good example is found in *Recovering Biblical Manhood and Womanhood*, where S. Lewis Johnson, Jr. maintains that "There is no reason to claim that Gal. 3:28 supports an egalitarianism of function in the church."[3] Johnson says historical orthodoxy concludes that Gal. 3:28 is inserted into the Bible to "affirm[s] the full equality of males and females 'in Christ,'"[4] which is a roundabout way of saying that equality is strictly in the unseen realm and has nothing to do with the functioning body of Christ.

This is like saying women and men are equal, but only up there and not down here. Are we equal *to* Heaven but not *on* earth? Are we equal only in an

---

[3] Johnson, S. Lewis, Jr. *Recovering Biblical Manhood and Womanhood.* "Role Distinctions in the Church, Galatians 3:28." Crossway Books, Wheaton, Ill., 1991, p. 164.

[4] Lewis, p. 163.

abstract, psychological way? Or are we equal in the eyes of God but not to each other? How can we be equal as Christians but not enjoy access to the same gifts and callings?

What does equal mean, anyway? It seems to me that if one-half of the Church is cut off from certain gifts or works of the Holy Spirit, then that is a most *unequal* position in the Body.

Further, Johnson fails to consistently apply his logic. He condones a functional application of the liberty granted to Gentiles in Gal. 3:28, that they come to Christ and become fully participating members of the Body, denied no ministry function. Likewise, Johnson condones a functional application of the liberty granted to slaves, that they come to Christ and become fully participating members of the Body, again denied no ministry function.

But when it comes to women, Johnson alters his interpretation of Gal. 3:28 to mean a strictly ethereal application. But if no reason exists to claim that Gal. 3:28 supports an egalitarianism of function in the Church, as he asserts, then to consistently apply his logic you must conclude that Gentiles and slaves also cannot expect egalitarianism of function. If Johnson is correct, then we have no grounds to claim that Gentiles and slaves can operate in any of the five-fold ministries, the same ones he suggests can be denied to women.

To be consistent in his logic, Johnson must agree that Christ has opened the doors of salvation to Gentiles and slaves but they, like women, have no new covenant claim to the royal priesthood. Or, perhaps, he means we now have two classes of priests, one restricted, one unrestricted.

I pose this question to Johnson and all who think like him: If the freedom granted to women in Gal. 3:28 is not functional, then what freedom does it grant *that they didn't already have?* Salvation? Jewish women had it. Temporal blessings? They had them. Access to God? They took the same route men did. The honor of being his chosen people? They had it. The honor of bearing his name? They had it. The law and the covenant? Yep, you guessed it, they had those too. (Although women were not formally trained in the law, they did hear it when it was read publicly.)

What was it that Christ gave women in Gal. 3:28 that they didn't have before the cross?

Just in case it isn't plain by now, I'll spell it out. *Before Christ, religious restrictions on women were strictly functional ones.* They were not allowed to serve in the temple or to handle the holy things of the priesthood. *Women were restricted only in service.*

> *That's what Christ purchased for them on the cross: Freedom to serve. The holy things under New Testament dispensation are God's Word and Spirit. If Gal. 3:28 can't be applied functionally to women, if they can't minister God's Word and Spirit, then they haven't been freed at all.*

That's what Christ purchased for them on the cross: Freedom to serve. The holy things under New Testament dispensation are God's Word and Spirit. If Gal. 3:28 can't be applied functionally to women, if they can't minister God's Word and Spirit, then they haven't been freed at all.

If Gal. 3:28 freed Gentiles and slaves to minister, it freed women, too. That's why Paul lumped the six classes together. When Christ removed restrictions from one class, He removed them from them all. Completely. Without limit. Forever.

Christ also removed the distinction of circumcision, which is more than symbolic. In the past the covenant signature was written upon the flesh of men alone. As with other religious exercises, women partook only vicariously. It's no small thing that now the priesthood demands spiritual circumcision of the heart, a

> *Circumcision of the heart is the great equalizer: no more is maleness a prerequisite to serve.*

similarly intimate submission of self, *but an experience that is available to everyone.* Circumcision of the heart is the great equalizer: no more is maleness a prerequisite to serve.

Now that the gender barrier is gone, you have all the evidence you need to say boldly that God is looking for a prepared heart, a circumcised heart, and not necessarily a man's, to do his work. The New Testament says the Holy Spirits gives ministries and spiritual gifts to whomever He chooses. The only birth distinction now is spiritual, the new birth of the Spirit.

Tucker addresses Johnson' illogical argument by comparing it to the dilemma of perceived worth of occupational roles in society:

> I do not know of anyone who would say there is a necessary relation between personal role and personal worth. A business executive, for example, has no greater worth than the night janitor who cleans the office. And, no one, I hope, would suggest that a White business executive is of greater worth than a Black janitor. But if someone were to suggest that "business executive" is a role limited to Caucasians, and that African-Americans cannot fill that role, then the issue of personal worth is very relevant. Why is the African-American denied a

particular role solely on the basis of
race? Is the African-American inferior
or less worthy in some respect? Past
generations have made this case, but
that makes it no less abhorrent.

The case for women is no
different. If all women are denied
certain roles solely because of their
gender, it does relate to their worth—to
their lack of equality—just as it does
for African-Americans. [5] (emphasis
Tucker)

Johnson supports his ideas about supposed biblical
restrictions on women by what he calls "historical
primacy." That is, "If the Christian church has held this
view for centuries with Bible in hand, then you may
presume that there exists some good reason for that
fact."[6] In other words, we've always done it this way,
so it must be right.

Jewish men of Jesus' time believed in historical
primacy too. For 2,000 years they divorced their wives
for any reason because that's what their fathers had
done. And White churches in America for 300 years
actively discouraged Black membership, citing the
Bible's curse on Ham and other reasons, until as
recently as the 1960s.

The Progression of Restrictions on Women

Johnson is wrong. The Church has not held this
view for centuries. The Church's attitude toward
women ministers has evolved considerably since the

---

[5] Tucker, p. 249.
[6] Lewis, p. 164.

beginning and they're still evolving. Some camps are becoming more liberal, others more restrictive. Witness the subtle changes over the centuries in Bible verses that deal with women:

1380 – First English Bible, Wycliffe Version:
"But I suffer not a woman to teach: neither to have lordship on the husband ..." At first, women were only forbidden to teach or have authority over their husbands, a proscription that complements the Gen. 3:16 curse and five New Testament verses that deal with wifely submission. Nor does it oppose Gal. 3:28. Wycliffe translated husband from Greek *aner*, which means two things: a male individual or husband. The Greeks used the one word to convey either concept. Remember this. It's important.

1611 – KJV
"But I suffer not a woman to teach, nor to usurp authority over the man ..." But then, 231 years later, a change. Translators now imply that women cannot teach or usurp authority from any man, not just their husbands, moving from one man to all men—a much more restrictive interpretation.

This one-word change created a cloud of confusion. People wondered, reasonably, if there were any unusual and acceptable circumstances when a woman could teach a man. On the mission field? When her pastor-husband dies? When she is older than her students and more respected or more trained? Some denominations allow women to teach men in these situations.

The real tragedy of this one-word change, however, is the stigma it puts upon women. If God doesn't want them to teach men, the thinking goes, there must be something flawed about them spiritually, mentally, or both. We feel compelled to explain this supposed flaw, trying to make sense of the restriction. This leads to all kinds of wild ideas about God, women, and the Bible. And amazingly, although no one can intelligently explain why women aren't fit to teach to men, everyone thinks the Bible supports the mystery.

1952 – Revised Standard Version
"I permit no woman to teach or to have authority over men ..."
1973 – New International Version
"I do not permit a woman to teach or to have authority over a man ..." Then, 340 years later, a subtle but insidious shift. Now the admonition is not aimed at women, instructing them to refrain from *usurping* authority. Instead, it's aimed at Church leadership, directing them not to *grant* authority to women, as women can only "have" authority that has been granted to them by another. The result is the exclusion of women from all teaching, administrative, and leadership positions over men. This further solidified the residual Old Testament notion that women, being somehow unexplainably an underclass, should be barred from teaching, except to teach children and other women. About this same period comes the most restrictive interpretation of all:

1970 – New English Bible
"I do not permit a woman to be a teacher, nor must woman domineer over man ..." Now it appears that women are so suspect that they can't be trusted to teach anyone at all, not men, children, or other women. Yet they're still allowed to prophesy, because God's Word is so plain in allowing them this freedom that a biblical mandate is beyond question.

Prophetess or teacher, what does it matter? What

comes out of a woman's mouth is reliable or it isn't. It's illogical to say a woman's prophecy is trustworthy but her teaching is suspect. It's the same vessel. Remember, all other verses that deal with teaching ministries make no restriction on women.

This narrow interpretation should not surprise. The translators of the New English Bible also maintain that a woman is "saved through motherhood." The result of faulty translation and interpretation is doubt and confusion about women in ministry, therefore fewer women to spread the Gospel.

Why do we twist ourselves into religious pretzels? We do it because the issue of authority dominates our thinking about women in ministry far more than it should. So much, in fact, that to continue our study of Gal. 3:28, we must detour here to look at the traditional view of women and authority. Because wherever women and ministry are the issues, the notion that women are born under universal male spiritual authority is right there to constrain it.

Listen carefully to the following arguments and you'll hear a familiar echo, the horrified gasp of the first Jewish Christians, passing down through the ages, bouncing back and forth off the canyon walls of ignorance ... "But she's a woman!"

Hiss #9: You Are Under Authority in a Way Men Aren't

> Wives, be in subjection to your own husbands.
> I Pet. 3:1

Several years ago I had a memorable conversation with the administrator of a huge, metropolitan, evangelical church. We were on the subject of women teachers and preachers when I asked him whether his church encouraged women to use the pulpit.

No, he said. Women must be under authority.

Women must be under authority. Women must be under authority. I mulled over that one for months. I had heard the line many times before, but it still bothered me. It was tough to accept that God had made me a member of the Church's underclass, born to be *under* authority to another group—always male.

But this time I was not sad but angry, angry at myself. The man's self-assured, cursory response provoked me. Something didn't feel right about it, but I didn't have the Bible answer that really satisfied, and that bugged me.

Many questions came to mind. What's the connection between authority and women? Why does a woman come out from under it when she ministers God's Word? Weren't women commanded to publish the good news too? Under authority to whom? God? Men? When and why were we put there? And where in the Bible is the blueprint for this type of submission?

I began a thorough search of the Bible, looking for a pattern of universal female submission to male authority. By that I mean I went looking for a pattern wherein I could see for myself that women, by gender alone, are under an authority that men are not under.

> *No pattern exists in the Bible that indicates that women, because they are born female, are under more authority, a different level of authority, or a different type of authority than men.*

I never found what I sought. No pattern exists in the Bible that indicates that women, because they are born female, are under more authority, a different level of authority, or a different type of authority than men.

But thank God, He has left us a clear, consistent pattern of female submission of a particular kind. And it's a good one, too. In fact, God's plan for female submission is easy to prove and easy to bear.

Thank God also that his Word always agrees with itself. You never have to strain to understand a difficult passage, using only that one as a key. The Holy Spirit confirms truth by complementary types in the Bible on every subject. If a hard passage seems to contradict an easy one, then you must go back to the hard one, pray, and research until they agree. Now let's look at his pattern.

Biblical Pattern of Female Submission to Male Authority

The earthly pattern of female submission to male authority is a picture of the heavenly, portrayed in both Old and New Testaments. It is marked by certain prerequisites. In every case, they are:

1) Blood covenant
2) An exchange of something valuable
3) A date when the covenant begins
4) Voluntary consent to submit, and
5) A fruit-producing union.

If any of the five prerequisites are missing, then you may have a biblical pattern of something, but it isn't a biblical pattern of female submission, which is ultimately the picture of Christ and his bride.

The first prerequisite, **blood covenant**, is the cornerstone of biblical female submission. In the Old Testament God made the first covenant with the Israelites, whom He called his wife, referring to Himself as her husband. He made it with Abraham and sealed it in the blood of an animal.

In the New Testament God made the second covenant with Abraham's heirs, also sealed it in blood, the blood of Christ, the Bridegroom. The Church is his bride. The earthly picture of the heavenly union is the marriage covenant between human husband and wife. They consummate their union by marital relations, which typifies the blood. In every biblical pattern a union as intimate as that between husband and wife is the picture God uses to portray the loving relationship He wants to establish with us.

Why a covenant? A publicly made covenant, or contract, is necessary to protect both parties. It assures mutual and exclusive commitment.

In both spiritual and earthly patterns, the female figure always submits to the authority of the male figure, and him only, with whom she made the covenant. For example, the Israelites entered into covenant with and were submitted to only Jehovah; the Church has entered into covenant with and is submitted to only Christ; and a woman enters into covenant with and submits to only her husband.

The second prerequisite is an **exchange of something valuable**, not necessarily in equal portions. It's an ongoing, mutual surrender of self for the benefit of the other.

In the Old Testament God offered the Israelites forgiveness, the material benefits of his Kingdom, victory over their enemies, and countless other blessings in exchange for worship and obedience.

In the New Testament Christ shed his blood to cleanse our sin, redeemed us from Satan's kingdom, promised to share his own with us, and gave us eternal life in exchange for worship and obedience.

In marriage, husband and wife vow to exchange love, honor, worldly goods, "for richer or for poorer," care for one another, "in sickness and in health," and so forth, until death.

The exchange must be a cognizant one. In spiritual and earthly patterns, both parties must understand the terms and obligations of the covenant before they confirm it. God never invites us to enter into a covenant with Him without first explaining his expectations of us and his obligations to us. God told Abraham what He wanted from Him and what He would do for Him in exchange. He does the same for the Church.

In many earthly jurisdictions, failure to be informed of or understand one's obligations renders a contract null and void.

In marriage, husband and wife also have mutual expectations and obligations (often discovered *after* the wedding).

The third prerequisite is a **set point in time**, a date on the calendar to which you can refer and say, "It began on this day."

A covenant operates like an insurance policy. It begins on a contractually agreed upon date and it ends on a contractually agreed upon date. Our new covenant with God is eternal, of course, but even it must be in writing. Your name is written in Heaven in the Lamb's Book of Life, granting you entrance to God's Kingdom, or it isn't, and you will be excluded.

> *No one is born into covenant; the day of your birth doesn't ratify a covenant. Even though Abraham had the promise, he had no covenant relationship until the day he accepted God's offer and they sealed it in blood.*

No one is born into covenant; the day of your birth doesn't ratify a covenant. Even though Abraham had the promise, he had no covenant relationship until the day he accepted God's offer and they sealed it in blood.

The same was true for Abraham's natural heirs. At birth they had only the promise of a covenant; Jewish ancestry did not ratify it. Until they made the decision to abide by God's law and accept the token of circumcision, they remained outside the covenant.

The second covenant is ratified exactly like the first. The promise of salvation is here, but it must be confirmed by a faith decision. Abraham's spiritual heirs, non-Jews too, can enter in, but until each person chooses the lordship of Christ, they live and die outside the blessings of the covenant.

The earthly pattern exactly mirrors the spiritual. A woman joins a man in marriage on a calendar date. Husband and wife know when their covenant began and if you ask, hopefully they'll be able to tell you the day.

Just as Jews had to enter into covenant on a certain date because Jewish birth was insufficient, being born female does not indicate covenant relationship to any man (or men). There must come a day when a woman chooses to enter into marriage. Heavenly or earthly, Old Testament or New, the date is always determined by when the recipient of the offer accepts it. A wedding is a public acknowledgement of a privately made covenant.

The fourth prerequisite is that **covenant relationship is voluntary**. In the Old Testament Abraham and his descendants were free to reject the covenant because participation was an offer, not a command.

In the New Testament salvation is a gift. We can take it or leave it.

The earthly pattern is the same. A man courts a woman and tries to convince her to marry him, but she is always free to say no.

Female submission must be voluntary because 1) first and foremost that is the biblical pattern; and 2) the nature of submission always puts the burden to comply on the person called to submit, not the person being submitted to.

> *Submission springs from a heart that respects, even loves the one to whom it submits. It is based on relationship and founded on liberty—freedom to submit or not to submit.*

Note that in all three scenarios, Old and New Testaments and the earthly, no one submits voluntarily unless trust is in place to support the decision and guide the relationship. Submission springs from a heart that respects, even loves the one to whom it submits. It is based on relationship and founded on liberty—freedom to submit or not to submit.

In I Pet. 3:1 and 5, Paul used the Word *hupotasso* to command the *wife* to be in subjection to her *husband. Hupotasso* is from *hupo,* a noun meaning a place beneath, and *tasso,* a verb meaning to assign or dispose to a certain position or lot. Paul commanded a wife to place herself in a position beneath, or under, her husband's authority. Feminists hate this, but it's a fact. A submitted wife is one who *places herself* under her husband's authority.

> *A submitted wife is one who **places herself** under her husband's authority.*

Repeat: God never directs his command to submit to the one in authority. Because submission is voluntary, a command to the one in authority would be a command not to submit but to enforce submission. *That would make submission involuntary, which is oppression.* The role of the male figure is to make the offer to provide leadership, not to demand submission to it. The burden to comply is always on the female figure and only after she has agreed to covenant relationship.

> *God never directs his command to submit to the one in authority. Because submission is voluntary, a command to the one in authority would be a command not to submit but to enforce submission.*

A biblical pattern exists, however, where submission to authority is involuntary, because there's no covenant to regulate it. Submission by slaves and prisoners is involuntary. Also, we know that eventually every nation and tongue shall bow the knee to Christ and confess his lordship. But they won't do so voluntarily because they love Him. They will do so because He is Lord, regardless of whether they have chosen to *hupotasso* or not.

The fifth and final prerequisite is a **fruit-producing union**. One of the first things God promised Abraham was that He would multiply his descendants as the countless stars in the night sky. God fulfilled this promise in Christ, for He is the firstborn among many brethren.

From the earthly union comes natural children, for God said He sought "godly seed" in his plan to unite a man and a woman.

God makes a covenant with a plan to reap an increase. That's (one of the reasons) why homosexual relationships are repugnant to God. They cannot reflect the heavenly pattern of a fruit-producing union.

The Traditional Interpretation

Now that we've seen the biblical pattern, let's look at the traditional. The heart of this teaching is the presupposition that by gender alone men have spiritual authority over women. Gender, not covenant relationship, is the controlling factor. That's why many denominations will not allow a woman, no matter how qualified, to fill a position that requires her to minister to men. The assumption is that those who have the pulpit have authority, and those who are on the receiving end are under that authority. If a woman ministers to a man, so the thinking goes, then she has "come out from under authority." In other words, she's left her lower place (*hupotasso*). They say a woman should be under authority because the man symbolizes the Head (Christ), and the woman symbolizes the Body (the Church).

This tradition is so widespread that we're as

unaware of it as oxygen. In any fellowship, you will find few that openly admit that men have universal authority over women. That is too hot to handle. But nearly all Christians are so confused about the scriptural validity of women ministers that they can't give you a logical explanation as to how or why women's ministry to men usurps authority. All they know is that *somehow* it usurps.

> *Nearly all Christians are so confused about the scriptural validity of women ministers that they can't give you a logical explanation as to how or why women's ministry to men usurps authority.*

But if men don't have universal authority over women, how can women usurp from men what they don't have in the first place? The problem is, when you say that a woman usurps male authority when she ministers to a man, you infer that the man has authority, the woman doesn't, and she's trying to steal it. And to say that women are under (male) authority infers that women are in a spiritual position below men.

Does our tradition reflect or reject the well documented scriptural pattern? Not sure? Then let's apply the traditional pattern closer to home.

Consider Mr. Schmoe and myself. I hardly know Mr. Schmoe. He's sitting next to me in worship service today. Tradition says he can teach me because, being a man, he has authority over me, but I cannot teach him because, being a woman, I must *hupotasso,* that is, assign myself to a spiritual place beneath him.

But I ask you, even in a symbolic way, when did we establish relationship and where is our covenant? When did I give consent? What do I get in return? When and how was our covenant ratified? What fruit will come of it?

As a person of free will, I can demand something

144

in return for my submission. But in this scenario, there is no return for my sacrifice.

My example is ludicrous, of course. But so is the vague, other-worldly notion that a "woman must be under authority." *It opposes the biblical pattern of female submission in every test.* And the biblical pattern is so *plain,* so repetitious, so well documented. It's absurd to think that a spiritual relationship exists between this stranger and myself other than the brother-sister connection we have in Christ. Aside from my husband, I have no more obligation to be under authority to Mr. Schmoe than I do to a flagpole.

> *To be scriptural, female submission to male authority is always marked by a woman's voluntary consent to be joined together to the spiritual head of her choice.*

That's because, to be scriptural, female submission to male authority is always marked by a woman's voluntary consent to be joined together to the spiritual head of her choice. And Mr. Schmoe is not my head.

The New Testament says that the husband is the head of the wife as Christ is the Head of the Church (Eph. 5:23). **Don't get masculinity mixed up with the head**. *The head, not masculine gender,* represents authority. When it comes to an earthly type, my only head depicted in God's Word is my husband. Any man who sits next to me in worship service or preaches from the pulpit is no more a picture of my spiritual head (authority) than any woman who sits next to him is a picture of his bride (his submitted one). **Don't get femininity mixed up with the Body**. *The whole body of Christ, not female gender, represents Christ's submitted bride.*

The earthly type of Christ's bride is always a wife submitted to her *own* husband.

145

I Cor. 11:3 says that the head of every man is Christ, but it does not say that the head of every woman is the man. The reason it does not say that is because "woman" here comes

*The earthly type of Christ's bride is always a wife submitted to her **own** husband.*

from *gune*, which means woman but specifically wife. *Gune* is the same word Paul used twice in I Pet. 3:1 when he said "... wives, be in subjection to your own husbands," and that unsaved husbands might be won over by the conversation (lifestyle) of the "wives."

Only one man can be the head of a wife, and this relationship has a definite beginning: a wedding day. So it's impossible that every woman has a man as her head because not every woman is married.

Genesis to Revelation: One head, one body. It's always that way in the Bible. God and his one people, the Israelites. Christ and his one people, Christians. And so it should be on earth, a husband and his one wife. To be scriptural, female submission must be one on one, one woman submitting to one man, one man providing leadership to one woman.

Marriage between a woman and a man is the only covenant that perfectly reflects the biblical pattern of female submission, therefore it's the only place where a woman, because she is a woman, must place herself under authority to a man, because he is a man.

The scriptural pattern we follow is the willing submission of the Bride-church to Christ, governed by a generous covenant of mutual exchange. Marriage between a woman and a man is the only covenant that perfectly reflects the biblical pattern of female submission, therefore it's the only place where a woman, *because she is a woman,* must place herself under authority to a man, *because he is a man.*

Just as Christ grants all people free will to choose to make Him their spiritual head for eternity, He grants women the free will to choose who (if anyone) will be their symbolic head for their time on earth.

Free will is dignity. But our perversion of God's design demeans women, short circuits teaching and preaching ministries, and causes resentment in the Body.

We've created a divisive spiritual caste, and who do you think is the author of this whopper of a lie? We've learned little from the Galatian Jews.

> *The traditional teaching that women must be under authority, that they are born into bondage in a way that men aren't, is a heinous insult to the Lord's personality. It isn't his* law *that makes us submit to Him. It's his gentle, loving nature that woos us.*

But that's not the worst of it. Here's the part that hurts women the most, the Satanic lie that eroded my trust in God's goodness, made it impossible for me to love Him with abandon, strangled my faith, and left me spiritually crippled for the first 18 years of my Christian walk. The traditional teaching that women must be under authority, that they are born into bondage in a way that men aren't, is a heinous insult to the Lord's personality. It isn't his *law* that makes us submit to Him. It's his gentle, loving nature that woos us.

Christ is the consummate gentleman; He forces his headship on no one. He reveals Himself to us, and then we want to know Him, serve Him, and give ourselves to Him. Of course, Christ is looking for obedience from his bride, but He desires obedience that flows from a heart that chooses to submit—*that chooses Him.* Peculiar to the biblical pattern of Christ and his Church is the bond of love. We submit because we love Him.

> *Peculiar to the biblical pattern of Christ and his Church is the bond of love. We submit because we love Him.*

Peculiar to the traditional pattern is the rule of law. It demands submission where no relationship exists born of love and respect. (How else but by the preaching of the law can you get people to submit if they're not motivated by love and respect?) Where Christ says, "Come away my beloved," and we run after Him, the voice of tradition says, "You will be under authority, woman!" And out of sheer obedience to what they think is God's will, women bow their hearts and try to accept with grace their lower position in the Church.

This is not Bible. This is bondage.

God forgive us. We call this monster a picture of the relationship between Christ and his bride. (I wince as I write this.) What an abomination we have created. We preach the letter of the law but ignore the spirit of it: mutual love and respect between the male and female figures that shine through every relationship where God is involved.

It's amazing: God respects us so much that He does not force us to submit to his lordship. We can choose to reject Him. By allowing us to choose, He esteems us, therefore we are elevated.

God respects us so much that He does not force us to submit to his lordship. We can choose to reject Him. By allowing us to choose, He esteems us, therefore we are elevated.

If God operated differently, if He forced us to submit to Him instead of inviting us to do so, we wouldn't be his bride. Our sins would be cleansed, yes. But we would remain in our low position; we'd still be in bondage. Instead of slaves to sin we'd be slaves to

Him.

Because when the biblical pattern of female submission is stripped of holy motivation born of love and respect, all that remains is obedience by written decree, the letter of the law. Only those in bondage, prisoners and slaves, submit to authority out of sheer, cold obedience. *It's their low position that robs them of freedom to choose.*

That's why the traditional pattern is so unscriptural. It sets women at a lower position in the Body. And somewhere along the way, their lower position becomes entangled with their identity, so that they no longer feel like equals, but lower-thans. They become *less* than because they are *lower* than.

They tell us that we must lower ourselves by submission to authority (that *is* what *hupotasso* means) but then tell us we are not lower and ought not to feel lower. But how can we feel anything but lower?

And if women lower themselves to men, doesn't that mean that men occupy a higher place?

It's nonsense to say that when a woman submits (hupotasso) to her husband's authority she lowers herself but when she submits (hupotasso) to universal male authority (by agreeing to forego ministry) she does not lower herself. This makes no sense, scriptural or otherwise.

It's nonsense to say that when a woman submits *(hupotasso)* to her husband's authority she lowers herself, but when she submits *(hupotasso)* to universal male authority (by agreeing to forego ministry) she does *not* lower herself. This makes no sense, scriptural or otherwise.

Friend, women are not stupid.

Somehow, intuitively, I understood these things for years. I knew there was something wrong with this teaching. But it wasn't until I thoroughly searched the Bible on my own that I understood why the "women must be under authority" teaching is so poisonous. I was led to believe that God had created two classes in the Church and that I was locked into the lower one for my entire earthly experience.

It's difficult for me to describe the deep and abiding hurt and futility this one thought bred in my soul. I couldn't understand why God, who is no respecter of persons, would play favorites. I couldn't understand why He had equipped and anointed so many women to teach but had no plans to let them. I was confused about his nature when I thought that God showed a respect to men that He denied to women.

The way I saw it, God had made men free agents, in a position to submit to whatever authority they chose, but He had birthed me and all women into a position of bondage wherein we were born under authority to another class and had no say in the matter.

I knew that because of this, men *and women* perceive women to be lower in the Church.

> *How could I love with all my heart a God who had called me to such humiliation? Surely prior to the Church's awakening regarding racism, Black Americans felt the same sting.*

How could I love with all my heart a God who had called me to such humiliation? Surely prior to the Church's awakening regarding racism, Black Americans felt the same sting.

Most painful of all, in my ignorance I believed that a God who would treat women in this manner must love them less than men and have fewer plans for them. How proud He must be of them, his sons, I would think, and all He is doing in and through them. I suspected that men were the focus of God's plan in the earth. Women were merely an afterthought, tolerated out of his compassion. After all, He created us. Surely He felt an obligation to include us, somehow, in his plan to redeem the world.

I am at rest now. I know the truth. And I love Him all the more for it. But how many women still feel the way I used to, that vague unease about God's love and plans for them? How many doubt that their heavenly Father loves them every bit as much as He loves men? How many discount their dreams of ministry because of this wicked lie of the devil? How many endure his chokehold on their faith in the name of obedience? How many suffer from low self-esteem due to this perversion of wifely submission? Will they ever feel utterly secure and at rest in his love?

Will someone please tell me what good fruit has come from this lying tradition?

Hiss #10: Only Half the Church Can Teach—Not Your Half

> Let the woman learn in silence
> with all subjection.
> But I suffer not a woman to teach,
> nor to usurp authority over the man, but
> to be in silence.
> For Adam was first formed, then
> Eve.
> And Adam was not deceived, but
> the woman being deceived was in the
> transgression.
> Notwithstanding she shall be
> saved in childbearing, if they continue
> in faith and charity and holiness with
> sobriety.
>   I Tim. 2:11–15

Here is a good example of how it pays to study God's Word instead of just glossing over it. Does this verse really mean that women can never open their mouths in worship service? Why did Paul put this strange restriction on women if there is now no male or female? And why did he drag the creation story into the

152

middle of it? What does childbearing have to do with teaching? Did Paul hiccup and lose his train of thought?

Misunderstanding of Paul's words about women, his "women bashing" some call it, has caused confusion for centuries.

As for myself, for years I disliked the man because his references to women seemed so condescending. In fact, I used to avoid reading certain passages because it hurt to think that God was pleased with this great saint who apparently thought little of women. (Remember: I was a hurting, spiritual orphan.) The way I looked at it, Paul's arrogant, cavalier attitude revealed a darkly misogynist side, a carryover, I presumed, from an earlier, machismo lifestyle. His comments made me feel more like a kingdom workhorse than a chosen vessel. I couldn't reconcile his hard words with the tender Spirit of Christ who greeted me softly during morning devotions. While researching this book I came across similar sentiment from other writers, men too, but usually women.

Everything in me told me that God loved me and wanted me to spread his Word. But many ministers I listened to and read put forth a Pauline interpretation that trivialized women and their ministerial role.

I vacillated for years, sometimes seeing myself as a member of the royal priesthood, other times succumbing to a nagging feeling that I was just second-class in the Kingdom, not called to anything spiritually big or significant. Confusion vexed me unmercifully.

Some denominations don't allow women to teach or preach primarily due to this passage. "Word" churches—those that seek to line up every facet of Christian service with the Bible—sometimes allow women to minister, but usually only to children or other women. Such ambivalence about women ministers stems from uncertainty about what God's Word says about them.

As a result, no matter where you worship, you find a common denominator in discussion of this passage: The hallmark of errant Bible interpretation is contradiction that leads to confusion. And a confused mind always says No.

To understand these verses, first we need to establish who is talking, Paul or the Holy Spirit. It's tempting to charge the Words to Paul, since he begins v. 12 with "I suffer (allow) not." But when Paul spoke from his own spirit, he was quick to say so (I Cor. 7:6, 12). Lacking Paul's admission then, we know that here he spoke by inspiration of the Holy Spirit.

With that said, we will examine the five verses one by one to get at the truth.

v. 11 *Let the woman learn in silence with all subjection.*

The most important point here is that women learn. This was a radical idea for the time, because we know that prior to Christ women were not formally trained in the Scriptures. This verse should be received with joy, not a groan, for Paul wanted women to study God's Word.

But why with subjection? Paul did not give the same commandment to men. Yet Paul was the one who denied a spiritual distinction between men and women.

In the New Testament, we frequently see wives commanded to be in subjection to their husbands (Eph. 5:22; Col. 3:18 et al.). And God commands all believers regardless of gender to submit to authority, one another, and elders. But as a rule, in every case where Paul singled out women for instruction on authority, he did so only when he was talking about wives and their own husbands.

New Testament writers usually used one word, *gune*, to mean woman or wife, but it specifically means wife. It was always up to the translator to determine from the context which idea the Holy Spirit meant. Sometimes *gune* was translated both woman and wife in the same passage, such as in pre-KJV translations of I Cor. 14. And we have already learned that the Greek word used here, translated "man," means male or husband.

Because of these facts, it's reasonable that when I Tim. 2:11 admonishes women not to usurp authority, Paul was speaking only to wives in relationship to their husbands. But more evidence exists.

v. 12 *But I suffer not a woman to teach, nor to usurp authority over the man, but to be in silence.*

Paul jumped from commanding women to learn to restricting who they teach. His inference is clear. Paul assumed that women who learn will teach. In Heb. 5:12 he complained to the whole assembly of Hebrew Christians, women as well as men, that after all the teaching they had received they should "now be teachers" but instead they still needed to be taught. Paul's rebuke echoes God's command that we give out what we have received, a theme woven through Scripture. God told Abraham He would bless him so that he would be a blessing. Jesus said we have freely received so we ought to freely give. Paul urged Christians to work to earn their own bread that they might have food to eat and to share with others. How contradictory of him, then, to urge women to be taught if he didn't intend for them to teach in return.

Teaching is the third ministry listed in I Cor. 12:28 of those God has set in the Church. In that context He makes no restrictions on women. The verse does not differentiate by gender but infers that God gives the teaching ministry to whomever regardless of gender.

Jesus Himself said that "whosoever" would do and teach his commandments would be called great in the Kingdom (Matt. 5:19).

Other passages confirm the neutrality of the teaching ministry. In I Tim. 5:17 Paul said, "Let the elders that rule well be counted worthy of double honour, especially they who labour in God's Word and doctrine." "Elders" here, from *presbuteros*, means an older person, senior, or presbyter. The term is gender neutral. If Paul meant only older men or only older women, he would have used the gender defining words *presbutes* and *presbutis*, respectively.

Paul told Timothy in his second letter to him (2:2) to commit the teachings he had received to faithful "men, who shall be able to teach others also." "Men" here is from Greek *anthropos,* meaning a human, male and female. No specific gender is implied. As you have already learned, if Paul meant that only men ought to teach, he had a specific word to say so.

In II Tim. 2:15 Paul instructed us all to "study to shew thyself approved unto God, a workman that needeth not to be ashamed, rightly dividing the Word of truth." Workman is from *ergon*, a derivative of *ergates*, meaning a toiler and figuratively, a teacher. No specific gender is implied. In v. 24, Paul said all the Lord's servants should be "apt to teach."

We also have the example of Priscilla. If Paul commanded women to refrain from teaching men, then he contradicted himself in Acts 18 when he failed to rebuke Priscilla:

> And a certain Jew named Apollos,
> born at Alexandria, an eloquent man,
> and mighty in the Scriptures, came to

156

Ephesus.

> This man was instructed in the
> way of the Lord; and being fervent in
> the spirit, he spake and taught
> diligently the things of the Lord,
> knowing only the baptism of John.
>
> And he began to speak boldly in
> the synagogue: whom when Aquila *and
> Priscilla* had heard, *they* took him unto
> *them*, and expounded unto him the way
> of God more perfectly. vv. 24–26

Priscilla wasn't shy about teaching a man. In fact, Priscilla had to be, in her own estimation, more mighty in the Scriptures than Apollos to teach him. Paul agreed with her. He was traveling with Priscilla at the time and had opportunity to discourage her but didn't.

Paul did outline one restriction on teaching, but he aimed it at men, not women. Older women, he said, ought to be the ones to

> ... teach the young women to be
> sober, to love their husbands, to love
> their children,
>
> To be discreet, chaste, keepers at
> home, good, obedient to their own
> husbands, that the Word of God be not
> blasphemed. Tit. 2:4–5

Theologians have used these two verses to "prove" that women ought to teach only children and other women. But Paul didn't intend to diminish women's new freedom. Look carefully at the areas of Christian growth that Paul said women should address: loving your *husband*, being a good *mother*, keeping a godly *home*. These are not precepts of the Word and doctrine outlined in Heb. 6:1–2 and confirmed in I Tim. 5:17 as the purview of elders of both sexes. These matters concern women only. It makes sense that older women provide guidance in things that pertain only to women. These verses do not restrict women. They restrict men by setting proprietary guidelines between the sexes.

With this in mind, again consider that Paul might have directed his comment in I Tim. 2:11 about learning, yet still being under subjection, to wives alone. I Cor. 14:35 commands a woman to take her doctrinal questions to her husband; I Tim. 2:12 reminds her that she shouldn't teach or usurp authority from him once she is trained in God's Word.

As for Paul's admonition that women not usurp authority, as we have seen, Scripture firmly establishes that wives are under the authority of their own husbands alone. The command was instituted in Gen. 3:16 and confirmed repeatedly in the New Testament. Scripture cannot be more plain: "Likewise, ye wives, be in subjection to your own husbands ..." (I Pet. 3:1). Wifely submission is an indisputable, scripturally defensible doctrine not voided by grace, because it was a command made prior to the law.

But believing women and men alike are also under the authority of their government, pastor, elders, and parents until marriage (Eph. 5:31). Women face no greater temptation than men to usurp authority from these, and the Bible forbids young men or women to instruct elders. Therefore, because men and women submit to the same authorities and are subject to the same temptation, it makes no sense that in this one verse Paul would single out women for instruction about usurping these authorities.

To usurp is to seize and hold power, position, or rights of another by force and without legal authority. It's worth repeating: How can a woman usurp authority from a man if he doesn't have authority over her to begin with? She cannot take what he does not have. And because Paul mentioned teaching and usurping authority all in connection with "the man," it

follows that the man she is not to usurp is the same man whom she is not to teach.

We know that the man Paul refers to in v. 12 of this passage is not a woman's pastor, elder, or father, because he would not single out women for special warning when both sexes are subject to these authorities to the same degree. And a woman is no more tempted than a man to usurp authority from them. So if the man Paul refers to is not just any man because just any man does not have authority over a woman, then logically the only man Paul is talking about here is the remaining man who does have authority over her, the only man in her life whom she would be tempted to instruct and seize authority from: her husband.

Remember, the Greek word *gune* from which the KJV translators rendered "woman" specifically means wife, and the Greek word *aner* from which they rendered "man" also means husband. Remember too that the first English version of the Bible, by Wycliffe, confirmed v. 12 to be concerned with only wives and husbands: "But I suffre not a womman to teche; nether to haue lordschip on the housbonde." ("But I suffer [allow] not a woman to teach; neither to have lordship on [over] the husband.") "The" as in "the man," is a definite article, indicating one particular man, not any or all men.

Here is more evidence that this verse is talking about the relationship between a wife and her husband, not all women and men. But there's still more evidence.

Read the following carefully. It's strategically important to understanding this verse.

The word authority here is not like any other rendering in the entire Bible. Thirty-five times you see the word authority, and in every case it's translated from Hebrew or Greek words that mean or imply *delegated* authority. It's the privilege to command granted by another person higher in rank than yourself, or directly from God. *But only here* does the Word authority come from a unique root, *authenteo*, meaning to act of oneself, to dominate or to usurp authority over.

KJV translators were on target in their literal translation: The kind of authority women are not to have is stolen, or *usurped* authority. Paul was admonishing women that they were not to take authority from their husbands and put it upon themselves. But he made no restriction to preclude women from having *delegated* authority, from their husbands, the Church or another governing body. Women are under no more limitations than men when it comes to *delegated* authority.

> *Paul made no restriction to preclude women from having* **delegated** *authority, from their husbands, the Church or another governing body. Women are under no more limitations than men when it comes to* **delegated** *authority.*

Because of the unique kind of authority spoken of here, usurped and not delegated, this verse speaks only to wives and their husbands, "the man"—not all men; therefore, the burden of compliance rests upon women and not church leaders. Paul restricted wives from *usurping* authority from their husbands; he didn't restrict the Church from *delegating* authority to women.

> *Paul restricted wives from usurping authority from their husbands; he didn't restrict the Church from delegating authority to women.*

The whole point of the passage then, is that as women grow in God's Word and become recognized teachers, they are not to wrest authority away from their husbands. Paul did not mean to put forth a new doctrine to restrict women in ministry. But he did mean to remind women that when their knowledge of spiritual things brings them to the level of being the Teacher and not the Taught, they still must subject themselves to their husbands' leadership.

The Contradictory Path to Confusion

Failure to conduct a careful exegesis of these verses has led to all kinds of ridiculous efforts to establish a doctrine to prevent women from teaching men.

We have churches where women can teach only children and other women. We have churches that allow women to teach men only when on the mission field (where men are often nonwhite—a policy tinged with racism). We have churches that allow women to teach only on a limited array of subjects, or only if the woman is older, or only if the woman is married to the pastor, and so forth.

In the 18th century Wesley was adamant that a woman should never speak or teach in a public assembly. He allowed women to speak, however, "if they are under an extraordinary impulse of the Spirit."[1] What is extraordinary is that he left this to the discretion of the woman, as he believed that not only is she more easily deceived, but that she "more easily

---

[1] Wesley's notes on I Cor. 13.

deceives."[2]

Some Christians maintain that a woman can teach but not with authority. Dr. Scofield maintained most illogically that a woman could teach but she couldn't claim to be an authority on matters of doctrine. To this I reply that only those who have the authority to teach, men or women, ought to teach, and if they can't claim authority then they ought to keep quiet.

Modern day cult expert, Dr. Walter Martin (*Kingdom of the Cults*), charged that the female teaching ministry has brought us nothing but "confusion, division and strife,"[3] and that Paul saw this centuries ago by divine revelation and tried to warn us. For women to teach, he said, is for them to usurp authority over their "male head." He named leaders of four cults: Johanna Southcutt, Mary Baker Eddy, Helena Blavatsky and the Fox Sisters, as examples. They were, he said, "... living proof of the validity of our Lord's declaration that 'if the blind lead the blind, both shall fall into the ditch.'"[4]

Yet in his book Martin chronicled countless *men* who have and still are leading millions of people into that infamous ditch. Despite his bold claim about Paul, Martin added that church "leadership roles should more properly be filled by men *where available* to meet this need"[5] (emphasis mine). Could it be that Paul was willing to condone a little deception when a male teacher couldn't be found?

Another strange but common interpretation is that

---

[2]Wesley's notes on I Tim. 2.

[3]Martin, Walter, Dr. *Kingdom of the Cults*. Bethany House Publishers, Minneapolis, 1985, pp. 249–250.

[4]Martin, W., p. 250.

[5]Martin, W., p. 249.

it's O.K. for a woman to teach a man if she teaches only one or two at a time, the example of Priscilla. *The Encyclopedia of Bible Difficulties* puts forth this idea in its editorial on I Tim. 2:12. According to Editor Gleason L. Archer, it's scriptural for a woman to teach one or two men together, but if a third man enters the room, suddenly some heavenly law is violated and heresy results.

If we followed this reasoning to its logical end, we would hold worship services primarily in private homes, or baptize converts in lakes or streams and not heated baptismal pools, as that is the way we see it done in the New Testament. People who think like Archer apply a spiritual test for the teaching ministry on the number being taught, when the true test is evidence of anointing.

Worse, Archer's interpretation doesn't reflect a heartfelt desire to get God's Word to the world but a poorly veiled attempt to keep the influence of women teachers to a controllable minimum. Why does doctrine from a woman's mouth become suspect only when she teaches a group? Do you really think God cares if it's one, two, or 122? It seems to me that God would be more glorified and the Church more edified if 122 and not two heard the Word, regardless whether the source is female or male.

Archer's fallacy is an example of the prevalence of small thinking I told you about at the beginning of this book. How is it possible that limiting women to teaching just a few at a time increases the fruitfulness of the Gospel? We have it backwards.

v. 13 *For Adam was first formed, then Eve.*

Theologians have made much of creation order, that Adam was created before Eve, inferring that Adam had preeminence with God and in intellectual and spiritual matters. Their arguments stem from this one verse alone, supported, they think, by the story of creation.

If their argument were reasonable, then Jews also could claim preeminence in the Church. After all, they were called to salvation before Gentiles. Does that mean that Christians of Jewish descent can secure offices and ministries by birth alone? No thinking Christian believes such heresy. Yet many think men have preeminence over women in leadership roles and ministries precisely because Adam, a type of all men, was created first. Of course, this thinking contradicts Gal. 3:28 and can only be inferred from one verse, I Tim. 2.

If this *one* instance in I Timothy, where attention is made to the order of human creation, is the irrefutable scriptural basis for the doctrine that men have universal spiritual preeminence over women, how much more evidence do you have from Rom. 2 and 3 to conclude that Jews still have universal spiritual preeminence over Gentiles, where in *three* instances Paul speaks of the advantage of their chronological status? Speaking of judgment day, Paul testifies:

> Tribulation and anguish, upon every soul of man that doeth evil, *of the Jew first*, and also of the Gentile;
> But glory, honour, and peace, to every man that worketh good, *to the Jew first,* and also to the Gentile ...
> Rom. 2:9–10 (emphasis mine)

And of the advantage of Jewish blood, he says:

> What advantage then hath the

164

Jew? or what profit's there of
circumcision?

Much every way: chiefly, because
that unto them were committed the
oracles of God. Rom. 3:1–2

Paul finishes with a clear and emphatic claim that
real Jewishness is not an outward manifestation but an
inward one, that circumcision is of the heart by the
Spirit and not of the flesh by human hands. Fleshly
circumcision is worthless, for we are all, Jews and
Gentiles, justified "freely by his grace through the
redemption that is in Christ Jesus" (3:24).

If you stopped reading at the above verses,
however, and didn't continue to read Paul's refutation
of the Jew's former preeminence, you would think that
having Jewish blood in your veins is what counts with
God.

Wesley was one of those who believed in the
preeminence of men based on creation order. He wrote
that because woman was created last, "woman was
originally the inferior."[6] Yet in his Genesis notes he
said humans were superior to animals because they
were created last!

Observe, 1. That man was made
last of all the creatures, which was both
an honour and a favour to him: for the
creation was to advance from that
which was less perfect, to that which
was more so: and a favour, for it was
not fit he should be lodged in the
palace designed for him, till it was
completely fitted and furnished for his

---

[6]Wesley's notes on I Tim. 2.

reception.[7]

Well, what's good for the goose is good for the gander. If I tried to make the case here that creation order supports the argument of advancement from "that which was less perfect to that which was more so," or that God did not see fit that Eve should be "lodged in the palace designed for (her) till it was completely fitted and furnished (with Adam) for her reception," then woman, being the last creation to appear ... well, figure it out.

But I don't feel like being stoned today, so I'll stay away from that. Again: The hallmark of errant Bible interpretation is contradiction that leads to confusion. If Paul did not mean to reinstate the subjugating yoke of the law upon women in this passage, then what did he mean when he said Adam was formed first? What advantage did that give Adam?

Chiefly this: Adam had more time to get to know God. From what we read in Genesis, Adam received face-to-face instruction about the tree and the regulations regarding it. Scripture is plain and so was God. He told Adam to leave the tree alone, and Adam was not deceived. Adam's advantage was the same as the Jews', "... that unto them were committed the oracles of God." But having the law—the mind of God—revealed to them, as Adam did, didn't benefit him or the Jews because neither obeyed it.

Scripture is not clear as to where Eve got her instructions, but we know that she had not yet been created when God spoke to Adam to avoid the tree of knowledge of good and evil (Gen. 2:17–22). Someone told her about the tree and the rules, for she spoke to the serpent in Gen. 3:2–3 and explained what they could

---

[7]Wesley's notes on Gen. 1.

and could not eat and why. Did God or Adam speak to her? As God does not waste words, it was probably Adam who clued her in (more on this later).

v. 14 *And Adam was not deceived, but the woman being deceived was in the transgression.*

Because she had spent less time with God than Adam and likely received secondhand instruction, Eve was more easily deceived. Secondhand news isn't as persuasive as what we get straight from the original source.

Both were guilty, of course. But Eve disobeyed because she was deceived. Adam was not deceived. He knew that to eat meant death, but he ate anyway.

Witness the appropriateness of their punishment. Adam showed contempt for God's provision by eating forbidden fruit even though every good food was within his reach, so he was condemned to hard work in order to eat again, a judgment against his physical body. Eve also showed contempt for God's provision and was condemned to suffer in her physical body (multiplied sorrow and conception).

But after taking a bite, Eve turned to her husband and urged him to eat also. For this second offense she condemned herself to be under her husband's authority. God won't allow a woman to exercise authority over her husband because her first attempt at leadership in the home was so egregiously irresponsible.

> *God won't allow a woman to exercise authority over her husband because her first attempt at leadership in the home was so egregiously irresponsible.*

Because Paul referred to Eve's deception (an act)

and not her nature, her punishment of subjection to her husband makes scriptural sense, as God would not punish her for being but for doing. God would not create a flawed being then punish her for that flaw.

That's why we know that the curse of subjection came upon Eve only as a result of a specific act of disobedience and not to curb a flawed nature.

In other contexts, however, Adam and Eve are portrayed as types for all men and women. But here Paul did not refer to their maleness or femaleness but to the unique relationship they had to one another that was marred when Eve drew her husband into sin.

Paul's focus on Eve's sin parallels God's treatment of it in Gen. 3, wherein God said to the woman, "What is this that thou hast *done*?" and to the man, "Because thou hast *hearkened* unto the voice of thy wife ..." (emphasis mine). In both Old and New Testament treatment of their sin, when it's stripped of its traditional interpretation, the focus is always on the mutual disobedience of two people and not on a design flaw in Eve's nature.

Traditional treatment of the first sin tends to blame mostly or only the woman. But the Holy Spirit used the Word *anthropos*, which means human creation (man and woman) but was translated "man," to describe the first sinner in Rom. 5:12, "Wherefore, as by one man sin entered into the world." Where traditionalists blame the woman, KJV translators blame the man [Adam], but the Holy Spirit ignores gender altogether and calls them "one."

As a result, we know that all women who come after Eve are in no more peril of inheriting a tendency to deceive or be deceived than all men who come after Adam are in peril of inheriting a tendency to sin knowingly. Rom. 5:12 says we have all inherited a sin nature without reference to a tendency to commit any particular type of sin.

> *The core of our tradition is that, since Eve disobeyed because she was deceived, women are more subject to be deceived than men, making them specious vessels of truth. The result is that they can't be trusted to teach, especially to teach men.*

But tradition has veered far from this simple truth. The core of our tradition is that, since Eve disobeyed because she was deceived, women are more subject to be deceived than men, making them specious vessels of truth. The result is that they can't be trusted to teach, especially to teach men.

These same Christians do not worry, however, that Adam's *knowing* act of disobedience might reveal a tendency in men to willfully disobey. In fact, in arguments that deny all common sense, men are said to be more trustworthy as teachers than women precisely *because* Adam sinned while knowing full well he was committing evil.

Letha Dawson Scanzoni's response to this convoluted logic:

> I remember a class at Moody Bible Institute in the 1950s where the professor told us that women are prohibited from pastoring churches or teaching doctrine in a school – although they could teach women and children. The reason? 'Eve, the woman, was completely deceived, whereas Adam sinned with his eyes open. The man, filled with the Spirit, is therefore a safer repository of doctrine.' How it's that 'sinning with one's

eyes wide open' makes one a 'safer repository of doctrine' makes no more sense to me now than it did then. And how a woman, who supposedly can be so readily deceived that she falls into doctrinal error, is nevertheless equipped to teach children and other women doesn't make sense either – unless women and children don't matter in the minds of those who spread such teachings.[8]

Tucker's conclusion is on target:

It's on this very issue of application that the traditionalist argument falls apart. If women were more prone to be deceived than men, how incredibly irresponsible it would be of church leaders to let them teach other women and little children, whose minds are impressionable. Far better to let women teach adult men, who would be better able to withstand the threat of heresy.[9]

If Eve can't be trusted to handle God's Word because He gave it to Adam first, should not this same principle be applied to Gentile Christians who received the second covenant?

Need I say it again? The hallmark of errant Bible interpretation is contradiction that leads to confusion.

---

[8]Quoted in Tucker, p. 118.
[9]Tucker, p. 118.

If all these Bible interpreters have concluded that women teachers are a deadly virus to the health of Christian doctrine, how can they in any way, at any time, for any emergency justify the substitution of a woman for a man in a teaching position? Better to have no doctrine taught than a suspicious one. This is like saying that adultery is always wrong except when your spouse is not around to fill the need.

> *If all these Bible interpreters have concluded that women teachers are a deadly virus to the health of Christian doctrine, how can they in any way, at any time, for any emergency justify the substitution of a woman for a man in a teaching position?*

v. 15 ***Notwithstanding she shall be saved in childbearing, if they continue in faith and charity and holiness with sobriety.***

This last verse is the stumper that has had theologians scratching their heads for years. One of the commentaries I looked into concluded that we will never know what it means, for God has left us with a timeless mystery.

Nonsense. If God didn't want us to know what it means, He wouldn't have put it there; the Bible isn't just pretty prose. It's God's message to the world. He does not send us on a wild goose chase. He does not command us to "study to shew thyself approved unto God, a workman that needeth not to be ashamed, rightly dividing the Word of truth" if He knows we will never be able to rightly divide it. He put it there because He wants to communicate truth. The passage is not deep or symbolic or prophetic. It's instructional.

So what does childbearing have to do with teaching and authority? Everything. It's the last and most convincing evidence that proves I Tim. 2:11–15 does not restrict women teachers. It's the Creation Connection that opens up the whole passage.

To understand what Paul was talking about, we return to Genesis and review the curses spoken over the woman:

> A) Unto the woman he said, I will greatly multiply thy sorrow and thy conception; in sorrow thou shalt bring forth children;
> B) *and* thy desire shall be to thy husband, and he shall rule over thee.
> Gen. 3:16

The verse outlines two curses: A) She will have difficulty (sorrow, pain, toil) in delivering children, and B) she will be under the authority of her husband. We have already looked at how Paul addressed the second part of the curse and its residual effect upon a postresurrection woman (I Tim. 2:11–12). Now we'll look at the first part.

At the beginning of v. 15, "notwithstanding" means in spite of or despite. You can't say "in spite of" without first establishing what it's that you are setting aside. In grammar we call the word "notwithstanding" a conjunction, meaning a word or phrase that connects other words or phrases. Its function here is to connect the thought in v. 14 to the one in v. 15. Verse 15 did not just appear here. It's not an aberration, which some commentators have inferred. It's tightly connected to the rest of the passage.

And "childbearing" does not mean that a woman is saved through the act of childbirth. We are saved only by faith in the atoning work of Jesus Christ.

Incredibly, translators such as Wycliffe, Tyndale, Coverdale, Taverner, and even modern ones have

172

translated v. 15 to mean that a woman is redeemed by a unique punishment put upon her body at time of delivery. They intimate a salvation of works whereby childbirth pain along with faith, charity, and holiness merit eternal reward. Considering how the entire New Testament is devoted to the Gospel of salvation by faith in the death and resurrection of Jesus Christ alone, this is amazing doctrine.

Men saved by faith, women saved by childbearing ... what could these men have been thinking?

Their translations reflect the inordinate burden of guilt traditionalists impose upon the woman. They saw Eve's sin in the garden as an act of treason so overwhelming that not even the death and resurrection of the Son of God Himself could fully expunge it. She would just have to keep suffering to pay for her sin.

As you shall see in Chapter 12, the inordinate saving power ascribed to the act of delivery and the absolving pain associated with it were behind the Church's insistence that women not seek relief during labor and delivery.

Likewise, no one is saved by "the Childbearing," referring to the birth of the Savior, along with works of faith, charity, and holiness, as the Amplified version would have you believe. It's the not the birth of Christ that purchased our salvation but his *death and resurrection* in which we hope. Even if they meant that his death and resurrection resulted from the divine birth, faith in it alone secures our salvation, and not the Childbearing along with works, and especially not the Childbearing along with works as applied to one sex over the other.

These convoluted, heretical translations were wrested from God's Word because translators didn't understand how this passage builds upon Old Testament truth. When they forgot that God's Word always agrees with itself, they were pressured to create new doctrine surrounding childbirth to explain Paul's comments about it, just as they did when they arrived at his comments in I Tim. 2 about women teachers. Had they committed themselves to the truth that God's Word always agrees with itself, they would have continued to search instead of devising obvious exegetic error.

What Paul is doing here is addressing the *first half* of the curse: sorrow, pain, and toil in childbirth. He already established in vv. 11–14 that a woman is still affected by the *second half*—the wife is under the authority of her husband. Now with his sobering restriction about continued wifely submission, he offers comfort and consolation regarding the first half when he says that a woman will be saved (protected) from harm in childbirth if she continues in faith. This is the only logical explanation of the verse. *It's the Creation Connection that confirms that Paul's injunction to women that they cannot teach or usurp authority over their husbands is merely his way of elaborating on the remaining effects of the Gen. 3:16 curse on women, more specifically wives, under the new covenant.*

Because traditionalists didn't acknowledge the Creation Connection in I Tim. 2, they also had trouble when they tried to interpret I Cor. 14:34–35. Instead of restricting women in teaching and preaching, this passage only confirms a limitation on women concerning the authority of their husbands. The connection is easy to prove:

> Let your women keep silence in the churches: for it's not permitted unto them to speak; but they are commanded to be under obedience, as also saith the law.

And if they will learn any thing,
let them ask their husbands at home:
for it's a shame for women to speak in
the church.

We have traditionally used this passage to claim
that women are never allowed to speak (preach, teach)
in the Church, yet we do allow women to speak in
tongues, prophesy, and pray publicly because of other,
plainer passages. After all, God said He would pour his
Spirit on his handmaidens in the last days and they
would prophesy; it's impossible for women to prophesy
if they're not allowed to speak. The same goes for
public prayer and speaking in tongues.

Yet Paul says women shouldn't speak in the
Church. So what kind of speaking is Paul talking about?

To begin with, I Cor. 14 says nothing about
teaching and preaching, as *laleo* from which we get
"speak" rarely infers preaching and never teaching. The
Greeks used other words to mean preaching and
teaching. Rather, *laleo* is interpreted in nearly every
citation to mean only to talk or utter words, especially
an extended or random harangue. For example, Paul
used *laleo* when he said that he spoke with tongues (I
Cor. 14:18) and when he said we should forbid not to
speak with tongues (I Cor. 14:39). Interpreters have
imposed their own restrictions on teaching and
preaching into the verse.

Although we have interpreted v. 34 in a narrow,
restrictive way, we don't similarly interpret v. 35. It
says that if a woman wants to learn anything, she
should learn it from her "husband." Does this mean that
she can learn *only* from him? And it says that she
should learn "at home," and in a similarly strict
interpretation, does this mean she can learn *only* at
home? If we applied the same strict interpretation to v.

35 as we have to v. 34, then we would restrict women in church to neither talking nor asking questions, prophesying, giving messages in tongues, sharing testimonies, and praying aloud. Clearly, this is not what Paul intended.

We have interpreted other verses that pertain to women in the same bizarre, restrictive way. For example, some denominations forbid women to wear jewelry or fix up their hair because of Peter's admonition in I Peter 3:3 that a woman's adorning not be an outward one of plaiting (braiding) the hair or of wearing gold. But the verse also says that a woman's outward adorning ought not to be the "wearing of apparel."

No clothes? Let's not go down that road.

How about Tit. 2:4–5 where elder *women* are admonished to "teach the young women to be sober, to love their husbands, to love their children, to be discreet, chaste, keepers at home, good, obedient to their own husbands?" Why do we purchase teaching materials that deal with these subjects when *written by men* or attend their seminars? We say women can't teach anything but these subjects and only to women. Yet Drs. Timothy LaHaye, James Dobson, and Ed Wheat have published extensively on some or all of these, and some have written explicit books that deal with the even more sensitive subject of marital sex. No one silences them.

Along with speaking of some kind, the verse also talks about learning and being under obedience (to whom?). Again we see Paul emphasizing that a woman should learn. Most people have no problem with that.

Fortunately, Paul's repetition reveals what bothered him about her speaking. Look at the beginning of v. 35. "And if they will *learn* anything ..." If a woman is set on learning something, does she do it by

176

teaching? By preaching? To learn, we study, listen, and ask questions. This is what women were doing then, too. But they were interrupting the services with their questions. Paul told them to take their questions home to their husbands. Logically then, these women had to be married, and so it was to married women that Paul spoke.

But this is not a new, unique translation. Remember, *gune* means woman but specifically wife. Tyndale, who was fluent in Greek, translated it to mean wives here, not women, meaning wives ought to keep silence in the Church and bring their questions home to their husbands. Earliest translations, such as Coverdale's, Matthews', and Taverner's, agreed. Whatever women were questioning in service was more fitting to be dealt with at home.

This is just another example of how translations have evolved to restrict women's freedom to minister.

And what is "the law" to which Paul refers? Even if there had been an Old Testament law silencing women, Paul of all people would not refer to it because he was the one who sermonized at length on how Christians are no longer bound by the law. And no New Testament "law" exists to silence women.

One law exists, however, that commands women to be under obedience, one that both predates and outlives Old Testament law. Gen. 3:16 commands women to submit to their husbands. Both the KJV and Amplified versions have reference marks after v. 34 advising that the law Paul refers to is Gen. 3:16. Yet while the reference marks are correct, both translations contradict their references by translating the passage to mean all women must be under universal submission to all men in addition to their husbands. The Amplified is especially contradictory:

The women should keep quiet in
the churches, for they are not
authorized to speak, but should take a
secondary *and* subordinate place, just
as the Law also says. [Gen. 3:16.]
(emphasis Amplified; Gen. 3:16 speaks
only of husbands and wives)

But if there is anything they want
to learn, they should ask their own
husbands at home, for it's disgraceful
for a woman to talk in church [that is,
for her to usurp and exercise authority
over men in the church]. vv. 34–35
(*Amplified translators expand the Gen.
3:16 to mean women are under
authority of all men, not just their
husbands – contradicting the Scripture
they used as a reference in v. 34.*)

The Amplified's interpretation of v. 35 suggests
that by speaking aloud a woman usurps authority and
that only men have authority to speak in a public
assembly. "Speak" in vv. 34 and 35 is from *laleo*,
which, remember, means only to talk or utter words, not
to teach or preach. Yet Amplified translators twisted
this to mean that her speaking is an attempt to "usurp
and exercise authority over men in the church." This
contradicts all other passages wherein Paul encouraged
every Christian to learn God's Word then teach it,
prophesy, give messages in tongues, recite psalms,
share revelations, and so forth.

Paul was familiar with Old Testament law and he
wrote most of the New Testament. So where in either
place did he find a law that puts women as a class under
submission to men? The word obedience in I Cor. 14:34
is translated from *hupotasso*, which we've learned

178

means to put oneself in a subordinate position. At least five other places in the Bible Paul instructs women to *hupotasso*, and *in every case* he speaks only of their relationship to their husbands. Observe:

- Wives, submit (*hupotasso*) yourselves unto your own husbands … Eph. 5:22
- Wives, submit (*hupotasso*) yourselves unto your own husbands ... Col. 3:18
- Likewise, ye wives, be in subjection (*hupotasso*) to your own husbands ... I Pet. 3:1
- ... the holy women also ... being in subjection (*hupotasso*) unto their own husbands ... I Pet. 3:5
- To be discreet, chaste, keepers at home, good, obedient (*hupotasso*) to their own husbands …
- Tit. 2:5

One other time we see *hupotasso* applied to a woman. In I Tim. 2:11, where women are commanded to learn in silence "with all subjection," they're commanded to be in *hupotage*, the noun form of *hupotasso*. If a woman is to *hupotasso* to anyone, it's her husband. Repeat: A woman is *never* commanded to submit to any man except her husband. Clearly, the law that Paul referred to is Gen. 3:16, the one that put a woman under her husband's authority and the only law concerning female submission still in effect after the resurrection. Not just any woman receives instruction from her husband at home. If you aren't married, there's no hubby at home. The command applies only to married women.

These two passages complement each other, as they should, since one person wrote them by inspiration of the Holy Spirit. Because earlier Bible translators (Tyndale, Matthews, Taverner) interpreted *gune* here to

179

mean wife and not woman, it's likely that centuries ago the Church put a restriction on wives alone, forbidding them from interrupting services with their questions. As a guide, Paul says, wives shouldn't teach their husbands the things of God (I Tim. 2:12) but husbands should teach their wives (I Cor. 14:35).

Paul's I Tim. 2:11–15 treatment of the Gen. 3:16 curse on women and how it was unaffected by their new status in Christ is complete. Though we are all redeemed from the curses of the law outlined in Deut. 28, Paul established that none of us are freed from the curses on Adam and Eve recorded in Gen. 3. Just as a man cannot point to the resurrection to claim that he is free from the bondage of hard work, a woman cannot point to her new status in Christ (Gal. 3:28) to claim that she is no longer under her husband's authority. And although the curse upon childbirth is still a nuisance, at least she can claim God's protection through the experience.

Jesus' last instructions were for us to go into all the world and preach the Gospel to every creature, making disciples of all. To this end, it's a shame how the Church has shot herself in the foot. She only has two of them, you know, to bring the good news, one male, one female. If we interpret I Tim. 2:11–15 to mean that women can't teach or preach, then we cripple ourselves for the journey.

Hiss #11: Real Women Are in the Kitchen

> But one thing is needful: and Mary
> hath chosen that good part, which shall
> not be taken away from her.
>   Luke 10:42

The Home

I am the mother of four grown children. In the
early years their care took up most of my day. And
there were other claims on my time, like my husband,
friends, writing, house, yard, and church. One of my
biggest problems as a working mother was to know
how to divide my time among all these people and
things. I asked God often to show me his priorities so
that the use of my hours pleased Him. I didn't always
receive an easy or quick answer. I still struggle to know
how to best spend my time.

I am, however, closer to wisdom than before. I
spent the first 18 years or so of my Christian walk
confused. I listened to everyone's opinion about a
woman's duties except the Holy Spirit's. A mother

shouldn't work outside the home. A woman should be teaching her kids *at* home. Don't worship your house. Don't neglect your house. Don't idolize your children. Don't neglect your children. A woman should take time to look her beautiful self. A woman shouldn't be concerned with outward adorning.

When it came to my daily priorities, my head was full of shouldn'ts, don'ts, and ought-tos.

But then one day I read Jesus' testimony of his friend Mary.

What Is Needful? What Is Good?

Jesus and his disciples show up at Martha and Mary's home one night around mealtime. Jesus is a friend of these sisters and their brother Lazarus, and they are happy to see Him.

But Martha is frazzled with all the things she must do to prepare a meal for this crowd. Slaughter a sheep, bake extra bread, go to the neighbor to borrow plates and goblets, get all the feet washed and the wine poured, all the while keeping her eye on the fire and making sure her guests have all they need to be comfortable.

Meanwhile the guests are sitting with Jesus, who is teaching them kingdom truths. Martha would like to be there too, but she feels obligated to work in the kitchen, as women customarily do. She starts to feel resentful of her sister Mary, who is in with the others and enjoying Jesus' visit to the full. "All the work falls to me," Martha grumbles to herself. "Everyone else gets to sit and listen. Jesus finally comes to town and I have to work while everyone else gets blessed."

Martha decides to take her complaint to Jesus. She hopes He will speak to Mary and make her return to the kitchen to help. But Jesus turns everything around in a few words:

> And Jesus answered and said
> unto her, Martha, Martha, thou art
> careful and troubled about many
> things:
> But one thing is needful: and
> Mary hath chosen that good part,
> which shall not be taken away from
> her. Luke 10:41–42

Martha was deceived. Jesus didn't want her to put her spiritual growth and relationship to Him on hold to serve others. He said so himself. Her problem, He said, was that her mind was "cumbered" (10:40) or taken up. Cumbered comes from Greek *perispao* meaning to be dragged all around. Mary had lost her focus.

Martha's second mistake was to think that the solution was to draw another person into her problem. "My work will be less," she thought, "if someone helps me." Doesn't that sound reasonable? And why didn't Mary offer help without being asked? Together they would have quickly finished the work. How equitable that sounds. How politically correct. And besides, how would those people be fed if someone didn't stop everything and prepare a meal?

Jesus was not moved. He told Martha something revealing about the call on a woman's life: "One thing is needful." "Needful" comes from Greek *chrei*. It means employment. It's a compound of two words meaning to furnish, to employ, or it needs. It infers necessary business.

Jesus said his Word was Mary's necessary business, her job, and He gave Martha the opportunity to make it hers also. He called it the good part of service to Him.

183

Jesus subordinated women's temporal, earthly tasks, "much serving," to the eternal work of learning of Him, and He invited Martha to step up to a new level of discipleship. By calling one (learning of Him) the good part, He inferred that the other (much serving) was not as good. By calling one needful, He inferred that the other was not as needful.

That Jesus subordinated our daily temporal labors to attendance to his Word may or may not be an earthshaking revelation to you. But Jesus has a revolutionary message for women that has been all but lost on the Church. The One who made such an issue of service to others subordinated this ministry to the all-important business of attending to Him and his Word. It wasn't serving but *too much* serving that got Martha in trouble. It overburdened her mind, causing her to neglect Jesus. Her intentions were O.K. Her priorities needed adjustment.

> *The One who made such an issue of service to others subordinated this ministry to the all-important business of attending to Him and his Word.*

For years I misunderstood this. I believed like Calvin, who in a 16th century sermon told his followers that, "A woman does well when she keeps house, makes her bed, sweeps, boils the pot, takes care of her children" because housework is a "sacrifice acceptable to God."[1] Wesley too thought the home was the center of the universe for women. He said they should be in it at all times, but for three exceptions: to perform works of necessity, piety, or mercy.[2]

It's true, housework can be a sacrifice to God (or just a sacrifice. It depends on your perspective. If I

---

[1] Quoted in Bouwsma, pp. 76–77.
[2] Wesley's notes on Tit. 2:5.

could find a way to put it on an altar and make a burnt offering out of it, I'd be the first to light the match). Everything we do we should do for the Lord.

But that mopping and dusting are a virtue in and of themselves, that a woman's chief ministry tools are a broom and dustpan, that cooking is to be exalted over evangelizing ... this is questionable doctrine.

But for a season, it was doctrine I found easy to follow. I used to idolize my home. Keeping it in pristine condition made me feel like a good wife. I wanted everyone who visited to admire it, sparkling clean, then go out and tell the world what a great housekeeper I was.

And I wanted my husband to be proud of me. The funny thing is, I've since learned that he doesn't *care* about shiny floors and crumb-free countertops.

Then I was unemployed for a while and the first thing I did was take advantage of the extra time to have an even cleaner, more orderly house. My house was going to be so clean! My church friends so impressed!

But one day God spoke to me, or rather, He gave me a vision. In it I was kneeling before Him, talking about my life on earth and what I had accomplished. At that moment, it occurred to me for the first time that Jesus wasn't going to be the least concerned about how clean I had kept my house. It wouldn't be a topic of discussion.

I got the message. My calling (and yours) in this world is not a temporal one of temporal duties. You and I were not put here chiefly as a caretaker of a certain house on a certain street. Though we have to devote time to these to live civilly, ultimately we are called to higher things than the mundane exercises of an earthbound life.

> Your calling in this world is not a temporal one of temporal duties.

God is looking for permanent fruit, lives changed by his Word and love. From that day forth I was free from the traditional, worldly attitude about homemaking.

Prioritizing Our Employment

Christ must be first. This means before family, job, housework, and volunteer work. A woman's first priority should be finding Him in prayer, worship, and Bible study. Once the foundation is in place, other pursuits fall naturally under the balance of the Holy Spirit. He will tell you how much time to devote to the other stuff. Confusion will flee.

> *Schedule is not at the center of the battle. Priorities are.*

I can hear the groans. We're all busy. But friend, schedule is not at the center of the battle. Priorities are. One of my closest friends is an at-home mother who has home-schooled five (yes FIVE) children. Whenever I visit her orderly home, I can't help but notice how busy she is with volunteer work and her children's activities.

You know what kind of woman I am talking about, because everyone knows someone like June. She does all the things that you associate with an old-fashioned mom. Her day is full, more so than most at-home mothers you know.

But this mother is more Mary than Martha. Whom do I call when I need prayer? I call June, because her relationship to the Lord is so strong and consistent, her life so filled with the Holy Spirit that I know I am sure to receive. June is not an exceptional mother because she stays at home with her children, or because she sacrifices much of her day home-schooling them. She's an exceptional mother because she's an exceptional

Christian with an intimate relationship to Christ. She's a good mother because she's a good Christian, not the other way around.

Then there's Beth. I admire few women in this world more than Beth. She is a school board member and the state director of a Christian women's political organization, which takes a great deal of her time and requires occasional travel. She does all the accounting for her husband's small company and is active in her church and local government. She is a working mother.

But I don't call Beth for prayer because she's so good at all these. I call her because I know she's a woman who jealously guards her relationship to the Lord. Prayer and Bible study are first in her life, and as a result service and spiritual blessing flow out of her at every turn.

Get the picture straight. Women, those who work outside the home and those who don't, and especially mothers of babies and small children, have *always* had full schedules. But because of strong, repetitious cultural images, we fall easily into the habit of serving, serving, serving to the neglect of our relationship to Christ, and we excuse ourselves under the guise of self-sacrifice and a servant's call. We pride ourselves on how much we do for God. We perceive that it's acceptable to be so busy, so we gravitate toward the traditional role for the praise and confirmation of other Christians. We're comfortable in the Martha role. It feels good.

Focusing on Mary

The Mary role is more difficult to comprehend. She put her relationship to Christ above everything else, even the physical comforts of others, and this disturbs us. Mary offends. She appears self-centered,

187

superspiritual, unwomanly. She knew everyone expected her to work in the kitchen. It was what women had always done.

But Mary chose (Jesus' word) to ignore tradition for her own spiritual enrichment. This causes us consternation now just as it caused Martha then. I have been saved since 1975, but in all those years I have heard only one sermon lauding Mary's decision.

> *It isn't that Mary refused to serve. It's that she refused to let anything get in the way of God's Word, not even service.*

Get the sermon here. It isn't that Mary refused to serve. It's that she refused to let anything get in the way of God's Word, not even service.

Jesus applauded Mary, but he chided Martha for her choice to spend too much time on temporal pursuits. If it had not been within Martha's ability to reverse that choice, Jesus would not have encouraged her to do it.

We must choose. If we believe that our schedule leaves us no room, then we are deceived, for God has called all of us to make his Word and prayer first place. You are in charge of your schedule, even if you have small children. We are all given the same 24 hours.

Make God's Word, worship, and prayer your first priorities. Then ask God for grace to let go of or reduce the activities that steal time. Often these are things that look good at the outset, such as church and community work, over-time hours, and so forth. Or maybe you just need a shorter commute. God can arrange it.

There's nothing intrinsically wrong with any of these things, just like there was nothing wrong with Martha's desire to serve her guests. But too much time devoted to them causes us to miss out on God's best. Again, it's a matter of priorities.

I've discovered two rewards that come from choosing the better part. First, when I put Christ first in my day, the rest of it goes smoother, because fewer obstacles appear to mess up my schedule and reduce productivity. (Or is it that the obstacles are still there but my response is saner?) I don't know how He does it. I just know He does. Second, I have more with which to serve: more patience, more grace, and especially more faith.

But I've also discovered the down side of the Mary role. When you say to "No" to people to achieve your spiritual goals, as Mary did, expect to offend someone.

The up side is that once you have your priorities right, knowing how to handle home, marriage, and children won't be a mystery. The Holy Spirit will lead you. He'll tell you what, when, how, and how much.

Marriage

Paul told the first Christians to consider the single life and only marry if sexual desire became a problem. He gave this advice (I Cor. 7:7–28) to free them from time-consuming marital duties, that they might serve the Lord singleheartedly and without the "trouble in the flesh" that Scripture promises. (I had a pastor once who liked to quip that "trouble in the flesh" was the only promise God ever gave to married couples.)

Paul's advice still applies. The first thing we should prepare for should be ministry, not marriage. Proverbs 24:27 says, "Prepare thy work without, and make it fit for thyself in the field; and afterwards build thine house."

Our Puritan brothers and sisters, often the butt of jokes for their strict holiness and supposedly ascetic ways, were correct in their estimation of the purpose and design of marriage. English-American clergyman and author John Cotton (1584–1652) wrote that husbands and wives ought not to aim "at no higher end than marriage itself," because their spouses were brought into their lives "not for their own ends, but to be better fitted for God's service and bring them nearer to God."[3]

Are you born to marry or are you born to serve? God commanded us to seek Him and his Kingdom, not a spouse. He promises that if you do this, He will make sure that all the other things important to you come your way. This includes a mate.

Motherhood

When we were in our early 20s, my husband and I decided to become naval officers. Before signing the dotted line, we met with our pastor for counsel. When it was my turn to talk, I told him how I had come from a military family, how I had always wanted to serve my country, how I had already been accepted into Officers' Candidate School, and how my husband and I were in agreement, and so forth. Then I stopped talking and waited to hear the "word" from God, confirming our decision.

His response was nothing like I expected.

"But," he said, cradling his arms as if holding a little bundle and directing his question to me, "Don't you want to hold a soft, little baby in your arms?"

I was utterly dumbfounded. Here I was talking about the culmination of years of hard work and desire, and he was talking about giving up babies.

Parenthood was not a big issue to the first Christians as it is to us today. In fact, it was such a nonissue that the New Testament mentions the parenthood status of only a few disciples (e.g., Philip, Acts 21:8). Neither was it used as an excuse from

---

[3]Quoted in Ryken, p. 49.

service. Remember, the first Jewish Christians had no concept of religion. Service to God was assumed.

It's safe to say that parenthood was also assumed. A few crude forms of birth control existed in first century A.D. None were as reliable as what we have today.

Many women, mothers too, left their homes to follow Jesus. Home was not their shrine of ministry. Luke 8:1–3 tells us that women traveled with Jesus and the disciples and ministered to them financially. Some were married mothers, such as Joanna, Mary the mother of James and Joses, and the mother of Zebedee's children (Matt. 27:56). Most likely these women were older and their children grown. God's Word encourages us to care for our families; these women would not neglect their young children. Nevertheless, they were not what you would call traditional mothers. Yet Jesus received their love and support.

My attention to these passages is not to say that I propose that women just jump up and leave their families to go out and preach. I'm just saying that the Bible provides a record of mothers who made sacrifices for the Gospel.

One of my big frustrations as a new Christian was trying to understand the Church's preoccupation with motherhood. I don't mean *children*. I mean motherhood. Motherhood as an occupation. Motherhood as a calling. It seemed that it was a woman's most important duty, more important than evangelism. Frequently I heard Christians speak of it as a "ministry," though I have never found it named as such in the Bible.

Motherhood, it seemed, was a religion within a religion. I read the Scriptures; I knew what they said about duty to one's children. But where did all this fuss about motherhood come from, above and beyond what the Bible said?

Nineteenth Century Treatment of Motherhood

Nineteenth century literature, religious and otherwise, abounds in praise of motherhood. In fact, the home took on a religious quality all its own during the Victorian period, about 1840–1901. The lasting influence of a committed Christian mother on the spirituality of her children is indisputable, but Victorians attributed metaphysical qualities to her that bordered on heresy.

Author Catherine Beecher described the work of mothers as that which will "bring forth fruits of good or ill not only through earthly generations, but through everlasting ages."[4] A popular theme in literature of this period is that of the mother as savior, especially of wayward sons and husbands. Women, they thought, possessed spiritual ability above others to mediate for the safety and salvation of their families. Even the writings of Augustine, (St.) Chrysostom, (St.) Basil and (St.) Louis were attributed to the spiritual influence of their mothers.[5]

Roman Catholic literature on churchwomen, especially Mary, also influenced Protestant thinking. As explained by Colleen McDannell in *The Christian Home in Victorian America, 1840–1900* (Bloomington: Indiana University Press, 1986), traditionally Catholic women exercised their devotion by cloistering themselves in convents outside mainstream society. Protestant reformers shut down many of them, yet the

---

[4]Quoted in Colleen McDannell, *The Christian Home in Victorian America, 1840–1900.* Indiana University Press, Bloomington, 1986, p. 128.

[5]McDannell, p. 129.

ideal of cloistered womanhood lived on in the lives of Catholic and Protestant mothers who were similarly shut away in the sanctity and repose of their homes. Spending hours with their children in routine domestic activities and religious training, their influence took on a spiritually mediative quality that transcended their earlier perceived angelic employment.

In *The Mirror of True Womanhood* of 1877, Father Bernard O'Reilly got straight to the point in describing the Victorian notion of the redemptive value of motherhood, "... true woman in every home is the savior and sanctifier of man."[6]

The Example of Mary

Speaking of Mary, Charles Ryrie (Ryrie Bible) embellished what the Bible says of her using his own imagination to describe the kind of mother she was. Mary had lessons to teach, he said, "mostly related to the home." Quoting James Hastings, he added:

> Mary was a of a retiring nature,
> unobtrusive, reticent, perhaps even
> shrinking from observation, so that the
> impress of her personality was confined
> to the sweet sanctities of the home
> circle ... You see in the little that is told
> of her what a true woman ought to be.[7]

To these questionable cultural conclusions about Mary's activities, Dorothy Pape responds,

> Mary may well have been retiring

---

[6]McDannell, p. 142.
[7]Quoted in Tucker, pp. 200–201.

and home-loving, but with the possible
exception of the angel's announcement
of the coming conception, the scriptural
record never shows us Mary at home.
She is hurrying off to Elizabeth, then
going to Bethlehem for the census, then
to Jerusalem for purification rites,
down to Egypt, back to Nazareth, then
to Jerusalem again for the Passover, to
Cana for the wedding, to Capernaum,
to a city near the Sea of Galilee with
her other sons to persuade Jesus to
come home, and finally to Jerusalem
again. It therefore requires an exercise
of imagination to learn from her
lessons 'mostly related to the home.'[8]

Ryrie was not alone in his vivid imaginings of the
activities that occupied Mary. Victorian writers saw her
as a role model for the at-home mother, describing her
"in the peaceful house of Nazareth, industriously
pursuing the ordinary avocations of a poor artisan's
wife."[9] However, I see nothing ordinary about the
miracles performed by the first believers, including
Mary, recorded in Acts. Mary was in the upper room
and not at home when the Holy Spirit arrived (Acts
1:14). Though Mary was not an apostle, Acts is a book
devoted to *acts*, with emphasis not on anyone's retiring
nature but the miracles they performed by the Holy
Spirit.

Even Jesus had something to say about Mary and
motherhood.

---

[8]Quoted in Tucker, p. 201.
[9]Quoted in McDannell, p. 142.

> Someone told him, Your mother
> and brothers are standing outside,
> wanting to see us.
> He replied, My mother and
> brothers are those who hear God's
> Word and put it into practice. Luke
> 8:20-21 (NIV)

Again,

> As Jesus was saying these things,
> a woman in the crowd called out,
> Blessed is the mother who gave us birth
> and nursed us.
> He replied, Blessed rather are
> those who hear the Word of God and
> obey it. Luke 11:27–28 (NIV)

There it is again, the simple message that God's Word is more important than earthly pursuits. Do you suppose Jesus repeated it for a reason?

Modern Marriage, Home, and Motherhood

No one exposed the Gospel of Home and Motherhood better than Betty Friedan, the feminist author so unpopular in Christian circles. Friedan provoked all women, Christian too, when she published her cataclysmic book, *The Feminine Mystique,* in 1963. Her words were the match to the gunpowder that exploded into the firestorm of the women's movement.

Friedan's exposé on the "problem that has no name," that indefinable, nagging sense of unfulfillment in housewifery was not lost on Christians. Relegated to the confines of the home, many felt a call of God to do more than just oversee the physical chores of a household. Though I disagree with much of Friedan's platform, her description of the feminine mystique is relevant:

> But the new image this mystique gives to American women is the old image: 'Occupation; housewife.' The new mystique makes the housewife-mothers, who never had a chance to be anything else, the model for all women; it presupposes that history has reached a final and glorious end in the here and now, as far as women are concerned. Beneath the sophisticated trappings, it simply makes certain concrete, finite, domestic aspects of feminine existence – as it was lived by women whose lives were confined, by necessity, to cooking cleaning, washing, bearing children – into a religion, a pattern by which all women must now live or deny their femininity.[10]

> *"A religion, a pattern by which all women must now live or deny their femininity."*
> —*Friedan*

I quake every time I read the ending of that paragraph. "A *religion*, a pattern by which all women must now live or deny their femininity." How right she was. *That* was what I battled in my early years of conversion. It was the religion of motherhood, legalistic, rigid, and confining. When I wouldn't cross over to their side, I remained *outside*.

So what's new? Religious zealots, in love with tradition, persecuted Christ. But is it really an either/or

---

[10]Friedan, Betty. *The Feminine Mystique*. W.W. Norton & Company, 1963, pp. 43-44.

196

proposition? Family v. ministry? Deborah the judge and prophetess did not think so. Mary did not think so. Joanna did not think so.

But many in the Church do think so. It still amazes me that with the announcement of each of my four pregnancies, I heard so many comments declaring surprise that I was having any (or more) children. The consensus was always the same. Everyone thought I was a "career woman"—a minister friend's exact words. They were puzzled that I had chosen to have (more) children, as they thought that serving God as a writer and raising a family were incompatible.

When I announced my fourth pregnancy in 1993, the comments were even more bizarre than they were at the first in 1982. One Christian friend was disturbingly silent when I shared with her what I thought was good news. Her response was so odd ... I just had to find out what she was thinking. Upon questioning her, I found out that she was reticent because she feared that perhaps the baby was an "accident," because, after all, I had "wanted a career."

But it gets more outrageous. While I was still in the debate stages ("Do I have another baby or don't I?") I was confiding my desire for a fourth with a Christian friend, a full-time, working mother, when she offered her advice that my desire to have one more was probably a big mistake. Why? God would surely find a way to keep me home, away from work and ministry. "He has a way of doing that, keeping new mothers at home, you know."

For a few days after that conversation I walked around overcome with dread and fear. What if this last baby frustrated my plans to work and minister? What if I regretted getting pregnant? What if I turned 40 and was still home, taking care of a baby, never realizing the things God had for me?

Then I came to my senses. The first 14 verses of Deut. 28 are a list of blessings we will enjoy if we "hearken diligently" to God, "observing to do all his commandments" (v. 1). Children are included on the list.

> And the Lord shall make thee plenteous in goods, *in the fruit of thy body*, and in the fruit of thy cattle, and in the fruit of thy ground, in the land which the Lord sware unto thy fathers to give thee. v. 11

Children are not our lives; they are gifts from the Lord *added* to our lives. Note the biblical order: Devotion to God first, children second.

> *Life **began** when God breathed it into Adam's body. Therefore, life does not **begin** at conception—it **continues** from one generation to the next.*

Children are part of our inheritance. "Lo, children are an heritage of the Lord" (Psalm 127:3). Heritage is from Hebrew *nachalah*, meaning something inherited, estate or portion. Because each of us carries within us reproductive life inherited from God, the source of life, our ability to bear children is like an estate passed from generation to generation. You can trace this estate all the way back to the Father, the first parent. Life *began* when God breathed it into Adam's body. Therefore, life does not *begin* at conception—it *continues* from one generation to the next.

Children are a reward from the Lord. "The fruit of the womb is his reward" (Psalm 127:3). I love the literal translation of Hebrew *sakar* from which we get "reward." It means payment of contract, salary, fare, or by implication, compensation or benefit. For serving Him, He repays us with little souls, sources of continual joy. Again note the order: service first, reward second.

Spiritual priorities are at the heart of the motherhood controversy. Where is our focus? Look again at what Prov. 24:27 says about choices when it comes to work, ministry, and family: "Prepare thy work without, and make it fit for thyself in the field; and afterwards build thine house." "House" is from Hebrew *bayith*, meaning your house or specifically, your family. It's believed to come from another word, *banah*, meaning to build or to obtain children. Building your house means to establish for yourself a family, to get married and have children. We are supposed to prepare ourselves for service first. Marriage and family come second.

A good example of the divine order is the story of Shiprah and Puah in Exodus chapter 1. Pharoah was determined to diminish the number of Israelites, so he called their two midwives and ordered them to destroy every newborn male. But they refused:

> But the midwives feared God, and did not as the king of Egypt commanded them, but saved the men children alive.
> And the king of Egypt called for the midwives, and said unto them, Why have ye done this thing and have saved the men children alive?
> And the midwives said unto Pharaoh, Because the Hebrew women are not as the Egyptian women; for they are lively, and are delivered ere the midwives come in unto them.
> Therefore God dealt well with the

midwives: and the people multiplied,
and waxed very mighty.

And it came to pass, because the
midwives feared God, that he made
them houses. Exod. 1:17–21

A note in my KJV at "made them houses" says that
God "gave them families." This note is correct, because
the Word houses here is from *bayith*. God rewarded
Shiphrah's and Puah's obedience by giving them
children, and the Bible calls God's action "dealing
well." And hey, they were working women!

With all this evidence of what children are to a
Christian, we can deduce what children are not. Though
rearing children is an important ministry, *it's not listed
in Scripture as one of the ministries we should seek.*
Scripture commands us to seek many things, chiefly the
Lord, but also his kingdom and righteousness; his will;
not our own but every other person's wealth; peace; that
we may prophesy; and that we may excel to the
edifying of the Church. Nowhere among these are we
commanded to seek children (or a spouse for that
matter, I Cor. 7:27).

Children are an invaluable addition to our lives of
Christian service, sent for a purpose. God wants to
reward us, and He seeks godly heirs. But once God
gives them to us, his commands to seek these other
things do not become null and void. Children change
the way we do things, but they shouldn't change the
things we do when it comes to spreading the Gospel.

When it came to deciding on a fourth child, I
began to remind myself of all that God had already
done for my family, but especially for me. I
remembered how He had made it possible for me to
finish graduate school after the first was born; how He
had provided outstanding childcare whether I was in

school or working; how He had provided finances whether it was one, two, or three children. What I saw, in a picture, was that when I had put God first, He had always taken care of the details and given me my heart's desire. Three times in the past God had made a way for me to stay involved in what was important to me, even though I was a mother. I was confident He would do it again. I have never believed that motherhood meant the end of service.

Christians should not pit children against ministry or career. Competition between them is unscriptural, humanistic, the antithesis of God's plan. He does not want us to choose ministry over children or children over ministry, or children over work or work over children. God wants us to choose Him and his will above all else. Then, as we faithfully serve Him, either at home, at school, in a ministry or a job or a combination of any of these, He is happy to reward us with children if we desire them. And He will give us the wisdom to know how to arrange our lives to best care for, train, and provide for them.

I started this discussion by relaying to you all the shouldn'ts, don'ts, and ought-tos that dominated my early years. I was just like Martha. I allowed all the stuff of Christian service, the small stuff, to drag my focus all around because, like Martha, I thought God's focus was on the small stuff too. I was burdened by obligation and fear of doing the wrong thing.

But when I switched my focus to Christ and his Word and quit worrying about what others thought women ought to do, I was set free from all that garbage. The biblical blueprint I was searching for I finally found, and it was *in Him*. Because in the end, it doesn't matter what you do, as long as you do what He tells you to do. God really will show you how to be happy, if you ask Him.

=

Hiss #12: God Didn't Really Mean Pain

Unto the woman he said, I will
greatly multiply thy sorrow and thy
conception; in sorrow thou shalt bring
forth children ... Gen. 3:16

The contractions started at five minutes after
midnight. I had gone to bed at the usual time Thursday
evening but couldn't sleep, so I was awake when I felt
the first mild one. I was in labor! The contractions
continued sporadically, but not uncomfortably, all the
next day until about 9 p.m., when it began to dawn on
me that this was going to be no cakewalk.

By 4 a.m. Saturday, I was receiving new revelation
from Psalm 116:3: "The sorrows of death compassed
me, and the pains of hell gat hold upon me." I shook my
snoring birth partner (Lamaze term) and told him we
had to get to the hospital.

Once there, they told me to get into a gown, make
myself comfortable (hah!) on a labor table, and that it
would be a while.

And it was a long wait. Apparently my body knew
how to contract but it didn't know what for, because

labor would not progress. Though it had begun 28 hours earlier, the nurse said I was still no way ready to deliver. The whopper contractions were accomplishing nothing.

My doctor couldn't be located, but the on-call doctor seemed like a nice fellow, so I wasn't worried. He ordered that I be given a drug to forward the delivery. It worked like a miracle, and within an hour serious labor began. But what the nurse gave me was not a painkiller, and I was beginning to think that the baby would come any minute because the contractions were getting difficult to handle. So I requested the common, safe anesthetic I'd prearranged with my regular physician.

> *Incredulously, the attending nurse informed me that I didn't need any anesthetic to deliver a baby.*

Incredulously, the attending nurse informed me that I didn't need any anesthetic.

Didn't need any anesthetic???!!! What???!!! I begged them repeatedly to give me something for the pain, but they just as repeatedly refused. The pain worsened to the point that I feared I was going to die right there on that labor table. But everyone kept insisting I didn't need anything except to calm down and "blow."

I have a not-at-all-vague memory of how labor progressed after this unsettling change in my carefully laid delivery plans. Sometime during the worst of it, I transmogrified into a green-eyed, venom-tongued hulk of a monster. I gripped my husband's sweater at chest level, his eyes big and round as half dollars, and with all the daintiness of Sampson I jerked him toward the table, ordering him quite unsubmissively that he MAKE them give me something for the pain, and like do it RIGHT NOW.

It didn't work. My husband later explained that the nurse had a way of making you agree that what she wanted to do was the best thing to do.

They continued to insist that all I needed was something to relax my muscles. But the relaxant they gave me made me feel like my joints were disconnecting and that I was floating. It did nothing for the pain. By now I was panicking, certain something had gone terribly wrong. My guts were splitting open, I was sure of it. I was dying, a slow, agonizing bloody death.

Oh well, I thought, *if they won't listen to me now, at least I know I'll be vindicated at the autopsy. They are going to be sorry they didn't listen to me!*

After what seemed like an eternity of increasingly more mind-bending labor, but was actually only history's longest five and one-half hour period, Juliet was born at 9:31 a.m., entirely without pain relief. The last thing I remember before I was wheeled out of the delivery room was my husband leaning over me, looking directly into my face. He was asking me something, though I don't remember what. I remember only that he was expecting an answer, but I couldn't speak. It was as if the portion of my brain that controlled speech had been temporarily paralyzed. I tried to respond, but my mouth wouldn't move. I remember feeling like I was watching all the activity in the room as if I were watching a movie. I didn't know it then, but due to the trauma and excruciating pain, I was in shock.

The next morning, the doctor who had attended me came by my hospital room for the routine follow-up visit. I'm sure he felt obligated to comment on my natural childbirth performance, as he had observed many Lamaze mothers struggle to keep the faith, gritting their way through the marathon of contractions and pushes to the cheers and morale-boosting pep talks of their devoted birth partners. Now that my Olympics were finished, he thought I expected congratulations, too.

With all the magnanimity he could summon, and absolutely no facial expression, he opened his mouth and lied. "Mrs. Welch, you did a good job."

I could have punched him.

*   *   *

Only weeks earlier I'd stupidly used the 'P' word in a question to our Lamaze instructor.

"Pain," she replied icily, "is not a word we use in this class."

I should have seen it coming. But I didn't understand then how deeply entrenched in the culture are our strange ideas about women, labor, delivery, and pain. Processes unique to women, they have had more than their fair share of interest by the primarily male community of clergy and primarily female community of midwives. Until only recently, the first saw themselves as guardians of the curse, determined that women did not relieve themselves of childbirth pain, while the second came in the back door and tried to overcome it by whatever means available.

In all centuries since Gen. 3:16 was penned, only beginning in the 20th do you see a reversal. Now it's primarily male physicians who seek to ensure a painless delivery and primarily female midwives who subordinate or even deny pain for a more spiritual (their term) birth experience. This flip-flop affected women, of course, but it also affected the Church.

Painkillers for Labor and Delivery

In 1591, Eufame McCalyean of Edinburgh, Scotland, and her friend, Agnes Sampson, were burned at the stake as heretics. Their crime? Eufame, pregnant with twins, asked Agnes to find a medicinal herb to relieve the delivery pain that would soon be upon her. Eufame and her babies survived the delivery, but when the clergy found out what Eufame had done, they burned her at the stake.[11]

Women continued to suffer. But then a professor of midwifery at Edinburgh University, Dr. James Young Simpson, discovered the anesthetic properties of chloroform in the fall of 1847. At first he used the substance at parties for entertainment; he enjoyed watching his friends roll under the dinner table. But when he gave it to the wife of a fellow doctor during delivery, he made history. She was so thrilled with the results that she named her little girl "Anaesthesia." Dr. Simpson soon began to administer chloroform to his patients, then launched a series of lectures and publications to spread the word about painless childbirth.

Although surgeons seized upon the heretofore unknown opportunity to perform painless surgery, other physicians and most clergy were outraged at the thought of laboring women having their equally painful situation relieved by a drug. And some doctors were reluctant to use a drug for a purely physiological (natural) function. But as women began to demand it, doubters capitulated and received training in its administration.

---

[11]Tucker, p. 52; see also "In the Name of God: Why Agnes Sampson and Eufame McCalyean Were Burned at the Stake." Ray J. Defalque and A.J. Wright, *Anesthesia History Journal*, Vol. 22, Issue 3., pages 11–14, 2004.

> *It was not uncommon for difficult labor to drag on for days, ending in the death or near death of both mother and child.*

Their ambivalence to providing relief is amazing when you consider that prior to that era women in childbirth suffered horribly. It was not uncommon for difficult labor to drag on for days, ending in the death or near death of both mother and child when the baby became asphyxiated in utero, or the woman's body became so exhausted that her uterus quit contracting altogether, or they both succumbed to sepsis. (My paternal grandmother died this way. She was 35, the mother of 10.)

Despite these tragedies, doctors upheld a callous double standard for laboring women, calling their unbearable, protracted pain normal and natural, therefore justifiably to be tolerated.

> *The Church of England called chloroform for childbirth pain relief the "decoy of Satan."*

When finally given a choice, to suffer or not to suffer, women, the medical community, and the clergy were forced to address the spiritual whys of childbirth pain for the first time. But where women interpreted painless childbirth as a blessing and rejoiced at God's mercy, the religious community condemned it, especially the Church of England, even more than the medical community. One minister called chloroform

> ... a decoy of Satan, apparently
> offering itself to bless woman; but in
> the end it will harden society, and rob
> God of the deep earnest cries which

arise in time of trouble for help.[12]

Whether God needs more cries for help in time of trouble is a question for theologians with too much time on their hands. But there was no question that religious society was already hardened toward women's suffering.

Dr. Simpson, however, had the last word. In his December 1847 rebuttal, he pointed out that even God showed mercy to Adam by putting him into a deep sleep before opening his side to remove the rib from which He made woman (Gen. 2:21).

Fortunately for medical science and all mothers to be, the intense opposition to aiding suffering women was checked by Queen Victoria, the highest authority in the land at the time. Letters dated late 1848 reveal that the Queen was searching for more information from other royalty in confinement (the Queen was expecting her seventh child) regarding the wonder drug. But it wasn't until the birth of her eighth that she used it. Of it she gushed, "Dr. Snow, ... gave that blessed Chloroform & the effect was soothing, quieting & delightful beyond measure."[13]

Because of the close relationship between the throne and the Church, the Queen's endorsement had an ameliorating effect on clergy and opened the way for other women to enjoy painless, guiltless deliveries. For a time, painless childbirth was so closely associated with the Queen that it was termed *chloroform a la Reine*,[14] (the Queen's chloroform).

---

[12]Quoted in Jessica Mitford, *The American Way of Birth.* The Penguin Group, New York, N.Y., 1992, p. 42.

[13]Mitford, p. 44.

[14]Rion, Hanna. *The Truth About Twilight Sleep.*

In the New World, Americans were busy building a new life and their memory of British rule too fresh to take any interest in the Queen or her opinion of chloroform, so it was slower to catch on. And besides, they had discovered ether. Fanny Appleton Longfellow in 1847 became the first American to use it during labor. She called it "the greatest blessing of this age."[15]

Ether or chloroform, American obstetricians responded like their British counterparts. Dr. Charles Meigs, a popular physician, called chloroform "meddlesome midwifery"[16] and was vociferous in his railing against any kind of painkiller for confinement. (Dr. Meigs was the same who insisted that no doctor could be the carrier of puerperal, or childbed fever, as doctors were recruited only from among "gentlemen" and, he maintained, gentlemen's hands were not dirty. Childbed fever killed thousands of women. It was the number one cause of death in delivery, especially in teaching hospitals in the centuries before the discovery of the microscopic organism that caused it. Physicians and students in training examined dead bodies, then went straight to a delivery without washing their hands, thereby infecting the woman and contributing directly to her agonizing death of pain and high fever in the following 72 hours.)

Led by Mrs. John Jacob Astor, politically active women took up the torch near the end of the 19th century and carried it into the next with a battle cry for a newer anesthetic, Twilight Sleep, (repeat hypodermic injections of morphine combined with scopolamine, a

---

McBride, Nast & Co., New York, 1915, p. 2.

[15]Quoted in Judith Walzer Leavitt, Ed., *Women and Health in America*. The University of Wisconsin Press, Madison. 1984. p. 160.

[16]Quoted in Mitford, p. 44.

powerful hallucinogenic and amnesiac, and pentobarbital sodium given every hour). Scopolamine dates to 1880 when Ladenburg discovered that the seed of a European plant, *Hyoscyamus niger,* contained hallucinogenic properties.[17] Different pharmacologists experimented with the crystalline substance, but the first physician to publish authoritative papers was a German, Dr. Carl J. Gauss. In his report he commented on the opposition he had come against in his efforts to use it: "... Gauss remarked that it was a most singular fact that the greatest opposition to the use of any narcotic in childbirth had come from the church."[18]

Some doctors liked Twilight Sleep because it gave them control over the mother, who was not actually put out but in a light sleep and only partially conscious of pain. Still, Gauss reported that the second but less violent opposition came from physicians. They'd heard of the more than 200 patients who had died from chloroform overdose. Others said that childbirth pain was physiological, that "It's not nice to fool with Mother Nature." This notion is still popular.

About 1915, Mrs. Hanna Rion published *The Truth About Twilight Sleep.* At the opening of her book she addressed the number one opposition to pain relief:

> Down through the centuries, while
> so-called heathen races, inspired by
> that sympathy which runs like a thread
> of gold through all humanity, tried by
> sorcery and primitive devices to
> mitigate the sufferings of maternity,
> you Christians alone opposed every
> effort made for a modification of what

---

[17]Rion, p. 67.
[18]Rion, pp.72–73.

you called the 'normal, physiological pains of childbirth.'[19]

Even with the threat of institutionalized opposition, the news of Twilight Sleep spread quickly as sympathetic newspapers and magazines influenced popular attitudes. In the same year that Rion's book came out, the Twilight Sleep Maternity Hospital was established in Boston. By the late 1930s Twilight Sleep was anesthetic of choice, administered routinely on the East Coast.

Because it was primarily women and often suffragettes who were loud about finding safe and effective anesthesia for childbirth, during the late 19th and early 20th centuries painless childbirth became associated with the vote, birth control, and other suspect movements that people, often women, perceived as threats to family and faith. Without the Queen's input and influential women such as Mrs. Astor, who had the respect and wealth to make their voices heard, painless childbirth might have remained a figment of the laboring woman's desire much longer than it did.

Oddly, though it took hundreds of years for safe, effective relief to be discovered and accepted, it only took about 70 years, the space of a woman's life, for it to fall out of fashion.

Natural Childbirth

The 1933 publication of the controversial book, *Natural Childbirth* (later, *Childbirth Without Fear*), by British obstetrician Grantly Dick-Read was the beginning of the end of the American love affair with medicated childbirth. Dick-Read maintained that

---

[19]Rion, p.2.

childbirth pain is primarily due to fear. Fear (of childbirth), he said, causes tension, and tension causes pain, therefore we must eradicate fear. To do this, he said, a woman needs prenatal instruction, exercises to keep her body supple, training in deep breathing, and delivery in a relaxed atmosphere.

Unlike his devotees that came several decades later and claimed to follow his methods, Dick-Read was quick to acknowledge that natural childbirth is not necessarily painless.[20] (He titled his book *Childbirth Without Fear*, not *Childbirth Without Pain*.)

Not long after Dick-Read's revelations came Ferdinand Lamaze's *accouchement sans douleur,* labor without pain, that also required prenatal classes in all disciplines Dick-Read suggested. Where they differed was that Lamaze preferred rapid, shallow panting over Dick-Read's deep breathing exercises.

Then came obstetrician Frederick LeBoyer and his water births. He believed delivery to be a violent process, upsetting to the infant, so the use of dim lights and a first crib of warm water, most like the uterine home, is the least traumatic way to bring baby into the world.

The explosion of interest in Dick-Read's later-called natural childbirth method was a logical if not foreseeable outgrowth from the 1960s and '70s back to nature movement. Natural was always better: natural make-up, natural hair styles, natural fabrics, natural materials in jewelry, natural foods, natural medicines

---

[20]Dick-Read, Grantly, M.D. *Childbirth Without Fear*. Harper & Row, New York, 1981, p. 22.

and vitamins, and so forth, and then came natural childbirth. Even in the 1990s natural childbirth was still around, hailed as a method to give women

> *In the 1970s, natural was always better, which led to the notion that childbirth is better if it is natural—no pain relief.*

more control over the labor and delivery experience and reduce the need for chemical relief.

The gospel of natural childbirth swept across the country with amazing speed and created a cult of female followers. Writers such as Britain's Sheila Kitzinger, Ina May Gaskin, and others lauded natural childbirth as the way to free women from the highly masculinized medical hierarchy and give them back command of the birth experience. What united them was their desire to help women regain dignity and control of the birthing process whether it occurred at home, in a hospital, or elsewhere. For this every woman should be thankful. Terms such as birthing rooms, home delivery, alternative birth centers and the like became familiar to all women of childbearing age as they raced to experience a more satisfying delivery.

Though initially much good came from the movement, even more good came from the highly informative prenatal classes that were spawned nationwide. To this day, expectant mothers who make their first OB/GYN appointment to confirm their condition are routinely encouraged to sign up for these classes, which likely reduce fear more than anything else.

The Folly and the Craze

Much mental and physical suffering resulted from

the follies of the natural childbirth craze and its insistence that a woman could be in total control of childbirth pain or eliminate it altogether. As the concept migrated around the country, Dick-Read's carefully prescribed steps for training the mother in mind and body and his insistence on a relaxed birthing environment were forgotten. A rigid, politically correct approach to childbirth began to dominate the medical community (much like the politics of nursing these days). Any birth that was unmedicated became a "natural" birth.

A rigid, politically correct approach to childbirth began to dominate the medical community. Any birth that was unmedicated became a "natural" birth.

The extreme treatment I received (or didn't receive) while hospitalized resulted from this mania. At no time in our history have sufferers of an equally painful physical condition had so many put so much pressure on them to forego pain relief as pregnant women did during the natural childbirth craze. For any other hospitalization for conditions involving mild to severe pain, analgesics or anesthesia are administered *not* because they aid in a successful operation and *not* because they speed healing, but solely out of compassion for the patient.

For any other hospitalization for conditions involving mild to severe pain, analgesics or anesthesia are administered not because they aid in a successful operation and not because they speed healing, but solely out of compassion for the patient.

We lay the lightest possible load on those already burdened with hospitalization. Why should childbirth be treated differently? Relief of suffering should be our goal, not political points.

As with so many other cultural movements that begin with good intentions and claim to be motivated by compassion, such as socialism or environmentalism, natural childbirth began as a way for women to gain control over their childbirth experience, which indisputably is and should remain women's domain. But it progressed in the hands of humanists to become a political tool, a feminist declaration of independence. Instead of freeing and elevating women, it ensnared them to another bondage, wherein adherence to the ideal became more important than their well-being. My unfortunate experience at the birth of my first child is an example.

If the goal of natural childbirth is to put the woman in control, who was in control of my birth experience? Certainly not me. Forty years earlier, before the natural childbirth movement swept over America like an insidious cloud of mind-numbing gas, denial of painkiller to a laboring woman who requested it would have been unthinkable, because concern for the woman, not the cause, was paramount.

But then, 40 years earlier she would also have had her arms and legs strapped to a table for 24–30 hours; been knocked out completely so that she had no memory of her child's entrance into the world; and been denied the comfort of a loved one's presence, all excesses caused by a medical community out of control. This was my mother's experience.

So it's understandable why natural childbirth proponents reacted so fervently to the indignities foisted on women who left the bedroom for the delivery room. Women wanted control again. But they went about it the wrong way.

Denial and Guilt

My experience is not unique. The two biggest complaints of women disillusioned with natural childbirth is that 1) They were led to believe that breathing techniques alone would significantly reduce the pain so that they could handle the "discomfort." (How can anyone call this adequate preparation for childbirth when these women weren't told that the process can be extremely painful? When the word *pain* was never used during training?); and 2) They were made to feel guilty if they changed their minds about natural childbirth and requested anesthesia at the onset of contractions. They were made to feel that they had failed both their child and their birth partner by putting their comfort above the perceived safety of the infant, a sure mortal sin in the prayer book of the natural childbirth preachers.

I have met women who have even experienced this misplaced guilt when they had to have anesthesia for an unplanned caesarian, a surgical delivery instead of a vaginal one! *How crazy can you get?*

Twentieth Century Religious Denial

We have come full circle. For four centuries we distorted the Bible to deny women relief in childbirth. Then in the 20th century we denied that women were cursed with childbirth pain in the first place. Even respected evangelical leaders have been so taken in by the so-called natural childbirth movement that they've described it as the divine plan for women, a testimony that we have for centuries misunderstood Gen. 3:16.

In Joyce Milburn's and Lynnette Smith's *The Natural Childbirth Book*, they cite Christian physician and teacher Dr. Ed Wheat to prove that we have been wrong all along about the curse:

217

Dr. Ed Wheat emphasizes that women are *not* cursed. Neither are men. If you look closely at Gen. 3:17 you will see that it was the *ground* God cursed. This was done for the benefit of fallen mankind—to give people work to do, since no one is truly happy in a state of idleness. In Prov. 14:23 we are told that 'in all labour there is profit.' The Hebrew root word for 'labor' in that verse (*etsev*) is the same word used to describe the work man exerts in 'subduing the Earth' and the effort women put forth bearing children. The word *etsev* refers to strenuous, intense toil or hard work, but *not necessarily pain* ...

God was, in reality, establishing a system whereby man could live most effectively in a sin-tainted world—a system that, when followed, causes the 'curse' to have no effect on us. This system includes, not pain in childbirth as many would have us believe, but toil— LABOR—climaxed with indescribable satisfaction and unspeakable joy. And the latter part of Gen. 3:16 explicitly describes how this labor is to be carried out: '... thy desire shall be to thy husband, and *he shall rule over thee.*'

It's not surprising, then, that methods of husband-coached childbirth are so effective. Although their originators did not realize it, the discovery that the husband's presence

218

and encouragement relieved pain in labor was actually the *re*discovery of a law of nature, set forth in Genesis.[21] (emphasis Milburn/Smith)

Dr. James Dobson, respected speaker and author whose books, tapes, and articles have helped to strengthen thousands of families, endorsed Milburn/Smith's book. Concerned Women for America President Dr. Beverly LaHaye endorsed it with a forward.

Dr. Wheat's conclusions regarding Gen. 3:16–17 are wrong. It's true that the man was not cursed and the ground was, though it makes no difference whether it was Adam or the ground, since Adam earned his bread from the ground and was directly affected by the curse upon it.

> *It's not true that God cursed the ground as a blessing in disguise to Adam.*

But it's not true that God cursed the ground as a blessing in disguise to Adam because he couldn't be happy in a "state of idleness." Before sin entered the world, God had set Adam in the garden to dress and to keep it (Gen. 2:15), so before sin Adam was not idle. The Hebrew word from which we get "dress" is *abad,* which specifically means to work, but also to serve or till. God doesn't confuse his blessings with his curses.

To a degree, Dr. Wheat is right when he defines "labour" from Prov. 14:23. The word *etsev* (also *etseb*) is the same root from which you get "sorrow" in Gen. 3:16 that describes the birth process. The word suggests toil, but specifically *painful* toil, also a *pang in body or*

---

[21]Quoted in Joyce Milburn and Lynnette Smith, *The Natural Childbirth Book.* Bethany Fellowship, Inc., Minneapolis,1981, pp. 26–27.

mind, grievous, labor, and *sorrow.* This doesn't mean a light day at the office for the working man, nor for mom a few pants, a delicate push, and out pops junior. God said the painful toil, pangs, and grievous labor of making a living and delivering a child would be greatly multiplied.

To trivialize or deny the curses, especially regarding childbirth, is obscene, a trap for women. Just because God didn't use the word *curse* when He addressed the woman doesn't mean that childbirth is not cursed. When Jesus cursed the fig tree in Mark 11:14, he didn't use curse, but that tree was *cursed.* In v. 21, Peter said, "Master, behold, the fig tree *which thou cursedst* is withered away." Indeed, in just a few hours the tree died.

> *Just because God didn't use the word curse when He addressed the woman doesn't mean that childbirth is not cursed.*

Likewise, God's words alone in Gen. 3:16 without the preface of "I curse" were sufficient to make the negative forces of sorrow and pain cling to women forever. All God has to do is speak something into existence and it exists, either cursing or blessing. Other examples of this appear in Scripture, especially the Old Testament.

However, God didn't curse Adam and Eve. They cursed themselves when they violated heavenly law, because their act of disobedience set in motion the law of sin and death. In Gen. 3 God explains this to them, He forewarns of what is to come. But like the supposed blessing in disguise of the curse on the ground, those who try to make Eve's curse into a blessing are just calling black, white, and white, black. It's faulty Scripture interpretation.

Consider the context: God's words in Gen. 3:16

were spoken immediately following our first mother's sin, an explanation of the result of her *sin*, therefore it's ridiculous to call this curse a blessing. Is it logical that God was explaining the *blessing* that would result from Eve's disobedience?

As for "thy husband shall rule over thee" being an impetus to the rediscovery of a law of nature in regard to husband-coached childbirth ... it's exceedingly difficult for me to read SO MUCH into ONE Scripture, especially because the notion of husband-coached childbirth is confirmed by no other Bible verse, AND because there are so many other verses that talk about the terrible pain Jewish women suffered in childbirth.

However, Gen. 3:16 has been used successfully as a foundation for the teaching that the husband is the head of the wife, a doctrine confirmed at least five other places in the Bible. Gen. 3:16 has nothing to do with husband-coached childbirth. If it did, the Jews sure missed it. As early as Genesis female midwives and not husbands assisted women in delivery.

Further, the "discovery that the husband's presence and encouragement relieved pain in labor was actually the *re*discovery of a law of nature," to this all I can say is, if this law exists, then I must conclude that it was in operation at the time of Juliet's birth. Natural laws operate regardless of our knowledge or ignorance of them. If my husband's presence helped relieve pain, I shudder to think what that day would have been like had he not been there. If I had to do it all over again, using only the natural "anesthesia" of my husband's presence (who, I should add, did everything to comfort and encourage me), I'd prefer to be konked on the head with a very BIG club and put out altogether.

The final insult to women, the one most likely to bring them into spiritual bondage, is set forth by Milburn and Smith in chapter 7, "Does It Hurt Yet?" By

221

their chapter subhead, "But refuse ... old wives' fables" (from I Tim. 4:7), they intimate that childbirth pain is indeed just an old wives' tale. They attribute pain to one or more of three causes: a *physiological* cause, something physically wrong with your body; *functional*, something you do wrong, such as not panting correctly or at the wrong time; or *emotional anxiety,* ignorance of the birth process causes you to *interpret* sensations of labor and delivery as pain. (This suggests that the average woman isn't bright enough to differentiate between a "sensation"—whatever that is—and "pain.")

Milburn and Smith impose a terrible burden upon the already stressed mind of a laboring woman. If she, along with her doctor, can discover no physical reason for her pain, then the only logical explanation is that she is laboring or thinking incorrectly. Her pain is her own fault.

But Milburn and Smith contradict their theory of the origin of childbirth pain in a telling anecdote in their book. One woman describes being awakened from sleep by a strong contraction. "This really hurt and I was scared!"[22] she exclaimed. The source of her pain couldn't have been physiological because there was no indication that she was in poor health; it couldn't have been functional because she was asleep when the contraction started. A person can't be anxious and tense due to fear of the next contraction while asleep. And it couldn't have been emotional anxiety because she was semiconscious. When asleep, women are unaware that they're in labor. Had it not been for the strong contraction she experienced, the woman would have kept right on sleeping, relaxed and ignorant of her physical condition. *And she said it hurt.*

---

[22]Milburn and Smith, p. 61.

Another, more celebrated case hit the airwaves during my childbirth years, wherein a woman experienced childbirth pain though unaware she was in labor. A Seattle, Wash. couple, James and Deborah Schodt,[23] had been unable to conceive for 17 years. They had given up hope when early one evening in March 1994, Mrs. Schodt began to suffer from what she thought was a particularly bad case of the flu. She described the pain as "excruciating." She was cramping so badly that she and her husband feared for her health and took off for the hospital. Much to their surprise and delight, 10 minutes after arrival Mrs. Schodt delivered a healthy, 6 lb., 1 oz. girl.

Mrs. Schodt had no inkling she was pregnant. She attributed the cessation of her period to stress due to her mother's recently diagnosed cancer and the death of her boss. A nurse confirmed her conclusion and told her that amenorrhea is common during times of great emotional upheaval. Nevertheless, painful labor contractions—not fear of them—sent her panicking to the hospital.

Helen Wessel's *The Joy of Natural Childbirth* (also titled *Natural Childbirth and the Christian Family* and *Natural Childbirth and the Family*) is well written and researched. She goes to greater lengths than Milburn and Smith to prove that Gen. 3:16 is not a curse of pain but of only long toil. She also says that it's primarily fear of pain that causes pain and that the many women who died in childbirth in the 19th century only increased that fear, leading to a 20th century obsession. To prove that God didn't curse women with childbirth pain, she spends many pages presenting her voluminous

---

[23]Bartley, Nancy. "Woman's Bad Case of 'Flu' "Turns Out to Be Healthy Baby," *Seattle Times*, March 5, 1994.

research, including references to Jewish texts.

According to Wessel, our western interpretation of the Old Testament is wrong: The Jews did not associate pain with childbirth. Hers is an odd conclusion, however, since the Old Testament contains nine references to childbirth pangs, and every one is used as an allegory to describe the profound suffering, affliction, and death that were prophesied and fulfilled upon the Israelites and others to punish their disobedience. Three of the four Hebrew words employed, *tsiyr, chebel,* and *chiylah*, literally mean the throes of childbirth; the fourth, *tsarar*, means a cramp, pang, affliction, or distress. Micah 4:8–10 says these pangs are caused by childbirth.

> *Even if you are of the camp that insists that "sorrow" in childbirth means only hard work and not pain, how do you explain why God used the example of childbirth to warn the Jews of the intense suffering and destruction that awaited them?*

Even if you are of the camp that insists that "sorrow" in childbirth means only hard work and not pain, how do you explain why God used the example of childbirth to warn the Jews of the intense suffering and destruction that awaited them? He wanted them to repent before it was too late. If the Jews didn't associate childbirth with pain and sorrow, then God sure picked a strange and ineffective way to motivate them to repent. And if the Jews didn't associate childbirth with pain, why did they have at least three words in their language to describe it?

Wessel studied more than Milburn and Smith did, but she too failed to prove the curse of pain to be anything but a curse. Sadly, her conclusions also blame women for their pain. She claims their problem is ignorance, laziness in breathing and pelvic exercises, or failure to relax.

> *First the Church called the curse on childbirth God's will, then it reduced it to just toil, then it said it never existed in the first place. But to make sense of Gen. 3:16, we must consider the context in which God spoke to Eve.*

Ironically, Christians who try to make a case for natural childbirth as the biblical way (from the beginning yet!) trumpet their own weakness for following cultural fads and ignoring plain truth from Scripture. First the Church called the curse on childbirth God's will, then it reduced it to just toil, then it said it never existed in the first place. *But to make sense of Gen. 3:16, we must consider the context in which God spoke to Eve.* Adam and Eve had committed a crime and were now receiving an explanation as to how their sin would work spiritual death in their lives and the lives of their descendants. How anyone can expound beyond this basic truth, denying the effect of sin and even calling it a blessing, is mind boggling.

It's All in Her Head

Secular writers also point to everything and anything, but usually the mother, to explain childbirth pain. In all the books I researched for this study, explanations for pain were the same. The Gen. 3:16 curse was ignored or referenced as a silly religious fairy tale; childbirth pain was blamed on the mother's poor education. The burden to alleviate it was squarely on the mother's shoulders.

In Sheila Kitzinger's *Home Birth*, she attributes one cause of childbirth pain to the way a woman is

225

treated by hospital personnel through use of rules, tests, and the "constant threat of obstetric intervention."[24] But some enter a hospital because they *want* intervention and the assurance of a painless delivery. These women experience relief, not fear, as they contemplate their hospital stay.

The hole in the theory that fear of obstetric intervention causes pain is obvious. Over the centuries when women only gave birth at home, attended by those who loved and tenderly cared for them, when they had no reason to fear unnecessary intervention and every reason to feel at peace in familiar surroundings, the experience of childbirth pain was universal.

Despite its suspect title, Carl Jones' *Mind Over Labor* refreshingly does not deny pain or promise a pain-free delivery. Certified childbirth educator Jones does claim that using "spiritual imagery" reduces fear and pain and makes childbirth a happy experience. A strong connection exists, he says, between a laboring woman's state of mind and what goes on in her body.

I agree that a connection exists between state of mind and physical health. But God said labor pain would be *greatly multiplied*, and I strongly suspect that spiritual imagery is not enough to counteract it. Jones' eight-step method includes the following imagery (sample) to help relax the mother, though what is spiritual about it escapes me. He

---

[24]Kitzinger, Sheila. *Home Birth*. Dorling Kindersley, Inc., New York, 1991, p. 19.

suggests that the following exercise be done before labor begins:

> Imagine that you are outdoors watching the snow fall.
>
> Catch a falling snowflake on the sleeve of your jacket. Look at it closely. The snowflake is perfectly symmetrical, an exquisite ice sculpture in miniature. As it melts and disappears on the surface of your jacket, see another replacing it—equally perfect but different from the one before.
>
> Stand quietly for a minute and observe the snow falling. There is nothing you need to do. Nowhere you need to be. But here. Now.
>
> As you watch, the snow falls in its own way, its own time, without your effort. All you have to do is observe the flakes forming endless patterns on the sleeve of your jacket.
>
> Now be aware that the same natural power that creates endless new forms is working right now within your womb, creating a form far more exquisite than the snowflakes: your child.
>
> Tell yourself: When my baby is ready to be born, the door of my womb will open so he or she can be born. It will open without my effort. There is nothing I need to do but let it happen.
>
> When you are ready, slowly count to five, take a deep breath, and open

your eyes.[25]

A more bizarre mothering mantra appears on page 86, where the woman is directed to imagine herself inside her womb with the unborn baby, where she is supposed to repeat "baby ... baby ... baby ..." with each exhalation.

You can make whatever you want of this. I'll take the epidural.

Gaskin's *Spiritual Midwifery*, that '70s, self-proclaimed "spiritual book"[26] prefaced with Gaskin's confession of coming into the spirituality of touch from association with a monkey, is a study in the heights of metaphysics to which a cult will ascend (descend?) to establish the religion of natural childbirth. Gaskin was the head instructor of midwives on a farm "church," located on 1,000 secluded acres of raw forest land in Tennessee. Her book is part instruction manual, part testimony, part anecdote. She includes firsthand accounts of deliveries, 225 pages of them, along with graphic photos of husbands massaging their wives' breasts to loosen up the vaginal opening, confessions of "psychedelic" birthing experiences, the need for telepathy between couples, the psychic energy provided to the baby through nursing, and photos of naked, delivering mothers.

Pain is absent from every account. Either Gaskin's devotees do not experience it, or Gaskin judiciously included only testimonies that support her claim of painless childbirth. Pain is mentioned in just seven citations, all in the last few pages of the book that deal

---

[25]Jones, Carl. *Mind Over Labor*. Viking Penguin, Inc., New York, 1987, p. 95.

[26]Gaskin, Ina May. *Spiritual Midwifery*. Paul Mandelstein, year and place not given, p. 11.

with complications. I did find pain on one page, wherein the laboring woman distinguishes between *perceived* pain and real pain. "And sometimes I had to override brief temptation to interpret that powerful earthy push as pain instead of as life force ..."[27]

To Gaskin's credit, the sacredness of childbirth is a theme that bursts forth on nearly every page.

The trouble with all these theories is that they trivialize or try to explain away a woman's "perception" of pain because no direct physiological cause can be found. In other words, if science can't find a scientific reason for the pain, then there is no pain, just a woman who imagines it. But does this mean that "perceived" pain does not hurt as much as "real" pain?

> *Men don't suffer from the prognosis of perceived pain nearly as often as doctors diagnose it in women.*

Men don't suffer from the prognosis of perceived pain nearly as often as doctors diagnose it in women. Other uncomfortable conditions related to a woman's fertility process have been attributed more to faulty thinking than faulty hormone production or faulty reproductive organs: menstrual problems, morning sickness (Gaskin maintains this is a problem primarily seen in upper-middle-class women with too much time on their hands), postbirth depression (baby blues), and menopause symptoms have all at one time or another been blamed on a woman's head.

What a tragedy that the joyful act of giving birth has been cast together with all these symptoms in the nefarious movement to persuade women that they author their own pain. The fruit of this fallacy is that they are denied useful, candid spiritual guidance and

---

[27]Gaskin, p. 179.

effective medical help when they need it most.

Natural or Unnatural Childbirth?

Natural childbirth is the condition in which God originally planned delivery to occur, in a sin-free, pain-free world. Natural childbirth is what Eve would have enjoyed if she had delivered before sin became a factor.

What is "natural" childbirth? I conclude that natural childbirth contains no elements of modern or pseudo-medicine such as counting exercises, breathing techniques, massages, water deliveries, mantras, alternative birth centers, or any other pain control methods. Natural childbirth is the condition in which God originally planned delivery to occur, in a sin-free, pain-free world. Natural childbirth is what Eve would have enjoyed if she had delivered before sin became a factor. *But that pain-free childbirth experience has been lost to us forever.*

God designed us to live and procreate in such a heavenly world. We were not designed to cope with stress, pain, guilt, sickness, disease, or any other fruit of sin. But we live in a stained world. What we call natural, life as we experience it now with all its negative aspects, is actually unnatural in every way compared to God's original design. Therefore childbirth in its most "natural" state is truly unnatural. The whole world and its processes were and are affected by the law of sin and death—why should childbirth be excluded?

We may have been translated into the Kingdom of his dear Son, but our bodies live on earth. It's a spiritual thing: The law of sin and death is still around, still operating down here where we live.

The world exalts nature, but nature can kill us.

The world exalts nature, but nature can kill us. When is nature predictably on our side? From Genesis onward we have been in a continual battle to tame it, and often we lose.

Natural childbirth proponents are trying to apply a natural, humanistic solution to a problem that is spiritual. They can't win.

We Hope in God's Word

So then, if a woman believes in a curse on childbirth, how does she approach labor and delivery? With her Bible, of course. Speaking directly to the issue of childbirth, God promises Christian women two things: 1) It has the potential to be unnaturally painful (Gen. 3:16); and 2) He will not forsake you but get you safely through it (I Tim. 2:15).

Ways exist to overcome the first, negative promise. If natural childbirth seems reasonable to you, then study well and find yourself an equally convinced birth partner, even if it's someone other than your husband. Your faith in God's goodness and support from your partner will help. If you take the alternative route, employing analgesics or anesthesia, you still need prenatal classes, support from family or friends, and faith.

The second promise is conditional. I Tim. 2:15 says women will be saved in childbearing "if they continue in faith and charity and holiness with sobriety." The Greek word from which we get "saved" does not mean eternal salvation but to be kept safe, delivered, or protected. But many women died in childbirth at the period that these words were written, and many women since, Christians too, have died.

Because so many Christians have died, it's hard

231

for some to depend on their Savior to get them through childbirth intact. I believe, however, in a literal interpretation, that Paul spoke of protection from mortal, not spiritual death. But as with all God's promises, He expects us to live righteously to enjoy their full benefit. And He expects us *by faith* to apply his promises to our situation. Faith in the written word—not the severity of the need—moves the hand of God. Many good Christians die daily from physical ailments for which God has promised healing. Christians likewise do without necessary spiritual and material blessings because they're unfamiliar with God's promises that speak to both. Others fall into Satan's trap because they're ignorant of their authority as believers.

God said that his people perish for lack of knowledge. I can only wonder what kind of teaching Christian women heard during former centuries and how spiritually prepared they were for childbirth. Judging from the Church's response and the literature examined here, I suspect they heard much on the curse of Gen. 3:16, the weakness of their gender to bear adversity, and their responsibility to quietly and humbly accept suffering and even death in childbirth. I suspect they heard little of the promise of I Tim. 2:15.

Does redemption guarantee a pain-free delivery? No. We have been redeemed from the curses of the law, and by faith we can overcome those listed in Deut. 28. But the curse on childbirth in Gen. 3:16 was not a curse of the law because the law had not yet been given. So, just like the Gen. 3:16–17 curses, wherein a woman must submit to her husband and a man must sweat to earn his bread, were not removed in Christ, the curse on childbirth wasn't removed either.

Methods exist, however, whereby we can almost overcome its effects. For some it's natural childbirth.

For others it's drugs. No matter: God never instructs us to lay down and let a curse roll over us. We must work to overcome it, expecting God to help us.

Which brings us back to the beginning of this chapter, where I discussed medieval attitudes toward laboring women and how the medical society and the Church were determined that women suffer in childbirth to somehow pay their debt for sin. Similar teaching on the curse concerning the man (or the ground) is nonexistent. Christian men always have and do now make every reasonable and sometimes unreasonable effort to circumvent the curse on the ground. They go into debt for college and graduate degrees to increase their earning power. After working hard all day, husbands and fathers attend night school to increase their chance of job promotion. Many attend Christian seminars on tithing, giving, and biblical laws of prosperity. Do we fault men for striving to better take care of themselves and their families?

Even if we approached the curse on the ground from a strictly agricultural perspective, when have we not sought more safe and productive farming methods? Irrigation, fertilization, insect control, organic production, hydroponics, and cross-breeding for more disease- and insect-resistant food plants have been elevated to prestigious places in scientific research. Does anyone suggest that we cease our search for knowledge because by doing so we thwart the curse?

Such a notion is ridiculous. And just as ridiculous are arguments that seek to separate women from pain relief, pressuring them to return to primitive means by denying that a curse ever existed. When unnatural is called natural, when women are pressured to use impotent fleshly tools against a clearly spiritual force, they will return to the bondage of fear. If we teach that there is no curse, then women will not prepare

233

themselves to exercise dominion over it.

Though she supports the pain-is-in-your-mind theory, I still like what Ellen J. Greenfield has to say when it comes to a woman's choice in childbirth and delivery:

> Birthing requires a tremendous amount of rigorous bodily exertion, much of which can reach undeniably painful levels in many, if not most, women.
>
> What seems most important is not to deny this, but to minimize its ultimate impact on the end result. Women deserve assurance that they will be able to handle any pain they experience, either through carefully practiced techniques with proven results in minimizing the perception of pain, or through the use of analgesics or even anesthetics, should they feel the need. No woman having a baby in this age should have to deal with any more discomfort than she feels that she can handle with dignity.[28]

---

[28]Greenfield, Ellen J, M.D. *You Can Have an Easier Delivery*. Contemporary Books, Chicago, 1988, pp. 8–9.

Hiss #13: God Didn't Really Mean Conception

> Unto the woman he said, I will
> greatly multiply thy sorrow and thy
> conception. Gen. 3:16

The Church always has something to say about sex. There's no shortage of material to reveal what it has taught from the pulpit through the ages; examples follow. Catholics and Protestants have approached the subject from every angle, and centuries later they still draw lines in the sand over interpretation of the same few Bible verses that deal with it. The common thread that runs through all their writings always leads back to the same question: Does sex in marriage without the intent of procreation thwart the purpose of God?

Some of you are chuckling right now at what appears to be an irrelevant, Puritanical way of looking at an issue that at first blush (excuse the pun) has such an *obvious* answer. But people haven't always thought that way. Consider: If you were a committed Christian in Augustine's time, you might be spending a good part of your waking hours determining the tricky business of how to come together with your spouse without expending any "passion" in the process!

Sex in Marriage

Jews of Old Testament times had no inhibitions about marital sex. They looked upon it as entirely right, good, and God ordained, as Scripture says only positive things about it. The Talmud contains a section called "Sanctification"[1] that discusses betrothals and marital relations; their approval of both is implied in the title. In other places in the Torah (the whole body of Jewish oral tradition, writings, and laws) married couples are encouraged to engage in several sexual sessions in quick succession, thus "guaranteeing" conception of a son.

Their ready acceptance of marital relations is logical when you consider that the first commandment God gave to humans was Gen. 1:28, "Be fruitful, and multiply."

A few Jewish leaders, however, veered from the simplicity of God's approval. Their reason is unclear. First century Jewish philosopher Philo of Alexandria (30 B.C.–45 A.D.) said that married love is redeemed only because it's necessary for procreation. It's difficult to attribute his shift in traditional Jewish thinking to the excesses of the Christian Church, as the Church was in its infancy at the time of his death and hardly could have made much of an impact on centuries of Hebrew teaching.

The earliest record of the Church's attitude toward sex is the New Testament, but I assume you're familiar with these passages. Since it was written, and especially in the Middle Ages—the 1000-year period from 476 when the last Roman emperor was deposed until about

---

[1]Neusner, Jacob. *Invitation to the Talmud*. Harper and Row, San Francisco, 1984, p. 80.

1456 when Constantinople was conquered by the Turks—attitudes took unusual turns from the biblical example as a thick shroud of spiritual darkness enveloped Church thought.

A common belief in Augustine's time was that all sex is inherently sinful, therefore Adam and Eve could not have indulged before the fall. Many gave their opinions as to the original, sexless mode of procreation that God would have encouraged in Eden had sin not entered.

Augustine disagreed with theories that described the mechanics of sexless sex. In his *City of God*, he said that Adam and Eve did have sex before sin, but it was without shame because it was without "passion." Their union, he explained, was no more or less evil than other simple body movements, such as flexing the leg or arm. But when sin entered so did desire, and the burden of the Christian was to strive for spousal relations without it. Augustine drew his conclusion from his interpretation of I Thess. 4:3–4, that a person should learn how to possess his or her body in sanctification and not in the lust of concupiscence. What good Christian, questioned Augustine, "... would not prefer, if this were possible, to beget children without this lust?"[2]

(Pope) Gregory the Great (c. 540–604), a leader in Christianizing Europe, said that married couples who have sex only for pleasure, without intent to conceive, "befoul" their coming together, and that any sexual encounter, including marital, demands penance.[3]

Others who followed agreed. Italian theologian and philosopher (St.) Bonaventure (c. 1217–1274) said that even couples who had coitus for the express

---

[2]Augustine, Book XIV, pp. 464–465.
[3]Ryken, p. 40.

purpose of begetting children were without sin only if they loathed the act.

In the same century, Aquinas condemned any effort to avoid conception as a serious moral failure: "In so far as the generation of offspring is impeded, it's a vice against nature ...."[4] His emphasis, not on the sinfulness of the act but the act without intent to conceive, was the beginning of the end of the Church's teaching on the inherent sinfulness of marital sex.

Yet so dominant was the notion of sex as sin, that in the 5th century the Catholic Church prohibited priests from marrying. Fifteen centuries later the ruling still stands. The Church went so far as to institute celibacy days during which married couples were required to refrain. But the number grew from year to year, until at one time half the year and sometimes more was set aside for chastity. Others suggested five days a week. Latin scholar and translator of the Vulgate, Jerome (c. 340–420) declared that God had refused to bless the second day of the week because the number two suggested marriage, which was sinful.[5]

The predominance of such teaching led to an inordinate glorification of virginity and disdainful treatment of the wedded state in period literature. Writers gave more attention to and celebrated adulterous more than married love in the Middle Ages. Considering how the Church worked so hard to take the fun out of the marriage act, this should come as no surprise.

Even Luther, whose wholesale break with Catholic tradition is legendary, was ambivalent about the rightness of sex in marriage. Though he called marriage

---

[4]Green, Shirley. *The Curious History of Contraception.* St. Martin's Press, New York, 1971, p. 7.
[5]Green, p. 41.

a "holy estate,"[6] and acknowledged that God blessed it, his concern about marital passion rivaled Augustine's:

> Now [after the fall] man is so
> burdened with the leprosy of impurity
> that when in marriage he begets
> children his passions become almost
> irrational and he cannot produce
> offspring in the fear of God.[7]

Refreshingly, the Calvinists and Puritans rejected what can only be termed a bad attitude about marital relations in their acceptance of the biblical admonition that "marriage is honorable in all, and the bed undefiled" (Heb. 13:4). Calvin was outspoken in his opposition to the notion that married sex was sinful, and likewise spoke against those who advocated celibacy because of the snare of temptation to "bestial abominations."[8] He also railed against those who led young women into convents before they were old enough to make up their own minds about celibacy.[9]

Despite all common wisdom to the contrary, the Puritans elevated marital sex to a state of poetic ecstasy not openly acknowledged by God's people since the Song of Solomon was penned. Puritan minister William Gouge made the point from I Tim. 4:1–3 that "... it's accounted a doctrine of devils to forbid to marry. For it's a doctrine contrary to God's Word."[10] Puritans promoted the revolutionary idea that the marital act is good and free from sin's shadow in their sermons and in

---

[6]Luther, p. 381.
[7]Luther, p. 35.
[8]Quoted in Bouwsma, p. 136.
[9]Bouwsma, pp. 137–138.
[10]Quoted in Ryken, p. 42.

some surviving personal letters between husbands and wives.

Milton hailed married love in his masterpiece, *Paradise Lost,* and justified his opinion from the Bible. He said that "they shall be one flesh" (Gen. 2:24) was inserted precisely

> ... to justify and make legitimate
> the rites of the marriage bed; which
> was not unneedful, if for all this
> warrant they were suspected of
> pollution by some sects of philosophy
> and religions of old, and latelier among
> the Papists.[11]

As Puritans held in contempt virtually all teachings of the Catholic (Papist) Church and were energetically reactionary to doctrine they felt was not grounded in the Bible, it was to the advantage of married love that it had been so vociferously vilified by Catholic priests.

Conception

If religious literature is considered, conception in marriage never suffered the evil reputation brought about by frequency as did the marriage act itself. But the desire to thwart conception, or at least slow it down, took centuries to disassociate itself from its connection to prostitution and adultery.

And everybody had an opinion about it.

Augustine bemoaned that propagation capacity in his time was not what it might have been before sin. He believed this despite the record of commonly large families (large in our 21st century estimation) of ten or

---

[11]Quoted in Ryken, p. 43.

more children throughout the centuries, and despite the Genesis record that original *sin* brought about *multiplied* conceptions:

> ... but from the whole race He has not withdrawn the blessing of propagation once conferred. But though not withdrawn on account of sin, this power of propagation is not what it would have been had there been no sin.[12]

Augustine concluded that, because the power to propagate remained after the fall, it proved God's mercy toward us. To Augustine, a more fitting punishment on mankind would have been sterility.

Though few Catholics today might agree that our ability to conceive operates at a substandard rate, at least officially, the Catholic Church has remained unswerving in its opinion that each conception is the intervention of divine will. To intentionally thwart God's will is sin.

Early in the 20th century the Catholic Church mobilized its first American lobby to create a national counteroffensive against social reformer and founder of Planned Parenthood Margaret Sanger's (1883–1966) efforts to legalize birth control literature and devices. The Church's adamant denunciation of contraceptives as a destroyer of the family, and its successful campaign to portray Sanger and others as subversives, represented the only organized opposition that Sanger was never able to overcome. Primarily because Catholic leaders insisted that followers refrain from using any kind of birth control method other than regular

---

[12]Augustine, Book XXII, p. 850.

abstinence, people still vaguely associate this teaching with all Christianity, including Protestants.

But some Protestants did oppose birth control. Luther:

> It's therefore barbarian cruelty and inhumanity if people, and especially the wealthy and noble, do not want to have children and rather forego marriage than have heirs and offspring.[13]

We can only wonder *who* was treated with barbarian cruelty if a person decided to forego marriage to avoid parenthood and why this was a greater sin on the part of the rich than the poor. Nevertheless, Luther's condemnation of abstainers reflected the widespread concern over what would happen if women could somehow gain control of their rate of fertility. People genuinely feared the human race would soon cease to exist. Their 15th century angst was carried by concerned ministers and social engineers straight into the middle of the 20th.

Luther didn't stop at warning Christians about the evils of foregoing marriage to avoid childbearing. You can practically hear the song in his voice when he explained how Eve likely received her news about multiplied sorrow and conception. "... She could bear children, and retained the honor of motherhood. Therefore her heart was no doubt full of joy despite her punishment ..."[14] Like Augustine, he thought her logical punishment would be loss of childbirth privileges altogether, and so he delighted that women retain the

---

[13]Luther, p.56.
[14]Luther, p. 82.

honor. Luther concluded that what Eve would have had, prior to sin, was childbearing and rearing *without pain*, and called hers a "severe chastisement" that "wearies" her.

Too bad that he focused only on the curse of pain and was silent about multiplied conception, leaving future generations nothing to work with.

> *Nearly all early Christian writers followed Luther's lead by confirming a curse of pain on delivery but saying nothing about a curse on conception.*

Nearly all early Christian writers followed Luther's lead by confirming a curse of pain on delivery but saying nothing about a curse on conception. Wesley wrote in his Genesis notes that God promised women sorrow in childbirth. He expounded on the word "multiply" and God's justice in giving women multiplied *pain*. He explained that the curse is observed when a woman is delivering, confirming that he interpreted it to be only a long, painful delivery and that it had nothing to do with frequent conceptions. Yet he too made his observations using quotes from the KJV, a translation that outlines curses on both.

From all their commentaries dealing with the Genesis curse on childbirth, but especially from their silence about the curse on conception, we deduce that Church fathers viewed closely spaced, multiple conceptions as natural and desirable, not a curse at all. Their interpretation followed a logical line of thinking: to voluntarily avoid conception was to willfully reject God's blessing of children, an unholy scenario reeking of ingratitude.

But their numerous messages condemning the use of birth control devices or the avoidance of marriage to

> *What was so objectionable about parenthood during these years that, without empirical evidence, Church leaders were convinced that women would stop or at least reduce bearing if only they had the choice?*

remain childless more than suggest that the people they led thought differently. What was it about the experience of these husbands and wives that caused them to go astray? What was so objectionable about parenthood during these years that, without empirical evidence, Church leaders were convinced that women would stop or at least reduce bearing if only they had the choice?

If anything, their alarm over contraceptive use among their followers confirmed their unspoken conviction that women who bore large numbers of children by frequent, closely spaced pregnancies did so not by choice, but precisely because they had found no way to avoid it.

The Politics of Contraception

The search for reliable means of birth control is a tired one. For centuries, the universal dilemmas of lack of control over family size and too-frequent pregnancies has led people to try all kinds of ingenious devices.

Before latex, condoms were made from linen and animal intestines, diaphragms were fashioned of cotton or wool, and there were home recipes comprised of boric acid, grease barriers, and who knows all what else.[15] Among women it has always been common knowledge that ways exist to avoid pregnancy, even if it's just *coitus interruptus*, a practice recorded in the

---

[15]Rowbotham, p. 149.

Old Testament. Desperate women have resorted to all kinds of unsafe practices to prevent conception. When those failed, the most desperate turned to abortion and infanticide.

In early 19th century America, some were more outraged about advertisements for contraceptives than abortion, a widespread and legal option at the time. When Robert Dale Owen published *Moral Physiology* in 1831, his instructions on how to avoid pregnancy were called a "Complete Recipe" for a "Strumpet."[16] He served hard labor for distributing it.

Six years later, Rev. John Todd, writing in *Serpents in the Doves' Nest*, complained about the high number of single-child homes and women's easy access to contraceptive information:

> There is scarcely a young lady in New England—and probably it's so throughout the land—whose marriage can be announced in the paper, without her being insulted within a week by receiving through the mail a printed circular, offering information and instrumentalities, and all needed facilities, by which the laws of heaven in regard to the increase of the human family may be thwarted.[17]

But if the number of single-child families was as notable as Todd claimed, it may have been that all those young ladies did not experience insult to the degree that he projected.

---

[16]Quoted in Green, pp. 13–14.
[17]Quoted in Green, p. 14.

It wasn't until the late 1800s and the advent of the industrial revolution that organized movements began in a big way to push for easy access to birth control. Prior to this, at intervals throughout the 1800s, some had tried to teach and publish information on contraceptives primarily as a service to the poor. But the lack of easy to use, 100 percent reliable devices worked against their efforts to command big audiences. This was true for just about every birth control proponent, whether his or her reasons for supporting it were compassionate, political, economic, or racist.

It was accepted by nearly everyone in Victorian culture that women were merely passive partners in bed and that they existed, at least sexually, only for the pleasure of the man of the house and to bear his children. So why would they need or want to prevent conception?

Also working against the efforts of birth control supporters was the Victorian notion that women were nonsexual beings. That is, they believed that women experienced no sexual desire. This was not a minority opinion. It was accepted by nearly everyone that women were merely passive partners in bed and that they existed, at least sexually, only for the pleasure of the man of the house and to bear his children. So why would they need or want to prevent conception?

William Acton wrote in 1857 that "Decent women have no sexual feelings."[18] One year later future president of the Medical Society of London, Dr. Isaac Brown, devoted his London Surgical Home to removing that part of the female anatomy associated with sexual pleasure. (Though it makes you wonder why surgeons thought this procedure necessary if they were convinced that women were, by design, unable to

---

[18]Quoted in Green, p. 164.

experience sexual arousal.) In 1867 the *New Orleans Medical Society Journal* published an article, "The Influence of the Sewing Machine on Female Health."[19] It wasn't carpal tunnel syndrome in all those seamstresses that they feared, but arousal due to rhythmical pressure of foot on treadle. Bromide was their solution.

Partly because Victorians believed women were incapable of sexual arousal, or at least were responsible to suppress it, they enacted ordinances making it illegal for a woman to resist her husband's advances. A woman who didn't enjoy sex, their thinking went, might be tempted to refuse. Others used the Bible as an authority, quoting applicable Scripture to remind women of their obligation.

But the Bible does not put a greater burden on the woman than the man. They have equal obligations to one another.

> The wife hath not power of her
> own body, but the husband: and
> likewise also the husband hath not
> power of his own body, but the wife.
> Defraud ye not one the other ...
>   I Cor. 7:4–5

Because it was unthinkable to Victorians that a married woman would desire sex for any other reason than procreation, they widely assumed (at least men did) that a married woman wasn't interested in obtaining birth control devices, not even to slow down conception to a healthy rate, say every two years instead of 11–12 months apart.

If a married woman did seek contraceptives, in

---

[19]Green, p. 164.

Victorian thinking it could only be to hide an illicit sexual relationship. The result of all this was that contraceptives were associated with prostitution, as prostitutes were much in need of an effective way to prevent conception. Contraceptives were likewise linked in people's minds to the detested practice of abortion, which, they assumed, was also a procedure primarily sought by prostitutes. It took decades for the associations to wane.

Nevertheless, as we saw from the quotes above, married women of means have consistently managed to secretly obtain devices from some source.

> *The average 19th century layperson and the Church saw birth control as a threat to the family. If a wife could gain control of her conception rate, so the thinking went, it would lead to sexual immorality on her part.*

Considering these facts, you can easily understand why the average 19th century layperson and the Church saw birth control as a threat to the family. If a wife could gain control of her conception rate, so the thinking went, it would lead to sexual immorality on her part.

But all these abstract moral issues surrounding birth control took a back seat in people's minds when the industrial revolution forced major socioeconomic changes on the family. The industrial revolution presented far more health hazards to women than childbearing ever did. Unlike today, when women of all socioeconomic levels can attend college then enter the work force to take various career paths, at that time most jobs for women were bottom-level factory slots filled by the poorest who often worked at dangerous, repetitive tasks as many as 14 hours a day, 6 days a week. Overworked, often malnourished women continued to deliver yearly and care for their children single-handedly, just as they did before taking factory jobs. Their pittance wages barely fed their children let alone made possible hired help or childcare.

Plenty of low-skill jobs encouraged immigration. Accordingly, it was not long after that poor, nonwhite immigrant women, along with poor white Americans, became the targets of the earliest birth control education campaigns. But America wasn't first. Britain's industrialization was several years earlier, and supporters had begun there in the mid-19th century to teach and speak in public places with impunity, especially to poor female factory workers.

From this point on, it's difficult to extricate economics from politics in late 19th and early 20th century efforts to make birth control acceptable and easily obtained. Late in the 1700s, English economist and minister Rev. Thomas Robert Malthus (1766–1834) declared that population control of the poor was necessary to stave off world starvation, promoting presocialist ideas about the natural distribution of wealth to the needy.

More than 100 years later, his chiefly economic reasons for limiting conception still enjoyed a following, but with a twist. Malthus condemned any means of artificial birth control outside of celibacy. He called the devices "improper arts to conceal the consequences of irregular connexions"[20]—the birth-control-leads-to-immorality argument. He promoted "moral restraint" alone to fight overpopulation.

But his followers ignored that part. Between 1910 and 1920, the Malthusian League freely distributed birth control information to Britain's working class. When the Malthusian League changed its name to the

---

[20]Quoted in Green, p. 10.

New Generation League, it also changed its constitution to accept as a member any person who believed birth control should be available to all classes, regardless of whether they were convinced that all were threatened by a perceived shortage of food. This opened the door to an ideological marriage between Malthusians and Marxists.[21]

Racism also played a big part in the push to distribute contraceptives to the poor and working classes. The notion of birth control as a solution to widespread social problems is tinged with racism, regardless of the respectability of the source or the personal disavowal of birth control as anything but a compassionate tool to empower the less fortunate.

> *The notion of birth control as a solution to widespread social problems is tinged with racism, regardless of the respectability of the source or the personal disavowal of birth control as anything but a compassionate tool to empower the less fortunate.*

Neville Chamberlain, Prime Minister of England 1937–1940, complained that easy access to birth control by upper-class females spelled disaster for the British ruling party when "The British Empire will be crying out for more citizens of the right breed, and when you in this country shall not be able to supply the demand."[22]

When Sanger follower Rose Witcop published Sanger's *Family Limitation*, she was accused of supporting a product "dangerous to the race,"[23] though at that time the only race in jeopardy was white,

---

[21]Green, p. 154.
[22]Quoted in Rowbotham, p. 144.
[23]Rowbotham, p. 150.

250

English-speaking Americans. At the turn of the century when *Family Limitation* was published, foreigners were flooding through Ellis Island at record rates. In a fascist publication of the 1930s, birth control was stressed to

> ... secure the production of
> children by the fit ... At present birth
> control is known and practised by the
> relatively well off. It's largely
> unknown and less practised by the very
> poor. The result is exactly the reverse
> of the national interest ... The unfit will
> be offered the alternatives of
> segregation sufficient to prevent the
> production of unfit children, or
> voluntary sterilisation.[24]

Considering recent Nazi history and the facts of the Holocaust, it takes little imagination to envision the number and types of people who would be cast into the outspread net of the "unfit." Earliest communist writings stressed the need for birth control so that female comrades, freed of time-consuming childcare duties, would have more time to devote to the cause.

---

[24]Quoted in Rowbotham, p. 151.

> *The underlying belief was that birth control, like the vote, would change a woman's autonomy and self-determination, negatively affecting the family unit as they knew it.*

Along with the fear that the right breed would birth-control itself out of existence, another fear was that access to contraceptives would mean loss of virtue of all women, not just married ones. This argument presupposed that the only thing that kept them tied to righteous living was not morals training but fear of pregnancy. Victorians also feared that birth control, like suffrage, would threaten family order. Contraceptives had the propensity to shatter the traditional role of a woman as primarily a man's monogamous sexual partner and secondarily his children's mother. The underlying belief was that birth control, like the vote, would change a woman's autonomy and self-determination, negatively affecting the family unit as they knew it.

(Don't be tempted to quickly assign this notion to Victorian hysteria. In Japan, where the government is almost exclusively dominated by men, birth control [other than condoms] was not legalized until 1999. Abortion on demand has been legal since 1949; Japanese women abort at an inordinate rate, roughly 300,000 abortions are performed annually, but that number has gone down a little bit since legalization of the pill [and other woman-responsible methods]. The bottom line is that when effective contraceptive control lies in the hands of only one party, in this case the man, it definitely impacts the family. In Japan that means the death of thousands of unborn children. When pre-20th century men had total control over fertility rates and when their wives were forced to submit to coitus by law and often had no devices to prevent conception, such a combination also had a profound impact on the family.)

Feminists interpreted resistance to legalized birth control as evidence of women's sexual slavery and oppression by a male dominated government. But even though feminists denied a connection between contraceptives and female immorality, illogically they used the same argument to condemn men. They asserted that male anatomy alone, and its concomitant freedom from fear of pregnancy, and not ignorance of hell fire contributed to the hordes of men who freely enjoyed extramarital relations.

The fear of rampant immorality that would result from access to contraceptives and the perceived irreligious quality of such products were behind the jailing of women who tried to teach or publish on the subject during the 1800s. Their work was labeled obscene. Sanger follower Rose Witcop was arrested for publishing *Family Limitation*. Annie Besant was jailed in 1877 and lost custody of her daughter for republishing "obscene literature," a book by Knowlton that discussed ways of avoiding pregnancy. Her accuser called it

> ... a dirty, filthy book ... the object of it is to enable persons to have sexual intercourse, and not to have that which in the order of Providence is the natural result of that sexual intercourse.[25]

Sometime after 1920, and largely due to Sanger's efforts, the stigma of obscenity waned, and the search for more reliable, comfortable, affordable birth control began.

The '20s also meant votes for women, which led to

---

[25]Quoted in Rowbotham, p. 74.

a new political awareness and self-image for women as people with control over their lives, laying the groundwork for feminism in the '30s. The suffragettes of the '20s had accomplished far more than just the vote. Not since the Civil War and the fight for abolition had so many women become so politically involved, and their numbers and solidarity energized them to move forward on other social issues, particularly those that directly affected women. Many birth control advocates were retired suffragettes or the daughters of suffragettes.

But before women got the vote and before many joined the fight for legalization of contraceptives, in 1917 Sanger was imprisoned for her one-woman campaign to educate women on the devices she thought would free them from slavery to biology.

Prior to entering the contraceptive campaign, Sanger had a radical, socialist past; in her salad days there was hardly a left-wing cause for which she would not march. Chief on her list of pet causes was the human suffering she saw as a visiting nurse in immigrant communities, suffering she contributed to capitalist inequities and injustices. In her 1915 book, *Women and the New Race*, Sanger gave her explanation of why more than an estimated 15,000 American women had died in childbirth:

> From what sort of homes come
> these deaths from childbirth? Most of
> them occur in overcrowded dwellings,
> where food, care, sanitation, nursing
> and medical attention are inadequate.
> Where do you find most of the
> tuberculosis* and much of the other
> disease which is aggravated by

pregnancy? In the same sort of home.[26]
   *Sanger suffered from TB; her
mother died of it.

True to her Malthusian roots, Sanger saw not
starvation wages[27], nor ignorance of sanitation practices
that resulted in disease, nor the problem of too many
unskilled people competing for too few jobs, nor
irresponsible husbands, nor alcoholism, nor lack of
adherence to biblical financial principles, but too many
children as the source of economic trouble in the home.
Though she chronicled the facts of what she observed,
and though the human suffering was real and
disturbing, Sanger's focus was always the "problem" of
the birth of new life:

>The deadly chain of misery is all
>too plain to anyone who takes the
>trouble to observe it. A woman of the
>working class marries and with her
>husband lives in a degree of comfort
>upon his earnings. Her household
>duties are not beyond her strength.
>Then the children begin to come—one,
>two, three, four, possibly five or more.
>The earnings of the husband do not
>increase as rapidly as the family does.
>Food, clothing and general comfort in
>the home grow less as the numbers of

---

[26]*Feminisim: The Essential Historical Writings*. Ed. by
   Miriam Schneir. Vintage Books, New York. 1972,
   p. 329.
[27] Women who crafted silk flowers for women's
   fashions from their homes were paid $1.00 a day
   for 14 hours of labor during this period.

the family increase. The woman's work grows heavier, and her strength is less with each child. Possibly—probably—she has to go into a factory to add to her husband's earnings. There she toils, doing her housework at night. Her health goes, and the crowded conditions and lack of necessities in the home help to bring about disease—especially tuberculosis. Under the circumstances, the woman's chances of recovering from each succeeding childbirth grow less. Less too are the chances of the child's surviving ...[28]

As most readers of this book may not be old enough to remember when contraceptives were illegal and largely unobtainable in the United States (the last state to legalize them did so in 1961), it's difficult to imagine the dire circumstances in which mothers gave birth early in this century. Client records kept by a "medical center" (birth control clinics were still illegal) in Illinois in 1923 confirm that the conditions in these homes were compelling and that Sanger did not exaggerate the seriousness of their circumstances. Of the first 500 women, representing 25 nationalities, who visited the clinic, 464 listed their occupation as homemaker and had working-class husbands. Those who worked did so almost exclusively because of a husband-provider who was alcoholic, a gambler, or ill. A few were newlyweds who wanted to get established financially before having children. Of the 304 who volunteered their religious affiliation, 147—almost half—were Catholic.

---

[28]*Feminism: The Essential Historical Writings*, p. 329.

The reasons they stated for desiring contraceptives were often economic, as Sanger related. But just as often their reasons reflected their lack of control over problems indigenous to the human condition, problems that would be compounded by the inordinate amount of care a newborn required, or the mother was ill. Sometimes the request came from a woman caring for an incapacitated husband or several sick or diseased children or both:

Case No. 3
Quite a tragic case. Man 37 years of age. The woman 36 years of age, married at 26, German-Protestant. In ten years she has had sixteen pregnancies, seven miscarriages, six induced abortions and three children. Reason—economic.

Case No. 59 – Referred by United Charities and Municipal Tuberculosis Sanitarium
The man is 54 years of age, street cleaner, Colored-Protestant. The woman is 40 years of age, married at 20 and in twenty years has had sixteen pregnancies. Of the fourteen children, whose ages range from seventeen years to eighteen months, seven died in infancy.

Case No. 186 – Referred – Newspaper
The man [is] 30 years old, not working. The woman, 30, married at 21, American-Protestant, has had four pregnancies, two miscarriages and two

children. The husband has spinal
trouble. The woman is very nervous.
One child has rickets and the other
tubercular glands.

Case No. 241
    The man is 23 years old, laborer,
no work. The woman is 19 years old,
and was first married at fourteen,
divorced after two months and married
again at the age of sixteen. She has had
three children, whose ages are four and
two years and seven weeks. Reason –
economic, and having children too fast.

Case No. 318 – Referred – United
Charities
    The man is 28 years old, laborer.
The woman is 20 years old, German-
Catholic, married at 19. Both feeble
minded. One child feeble minded.

Case No. 451 – Referred by Mental
Hygiene Society
    The man is 37 years old, cannot
work. The woman is 38 years old,
American-Protestant, married at 26 and
has had seven pregnancies, four
children, ages ten, eight, six and four
years. She teaches to support this
family. The husband is insane—
diagnosis dementia praecox—and has
been sent home from the Elgin Asylum
on probation. The wife is in terror for

fear of another pregnancy.[29]

A League worker added:

> This gives a clear record of the
> family history. The reason given by the
> mother for wishing information is *that
> she is too poor, worn out and very
> tired.* When one stops to think that this
> reason is given by a young woman of
> 29, it seems sad beyond words.[30]
> (emphasis worker)

Sanger's own experience as a poor immigrant child
cultivated her sensitivity to women without means. She
was sixth of 11 children born to an Irish stonemason
and his homemaker wife. Her father—a talker, a drunk,
a brawler who despised all authority (especially the
Catholic Church)—was never able to provide for his
family. Ironically, it was church food baskets and her
older brothers' wages that kept them all from starving.

Though Mr. Sanger discouraged attendance at
Mass, his wife remained devout, carrying on her private
devotions at home. A hard-working and caring mother,
her health was broken by disease; she died at age 48
(some records say 50). It's significant that Sanger's
earliest memory is that of peering through a ground
floor window at her mother, lying pale and helpless,
probably from an especially hard labor and delivery, a
concerned neighbor leaning over her bed. Sanger was
about three at the time.

----

[29]Dennett, Mary Ware. *Birth Control Laws: Shall We
    Keep Them, Change Them, or Abolish Them.* Da
    Capo Press, New York, 1970, pp. 276–277.
[30]Dennett, pp. 277–278.

Sanger was instructed in Catholicism as a child, but later in life became a self-confessed atheist. She also dabbled in Rosicrucianism, "the god within," a mystical, international fraternity linked to Egyptology.[31]

Though the poverty, disease, and ignorance rampant at the bottom of the capitalist pyramid repelled her, Sanger never gave up entirely on the system. She hoped it would ultimately right itself on its own. But she did give up the idea of forceful social change. Instead she believed that thousands of educated women, freed from bondage to yearly childbirth and able to work at more than just the lowest paying manufacturing jobs, would eventually have the economic impact on society that revolutionary European workers had never had by violence. She also expected lower birth rates to reduce the labor supply, thus favoring workers.

But Sanger had ignoble hopes for contraceptives as well. Namely, she hoped that women "would achieve personal freedom by experiencing their sexuality free of consequence."[32] "Free love" is what we call it these days. Using her own definition of morality, she went beyond the teaching of sexual freedom (from unplanned pregnancies) for married women and sought for single women the same freedom from the consequences of fornication that she envied in her philandering male

> *Over time Sanger's plans for contraceptives became ignoble. Namely, she hoped that women would achieve personal "freedom" by enjoying sexuality free of consequence. "Free love" is what we call it these days.*

---

[31]Chesler, Ellen. *Woman of Valor, Margaret Sanger and the Birth Control Movement in America.* Simon & Schuster, New York, 1992, p. 135.
[32]Chesler, p. 14.

acquaintances and lovers. Worse, she preached her gospel of free love loudly and with unabashed defiance of moral codes of her day. Her many sexual liaisons are well documented, and even complementary biographies do not whitewash her lascivious life.

Worse yet, her mothering skills (or lack of them) in relation to the three children she abandoned[33] provide her no excuses. She was a lousy role model for the women's movement to which she was closely allied.

Sanger did not begin her campaign on such a radical platform. Her original focus was poor *married* women who had all the children they wanted but no power to harness nature. Though contraceptives were illegal at the time, Sanger knew that educated women of means somehow managed to get them. But Sanger found through interviews with the poor that not only could they not find nor afford contraceptives, often they didn't know such products existed.

And at least originally, Sanger did not promote abortion. She acknowledged it to be murder and worked to keep women from seeking it. In the early years she was moved by the long lines of women, sometimes as many as 50, who waited outside abortion clinics for a $5 operation that was legal early in the 20th century but unregulated and unsafe. The headlines of a handbill she circulated in a Brownsville, Brooklyn neighborhood to advertise her new clinic read, in several languages:

MOTHERS!
Can you afford to have a large family?
Do you want any more children?
If not, why do you have

---

[33]Chesler, p. 18.

them?
DO NOT KILL, DO NOT
TAKE LIFE, BUT PREVENT[34]

Sanger's opinion of the body was that it belonged to self (certainly not God). Eventually self and not the developing child became the focus.

But to Sanger and her colleagues, abortion soon became an acceptable back-up for contraceptives that failed or were not diligently administered. Eventually they began to demand that the operation receive legal protection as a "right." Sanger's opinion of the body was that it belonged to self (certainly not God). Eventually self and not the developing child became the focus. As distasteful as this philosophy is to Christians, it's in line with "No Gods No Masters," the motto of Sanger's feminist circular, *The Woman Rebel*.[35]

Why all this attention to Sanger? The Sanger Factor cannot be separated from the controversy around contraceptives and the fight to legalize them. To Christians, Sanger means Planned Parenthood, the nationwide network of women's clinics she founded, and Planned Parenthood is synonymous with abortion. And to many, a person, especially a woman, who supports birth control education is linked with the 'A' word, Planned Parenthood, and ultimately, the radical feminist program Sanger espoused.

Despite that *some* good resulted from her work, birth control education cannot be separated from Sanger's ignominious shadow.

---

[34]Chesler, no page given, center photo inserts.
[35]Chesler, no page given, center photo inserts.

The Evangelical Factor

> *Christians are reticent to offer any authoritative, reflective teaching on the subject, but confusion about what the Bible says on the matter hasn't helped either.*

As you can see, before contraceptives became acceptable, they were the intellectual property of groups considered rebellious and irreligious by most Christians. It has been socialists, Planned Parenthood, racists, and feminists who have been the most vocal about the importance of easy access to reliable birth control. All of them espouse philosophies repugnant to Christians, so it's no wonder that the issue gives many a bad taste. *This is why Christians are reticent to offer any authoritative, reflective teaching on the subject*, but confusion about what the Bible says on the matter hasn't helped either. Lack of assurance about any issue, and especially a controversial one, makes us timid about sharing what we believe.

Sadly, by its silence the Church has left a big hole in our thinking, and all the wrong people have jumped in to fill it. Because the truth is, women want information on birth control, and they *will* get it from somewhere.

Nowadays you may know nothing about the Malthusians, but you have heard of the free abortions performed in communist countries, and hardly anyone hasn't heard of the nationwide contraceptive and abortion services Planned Parenthood provides. Few Christians, however, can answer, "What does the Bible say (or your church teach) about birth control and why?" with more than a shrug and a subjective, "Well, I guess it's just left up to each of us to decide."

For some, that's OK. Guidance based on mental reasoning, culture, custom, and the need of the moment is enough. But for Christians who seek God's will in every area of their lives but have a weak conscience about birth control due to ignorance of the Bible, the information gap causes moral angst. I know because 20 years ago I was one of those distraught Christians. In a way, those who decide based on the world's reasoning appear to have an advantage over those who go to the Church for answers. Because those who go to the world will get a ton of information, but the conscientious, questioning Christian likely will get nothing.

> *In a way, those who decide based on the world's reasoning appear to have an advantage over those who go to the Church for answers. Because those who go to the world will get a ton of information, but the conscientious, questioning Christian likely will get nothing.*

Spirituality v. Nature

Because the Church has been silent and allowed the world to do the talking, modern Christians treat conception and birth control as natural, not spiritual issues. This generation has forgotten that everything has a spiritual origin and dimension. Modern marriage manuals do not touch upon the Gen. 3:16 curse on conception. It's not *why* a woman will conceive repeatedly and frequently, it's only the scientific fact that she will if she does not take precaution. In their popular (2.5 million copies sold) Christian sex manual, *The Act of Marriage*, Tim and Beverly LaHaye acknowledge that a woman can have up to 20 children in her lifetime. But their silence as to the spiritual reason for this fact treats too closely spaced births as primarily a biological phenomenon. And yet their book is considered a spiritual publication, written to help Christians view their sexuality from a biblical perspective.

We have come full circle from dealing with the problem from a strictly spiritual standpoint to dealing with it from a strictly scientific standpoint. Contraception has become not so much a problem of working with or against spiritual laws but working only with natural laws to achieve a desired end. And what was once regarded as a topic to be explained by the Church has become a spiritual nonissue, implying that God has little or no interest in it.

The shift has created two problems. First, we answer to God, not nature. The life that flows through nature is merely an expression of its source. Nature is under his thumb. If we look to nature, that is, science, for an explanation of our fertility and guidance in how to deal with it, then we misplace our spiritual focus; we remove Him from the throne of our hearts. Which leads to the second problem: Though we have free will, as with every decision we make, we are not the master of our own fertility. He is our maker. We do not own ourselves, not even our bodies. Whether we conceive or don't conceive is his purview, because He is involved in every detail that concerns us.

Therefore we must consult God and his Word when making decisions about birth control. If we don't, we've taken the worldly approach to the problem, an influence that stems from a corrupt culture that desires to eradicate God from all of life, including and especially fertility.

Lacking logically and spiritually satisfying answers from the Bible, it's not surprising that Christians and non-Christians alike have sought their own workable solutions to their conception problems.

We should not be too quick, however, to point fingers at confused Christians. God to nature role reversal was practically inevitable. Lacking logically and spiritually satisfying answers from the Bible, it's not surprising that Christians and non-Christians alike have sought their own workable solutions to their conception problems. And for those with an active conscience, it makes sense to justify their actions with a belief system that appears reasonable, logical, and moral. If the Bible appears to be silent and the Church appears to be confused, then you can rightly predict that Christians will do what they think best. The problem is too great to be ignored.

But must we conclude that God has left us no guidance? Is the Bible truly silent? And since when is Scripture subject to personal interpretation as to the part we play in procreation? Do most evangelicals use or refuse birth control? Considering the small size of most evangelical families I see, I strongly suspect that nearly everyone uses something to inhibit conception. But do we do it in faith as the Bible commands (Rom. 14:23)?

Finally, is it possible to divest contraception from the debate over Catholic and Protestant issues; the stigma of its economic, political, and racist history; its association with immorality; and its connection to radical feminism and abortion?

I believe it's possible.

Modern Treatment of Gen. 3:16

Bible scholars have written little about the curse on conception for several reasons:

1) As many ancient commentaries attest, church fathers believed that Eve was created primarily for procreation. Therefore it seemed a small thing, hardly a curse at all, that women were burdened with annual deliveries. As Church fathers saw it, women were accomplishing the one thing they were created to do, howbeit more painfully than they would have prior to sin.

2) The tendency for Old Testament characters to disregard the law and marry more than one woman had the effect of relieving their wives of the burden of bearing more often than was healthy, though in no way did the benefit justify the means.

3) From earliest biblical times large families were considered a sign of divine blessing. Many children also meant many helping hands for primarily agricultural societies.

4) In Old Testament times, every conception meant another chance to deliver a son, which heightened a couple's esteem in their community. A son also meant a father's worldly goods would be passed on in accordance with Jewish law.

5) Traditional teaching has supported the notion that women should submit graciously to Eve's punishment, accepting their biological lot as from God's hand. That's why, as late as the beginning of the 20th century, women who supported contraception were accused of speaking against nature and Heaven, a heresy condemned by both Catholics and Protestants. This served to muzzle (but not stop) women who lived in fear of social and spiritual consequences.

6) Because I Tim. 2:15 was commonly mistranslated to imply that a woman obtained salvation through childbearing, multiple pregnancies seemed like a good thing.

7) It was a man's world. Women's concerns just weren't important enough to merit much space in biblical commentaries.

A good example of the last is Wesley's notes on Gal. 3:28. When he arrived at "neither male nor female," he wrote that circumcision was now "laid aside, which was peculiar to males, and was designed to put a difference, during that dispensation, between Jews and gentiles."[36] Of course, it also put a spiritual difference between males and females. But Wesley devoted not a word of his Gal. 3:28 commentary to the gender question.

8) English to English translations of Gen. 3:16 from the beginning of the 20th century until now have radically altered our idea of the curse upon Eve.

I discuss this last point here because the present Church, especially those under age 40, is influenced greatly by 20th century translations. Because there is so little commentary written about the curse on conception, and because it's not commentary but God's Word that concerns us, we will go straight to the literal translation of the Hebrew to begin.

Literal Translation of Multiplied Conception

KJV translators rendered "multiply" from Hebrew *rabah*, which means to increase, bring in abundance, enlarge, more in number, multiply, and so forth. God used it three times in Gen. 1 when He spoke to the lower creatures, then Adam and Eve, to multiply. Translators rendered the word "conception" from

---

[36]Wesley's notes on Galatians 3.

Hebrew *herown* or *herayown*, which means only pregnancy or conception. The word is translated in the Bible three times (Gen. 3:16; Ruth 4:13; and Hos. 9:11) and in each citation refers to the act of impregnation.

So we know that "multiplied conceptions" is the exact meaning, a correct translation into English. Translations of both "multiply" and "conception" were rendered using the Masoretic Hebrew text, employing 54 of Britain's greatest Hebrew and Greek scholars. This is important, as all but the Geneva, Douay-Rheims, and Bishops bibles that came before were the work of only one man. It's the counterbalancing selection of learned translators and devotion to literal translation of Hebrew and Greek manuscripts that make the KJV still the most reliable to date.

Prior to the KJV, eight other versions rendered a close-to-literal translation of *rabah herown* to mean multiplied conception. For 521 years English-speaking people had a scriptural foundation for a curse on women's conception rate. Observe:

1380 - Wycliffe (translated first complete Bible, probably from Latin)

"To pe womman forsop god seide/I schall multyply (multiply) pi myseysez (miseries); & *pi conceyuynge* (conceptions) ..."

1535 - Tyndale (translated from Hebrew and Greek; he was fluent in seven languages)

"And vnto the woman he sayd: I will suerly encrease thy sorow *ad make the oft with child*, and with payne shalt thou be delevered ..."

1535 - Coverdale (translated from Latin Vulgate, Luther's German Bible and Tyndale)

"And unto the woman he sayde: I will increase thy sorow, whan thou art with childe: with payne shalt thou beare thy childre ..."

269

*1537 - **Matthews*** (later revised and called the Great Bible)

"And unto the woman he said: I will suerly encrease thy sorow, and *make the oft with childe* ..."

*1539 - **Cranmer*** (most of his material was taken from Coverdale and Tyndale; he spoke no Hebrew)

"But unto the woman he sayde: In multplienge will I multiplye thy sorowe *a thy concepuinge*: In sorowe shalt thou bringe forth children ..."

*1539 - **Taverner*** (sole translator)

"And unto the woman he sayd: I will encrease thy sorowes/and *make the ofte with child*/and with payne shalte thou be delivered ..."

*1557 - **Geneva*** (translated by scholars in Geneva from Hebrew and Greek)

"Unto the woman he said, I wil greatly increase thy sorowes, *& thy conceptios*. In sorowe shalt thou bring forthe childre ..."

*1568 - **Bishops*** (official Bible of the Church of England; translated from Hebrew and Greek by a committee at the command of Anglican authorities)

"But unto the woman he sayd, In multplyng I will multiply thy sorowe *and thy conceptions*. In sorowe thou shalt bring forth children ..."

*1582 - **Douay/Rheims*** (translated from Latin Vulgate by the English College first at Rheims. Most of the Old Testament was translated by Gregory Martin and published in 1609 at Douay when the College had moved to that location; also called the Rosin Bible)

"To the woman also he said: I will multiply thy sorrows, *and thy conceptions*: in sorrow shalt thou bring forth children ..."

1611 - KJV (translated from Hebrew and Greek by 54 British scholars)

"Unto the woman he said, I will greatly multiply thy sorrow *and thy conception*; in sorrow thou shalt bring forth children ..."

1808 - Thomson (sole translator)

"And to the woman he said, I will greatly multiply thy sorrows and thy anguish. With sorrows thou shalt bear children ..."

1885 - English Revision (54 British scholars employed to revise the KJV)

"To the woman he said: I shall give you great labour in childbearing; with labour you will bear children ..."

1901 - American Revision (or American Standard) (translators employed to revise the KJV)

"Unto the woman he said, I will greatly multiply thy pain *and thy conception*; in pain shalt thou bring forth children ..."

Twentieth Century Interpretation

Only in the 19th and 20th centuries do we consistently see "and thy conception" missing from Gen. 3:16. After the American Revised Version of 1901, the line disappears, whether the version is translated from the Hebrew Masoretic, other Semitic manuscripts discovered after 1611, strictly English texts, or a combination. Note the absence of the strategic line:

1952 - Revised Standard (32 American translators; considered most controversial of American bibles; essentially a revision of the American Standard Version of 1901)

"To the woman he said, 'I will greatly multiply your pain in childbearing; in pain you shall bring forth children ...'"

271

1954 - Amplified (literal translation using an extensive list of English versions of the Old Testament for comparison and Westcott's Greek text)

"To the woman he said, 'I will greatly multiply your grief and your suffering in pregnancy and the pangs of child-bearing; with spasms of distress you shall bring forth children ...'"

1966 - Jerusalem (28 translators used the Hebrew Masoretic, *the same text used by KJV translators*, also the Greek Septuagint, Dead Sea Scrolls and other texts)

"To the woman he said: 'I will multiply your pains in childrearing, you shall give birth to your children in pain ...'"

1970 - New American Bible (50+ scholars employed, 26 years to complete, primarily a Catholic version)

"To the woman he said: 'I will intensify the pangs of your childbearing; in pain shall you bring forth children ...'"

1970 - New English Bible (50+ scholars employed, 24 years to complete, translated from Hebrew and Greek texts)

"To the woman he said: 'I will increase your labour and your groaning, and in labour you shall bear children ...'"

1971 - New American Standard (54 Hebrew and Greek scholars employed; 11 years to complete)

"To the woman He said, 'I will greatly multiply your pain in childbirth, in pain you shall bring forth children ...'"

1971 - Living Bible (translated by Kenneth L. Taylor using American Standard Version of 1901 with help from Greek and Hebrew consultants)

"Then God said to the woman, 'We shall bear children in intense pain and suffering ...'"

272

*1973 - **New Revised Standard*** (revision of the Revised Standard of 1952)

"To the woman he said, 'I will greatly increase your pangs in childbearing, in pain you shall bring forth children ...'"

*1978 - **New International*** (transdenominational group of 100+ scholars, from Hebrew, Aramaic, and Greek texts)

"To the woman he said, 'I will greatly

> *As consistently as a curse on a woman's conception rate appears prior to 1901, just as consistently it disappears from bibles published thereafter.*

increase your pains in childbearing; with pain you will give birth to children ...'"

As consistently as a curse on a woman's conception rate appears prior to 1901, just as consistently it disappears from bibles published thereafter. This change is no small matter. For without question, if there is a curse on a woman's conception rate, it will have a profoundly negative impact upon her life to the same degree as the curse on the ground has profoundly and negatively affected every man.

The problem is that the first 428 years of English bible commentary (1380–1808) left us with a shaky scriptural foundation. Evidence of a curse on a woman's conception rate was always there, of course, but commentators ignored it or turned it upside down to mean the opposite of its literal translation: they taught that multiple, uncontrolled conceptions were a blessing. And because primarily agricultural communities benefited from many hands, translators and the Church at large sought to interpret a woman's plight from a pragmatic perspective. They tried to make sense of it.

They tried to find good in it. They linked the Old Testament curse on conception to errant New Testament translations that linked a woman's salvation to motherhood, straining to make a good and agreeable translation "fit."

This is similar to the mistake our forefathers made with slavery. They tried to make a scriptural fit between the curse on Ham in Gen. 9:25, wherein he and his descendants were cursed to labor as servants forever, and the need to religiously institutionalize their economic dependence on cheap labor. They failed, but not before they had planted a crop of corrupt opinion about African-Americans and their place in society.

This faulty reasoning is similar also to the practice of justifying disease and sickness. People know that God is loving and just, so when they are seriously sick or diseased, they look for reasons why God might have "afflicted" them, in his love, with such a "gift." People who think like this may love God a great deal, but they aren't well acquainted with his nature or his Word.

From the evidence of how the "multiplied conception" line fell off the face of the earth after 1808, appearing only once in 1901, we know that 19th and 20th century translators were befuddled. They were unwilling to deal with the sticky problem of uncontrolled fertility and its close correlation to the equally sticky, popular clamor for contraceptives. Perhaps they thought that if the troubling words went away, the problem would go away. But it did not go away. It's a disturbing coincidence that, in the 1800s and into the middle of the 1900s, when women for the first time became numerous, political, and vocal about legalizing contraceptives, the one passage in the Bible that indicates there is something wrong with a woman's frequent rate of conception disappeared from all translations but one.

Was the omission intentional? I don't know. We do know that in the centuries when the line was still in print, Church fathers refused to acknowledge it or taught that it was a blessing. So if they saw multiplied conceptions as a blessing, it doesn't make sense that they would want to remove scriptural evidence.

Neither can I make the case that women themselves were using Gen. 3:16 to prove that there was a curse, because as far as I can tell, no denomination was teaching such a thing. And though women were adamant that there was a problem, from the evidence it appears that they were more concerned with a finding a solution than a cause.

Therefore, though I can't prove that removal of the line was a political response to women's agitation for legalized birth control, I will always be suspicious of the collision of both historical facts.

I do know that its removal was a dark day for Christian women, the day in which the one dim spiritual light was turned off, the light that could have helped them understand the reason behind the burdensome nature of their fertility. Married women have always known that they have a problem, but due to lack of objective, scriptural teaching they have not known why nor God's solution. A Christian woman who looks into a modern Bible translation will find nothing there to guide her.

Long before I married and faced this dilemma, I used to look ahead and imagine myself in their position, so I was also affected by the spiritual vacuum. I used to wonder about the nature of the curses on women, as no one was able or willing to give me a

> *You can't speak about the curse on women's conception rate without someone assuming you are against large families.*

275

reasonable explanation. It seemed that there was a book written to answer every hard scriptural problem but this one. Well researched, thoughtful, modern commentary is hard to find on the subject, because even nowadays you can't speak about the curse on women's conception rate without someone assuming you are against large families.

That's why so few Christian women are willing to publicly admit that uncontrolled conception is a burden to them. To complain is to imply we're sorry we're female or we're unhappy with God's "divine plan." A faint odor of feminism lingers around such thoughts, too.

> *Scripture is plain. Large families are a blessing, not a curse. God Himself is trying to build a very large family for his own heavenly home.*

The Paradox

Scripture is plain. Large families are a blessing, not a curse. God Himself is trying to build a *very* large family for his own heavenly home. The first thing God told Adam and Eve to do was multiply. Because God's Word always agrees with itself, you can't logically claim that God *blessed* the first couple with many children and simultaneously claim that He *cursed* them with many children.

When God told Eve to multiply, she already had the ability to do so or He wouldn't have made the command. Because she had not yet committed sin, her ability to bear many children was a blessing only, for before sin she was under no curse. Therefore we know that the number of children granted to a couple is not the focus of the curse. (But it may sound like the same thing. It isn't. Keep reading.) *After sin entered the world, God did not say her children would be multiplied—that promise was already given her in the form of a blessing. In the curse He said her* **conceptions** *would be multiplied.* It was *control of conception, its frequency*, that was cursed. In this regard, Eve was more affected than Adam.

Think about the nature of the curse upon the ground, the curse that most affected Adam. He who once reigned as king of Eden forfeited control of earth and the forces of nature to become a slave to his appetite, forced to toil long hours to provide for himself and his family. Nature, as often as not, now worked against him, and not even the resurrection nullified its impact. We still must work to eat. Work itself is good; God gave Adam work before the fall. But that which Adam once rejoiced in he was now in bondage to as he discovered how difficult it is to prosper in a broken world. Survival is hard.

Likewise Eve, who once reigned as queen of Eden and who would have borne children in safety and ease, lost control over her rate of fertility as her conceptions were multiplied beyond her endurance, till she was worn out in body and mind. Pregnancy, once a pleasure, became a burden, even a grief to her as multiple conceptions threatened her health. Conception itself is good; God commanded Adam and Eve to multiply before the fall. But the fertility rate she might have rejoiced in now she was in bondage to as she discovered how exhausting it is to conceive one child after another. Mothering is hard.

No one knows what her rate of conception was before sin. Once a year? Every two years? Every five years? Eve was created to live in Eden forever. Before sin she had eternity to populate the earth, so why hurry? Bearing every decade would hardly be interpreted as spacing her deliveries too far apart. Had death not entered the world, Eve would only have had to bear two girls and two boys, and each couple bear the same, to quickly populate the earth.

Sanger said that women are slaves to biology, "forced motherhood" she called it, and in this one point she was right. Again, it all goes back to when Adam and Eve voluntarily forfeited dominion over the earth, when they disobeyed God and followed their appetites. Without God's help and human intervention, the curse on the ground and the curse on the rate of conception harm the body. We are still slaves to our flesh.

Failure to Acknowledge the Spirituality of Fertility

Failure to acknowledge women's crushing fertility rate as a spiritual problem can be compared to the dilemma of the poor but good man who goes to his church for help to feed his children. "My children are starving," he says. "I've done all I know, but still I am unable to take care of them." His church responds with a fatalistic, "It's hard to make a living, but you must make the best of your lot." The man goes home with a sack of groceries but no long-term solution, though the Bible offers many. Disappointed but determined, he vows to find a better way to feed his children. He must find a way. They'll be hungry again tomorrow.

He never gives up. He may even steal. God has put pursuit of dominion in every heart, and there are few whose despair is so deep that they lose the drive to obtain it, by whatever means. But a man tires of begging bread. Eventually he'll look to the world for answers, turning away from the God he interprets to be uncaring.

> *God has put pursuit of dominion in every heart, and there are few whose despair is so deep that they lose the drive to obtain it, by whatever means.*

Dominion over lack was purchased at the cross for this man, therefore his poverty is more spiritual than physical. But he needs a knowledgeable representative of Jesus Christ to point this out and share with him the biblical solution to lack.

When the Church has no answers for multiplied conceptions, its silence sends a message, one that attacks God's goodness. Our silence declares that we believe the problem is not a problem, or not a serious one, that it requires something other than a spiritual solution, or that God's Word does not provide one.

But worst of all, our silence says that God is not concerned with women's suffering, that He doesn't care about women. But every woman knows she has a problem. She deserves to know also that the Bible calls it a curse and that there is no sin in trying to overcome it.

Women will continue to strive for control of their fertility, because the drive for dominion burns in their hearts, too. If they can't get answers in the Church, they'll get them in the world. Christians will quietly find what they need in the marketplace. The disappointed will turn away from the God who they believe does not feel their suffering.

And like the poor man who steals to feed his children because his need is great but his faith is weak, the desperately pregnant will resort to abortion, legal or not, as they always have done.

Hiss # 14: Eve's Deception: Your Legacy

> But the woman being deceived
> was in the transgression.
> I Tim. 2:14

Eve has been vilified for centuries for listening to the serpent. Why did she do it? Why did she believe him instead of God? What made his story more trustworthy?

To answer these questions, we must return to the garden in Gen. 3 to refresh our memories about the first human tragedy, the deception of Eve.

* * *

The liar: "Now the serpent was more subtil than any beast of the field which the Lord God had made" (v.1). "Subtil" here means cunning, usually in a bad sense, or crafty. This distinguishes the serpent (Satan). Everything that comes out of his mouth is a lie.

The first thing he said: "Yea, hath God said, Ye shall not eat of every tree of the garden?" (v.1). Note the method Satan used on Eve: He attacked the validity of God's Word. "Did God say you couldn't eat of all the trees of the garden? Is that *really* what He said?" This is still Satan's chief method to undermine your faith. He plants a seed of doubt, hoping you'll nurture it. If you don't immediately reject it, it begins to grow in your mind. You fall into the sin of doubting God's Word and eventually reap death. Eve knew what the eating restrictions were, because in v. 3 she quoted God's words to Adam. But look how boldly Satan used to his advantage the little knowledge she had.

The liar: "And the serpent said unto the woman, Ye shall not surely die" (v.4). This was a bald-faced lie, told with a straight face. This is easy for Satan. He's had lots of practice.

The liar: "For God doth know that in the day ye eat thereof, then your eyes shall be opened, and ye shall be as gods, knowing good and evil" (v.5). He attacked God's integrity. He hinted that God is selfish, that He does not want to share his Kingdom with his creatures. Satan still uses this tactic. In fact, it's his biggest lie!

> ### SATAN'S CENTRAL MESSAGE TO YOU NEVER CHANGES:
> *"God does not love you as He says He does, and because He doesn't love you, He withholds good things from you."*

But the central message buried in this lie, the one that moved Eve to disobedience, the message to you that never changes, THIS is the hiss from Hell I heard for the first 18 years of my Christian experience:

God does not love you as He says He does, and because He doesn't love you, He withholds good things from you.

Satan's goal has never changed. He wants to destroy your love for God. He does this by planting a seed of distrust in your mind. And then:

And when the woman saw that the
tree was good for food, and that it was
pleasant to the eyes, and a tree to be
desired to make one wise, she took of
the fruit thereof, and did eat, and gave
also unto her husband with her; and he
did eat. v. 6

Eve should have rejected the lie. The Bible calls it
casting down imaginations that exalt themselves against
the knowledge of God. But instead she watered the seed
Satan planted in her mind by gazing on the tree and
musing on how good its fruit might taste.

First, she accepted the seed (the lie). Second, she
watered it by contemplating the act of reaching for and
tasting the attractive fruit. Third, she plucked and took a
bite, performing the act physically that had been
planted as a thought seed, mentally. (The KJV says she
gave to her husband *with her* [v. 6]. Did Adam observe
all this?) Eve had a choice. She had heard God's Word
and she had heard Satan's. But she decided Satan's was
more reliable. Why? Because she had received
secondhand instruction about the tree.

Adam received firsthand instruction regarding
what they could and could not eat in the garden. He
knew that to eat of that particular tree meant death,
because he had heard it straight from God. Adam had
this advantage over Eve, and that's why Satan set out to
deceive her and not him. When Adam willfully ate (he
was not deceived) he just made Satan's job easier.

But Eve never went to the source for instruction.
The instruction she quoted to Satan in vv. 2–3 she had
received secondhand from Adam, therefore making it
less impressive and forceful than the instruction Adam
had received. For this reason alone, she was more easily

deceived.

This is logical if you think about how God operates. He doesn't waste words. If He repeats Himself to someone, He does so only to confirm a future event. God gave Joseph, for example, two dreams foretelling his reign over his family (Gen. 37). Pharaoh dreamed two dreams in one night that confirmed a coming famine (Gen. 41:32). God gave the 10 commandments to Moses who was responsible to give them to the Israelites. God spoke the terms of the covenant to Abraham but did not repeat them to Isaac until Abraham died (Gen. 25 and 26). God repeated the promises to Jacob only after he was geographically separated from Isaac (Gen. 28).

Because God had given explicit instruction to Adam regarding the tree, He didn't need to repeat it to Eve. That was Adam's job.

So Eve knew the rules. But lacking the strong impression of receiving them from the source, and further swayed by a face-to-face encounter with *the* source of falsehood, Satan's words were more convincing and seemed more reliable than God's. The power of truth was diminished because it had been received secondhand; the power of the lie was strengthened because it had been received face to face. Receiving instruction secondhand made Eve the weaker target. This is the only reason Satan aimed his arrow at her.

Satan's battle for your mind still rages. When you fail to go to God's Word, you set yourself up to be deceived by Satan. In this regard, men are just as likely to be deceived as women. If you would spend the necessary time digging out the truth from Scripture for yourself, providing yourself a face-to-face encounter with the real thing, you would have the knowledge and faith it takes to recognize and reject Satan's lies.

And he never quits lying to you, not until you leave this world for the next. If you don't daily renew your mind with God's Word, Satan's testimony will begin to look more believable than God's. It's true: If you don't daily read and meditate on God's Word, it fades into the background of your consciousness, just as it faded into Eve's. When that happens, its influence fades as well.

Paul wrote in II Cor. 11:3 that he feared the Corinthian believers' minds would be corrupted in the same way Eve's was, that they might move away from the "simplicity" or singleness of Christ. He wrote in Rom. 12:2 that believers should transform their worldly minds by renewing them in God's Word. He wrote in Eph. 4:23 that they should be renewed in the spirit of their minds.

> *You must guard your mind, because that's what Satan's after. The battle is in, and for, your mind.*

You must guard your mind, because that's what Satan's after. The battle is in, and for, your mind.

Psalm 19:7 says God's Word is perfect and sure, able to convert, or turn back the soul, meaning the mind. This thought is echoed in the New Testament. Jas. 1:21 says to "receive with meekness the engrafted word, which is able to save your souls," again referring to the mind. "Engrafted" comes from two words, one meaning to set into position or to set at rest, and the other meaning to germinate or sprout. Jesus said God's Word is the seed (Luke 8:11). You should consciously put the seed of God's Word, verse by verse, into your mind and keep it there, giving it time to germinate, so that it can produce a harvest.

That's what meditation does. Meditation in God's Word causes the seed to travel beyond your mind into your spirit, where it germinates and sprouts into spiritual fruit: the good changes that come about in your heart and life. Meditation is something *you* must do; God will not do it for you.

It doesn't happen by mere passive listening to ministers of the Word. When you decide to meditate on God's Word, you plant the seeds for your spiritual harvest. And like industrious farmers, the more seed you plant, the more abundant life you reap.

Not meditating on God's Word leads to "mental assent." Eve made this mistake. She received God's Word in a casual, shallow way. She knew in her head what God had said but she didn't take it into her heart. Deep down inside of her, she was not convinced of the credibility of God's Word. Paul made this distinction when he wrote to the Thessalonians:

> For this cause also thank we God
> without ceasing, because, when ye
> *received* God's Word which ye heard
> of us, ye *received* it not as the Word of
> men, but as it's in truth, the Word of
> God, which effectually worketh also in
> you that believe. I Thess. 2:13

Though the repeated use of "received" appears identical in meaning, in this verse they're translated from two different Greek words and mean two different types of receiving.

Paul applauded the way the Thessalonians had received God's Word by using the word *paralambano*, which means to receive or take near to oneself, to associate with oneself in any familiar or intimate act or relation. The people took God's Word and planted it inside of themselves, in their hearts. They took it personally. They esteemed it to be God's personal message and treated it with respect, as something valuable.

To illustrate the *paralambano* way of receiving, let me tell you a story about a young soldier on deployment, thousands of miles from home. Three weeks have passed since he's heard from his sweetheart (imagine too that this was before telephones and e-mail). A letter finally arrives. He reads the details of his girlfriend's current happenings and so forth, until he comes to those sweet words on the last page where his dearest has written of her love for him, how much she misses him, how hard it is to be apart.

He rereads that last, sweet section of the letter. Then he reads it again. Then again. The words on the page make her presence seem very close. It's as though she is talking directly to him. In his mind he can hear the voice of his loved one speaking the words aloud. It's almost as real as hearing her in person. He clings to the impress of those words for days, and without even trying, he finds he has memorized his favorite few lines. They speak straight to his heart. This is receiving according to *paralambano*.

Paul contrasted this way of receiving to those who receive God's Word as it if were that of a mere human. The word he used for the second type of receiving is *lambano*, which means only to take, as if someone just casually handed you an object. It doesn't imply a binding up of oneself with the thing received. It's a detached way of receiving, and this type is at the core of mental assent. It's an example of God's Word received only into the mind and not the heart. It does not suggest an intimate relationship with the receiver as does *paralambano*.

To illustrate the *lambano* way of receiving, imagine you go out to your mailbox and there you find a letter from your insurance company, addressed to you by name, Mrs. Jane Smith. "Dear Mrs. Smith," it begins, and as they explain the upcoming changes in your policy, important ones that require your attention, they open each paragraph with "Mrs. Smith," to try to make the correspondence more personal. But you don't feel a personal touch to the prose because you know that the Mrs. Smith part is computer generated and every other policyholder gets a "personalized" letter just like it. But you make a mental note of how the changes will affect your coverage and your pocketbook, remind yourself to tell your spouse about it, then file it away.

You read it, remember the most important parts, but at an emotional level are unmoved by it. You take it into your mind only, not your heart. This is receiving according to *lambano*.

Lambano is characterized in your life by a lack of spiritual fruit, because Paul said that receiving God's Word in accordance with *paralambano* is what brings results, the inner change God seeks. Spiritual fruit is a result of the seed of God's Word first resting in your heart—resting long enough by meditation to germinate—then sprouting into a harvest. Eve allowed Satan's words to germinate in her heart, they took root, then sprouted into sin. She elevated the serpent's word above God's, whose words never traveled beyond her head. As a result, God's Word bore no fruit in her life, or Adam's for that matter.

> *Adam and Eve both sinned when they subordinated God's Word to someone else's.*

Do you remember what sin it was that God faulted Adam for first? It wasn't eating the fruit that God referred to. It was hearkening to his wife's words instead of to God's. Gen. 3:17, "And unto Adam he said, Because thou hast hearkened unto the voice of thy wife ..." Hearkening to

287

his wife instead of God was the first mistake that instigated the second, more infamous one. Adam and Eve both sinned when they subordinated God's Word to someone else's.

You must *paralambano* God's Word. You must read it, study it, meditate on it, and speak it, treating it as the most important message you've ever received, **because it is**. Your response elevates or subordinates it. When you elevate God's Word, death-producing deception is exposed, its power to bind you is broken, and spiritual fruit (abundant life) manifests in your situation. **His Word in your heart (and mouth) will do what He sent it to do**.

You must also walk in more than just secondhand revelation. You should be involved in a local church where you receive God's Word from committed teachers and ministers, but that's not enough. Get into the Bible for yourself. Ask the Holy Spirit to make the Word alive to you, and it will become real and personal just as if God Himself were sitting beside you, telling you of his will for you, opening up his mysteries. This is critically important to your spiritual growth. If your light is only what you receive from others, then you condemn yourself to always living in the shadows of the knowledge and wisdom hidden in Jesus Christ. And, like Eve, God's Word will not be as persuasive in your

---

If your light is only what you receive from others, then you condemn yourself to always living in the shadows of the knowledge and wisdom hidden in Jesus Christ. And, like Eve, God's Word will not be as persuasive in your thinking as you need for victory.

---

thinking as you need for victory.

I can't emphasize this last point enough. You must discover God's truth on your own. The risk of falling into deception is a greater temptation for a Christian than the risk of overt sin. Do not steal, do not kill, do not commit adultery. Even nonbelievers acknowledge moral absolutes. As a Christian, you are aware of their warning signs and take steps to get out of the way.

But deception is smooth, cleverly camouflaged. Often we discover the lie after it's too late to change course. As a result, and because of our lack of knowledge of God's Word, we find ourselves in all kinds of earthly trouble and wonder sincerely how we got there. "My people are destroyed for lack of knowledge," says Hos. 4:6.

Getting that knowledge is your responsibility. It's not your pastor's, not your Sunday school teacher's, not your spouse's. These are helpers, and you need them, but their input is secondhand revelation. Only by searching God's Word for yourself will you build a sturdy persuasion into your spirit. With it comes boldness, because you'll know that you walk in God's will.

God tells us, you and me, to "study to show thyself approved unto God, a workman that needeth not to be ashamed, rightly dividing the Word of truth" (II Tim. 2:15). You must study, not just *read* but *study* God's Word so that you will not be snared by the deceptions Satan tries to cast over your mind. You must study so that you can correctly divide the Scriptures.

The word "dividing" means to make a straight cut. When you remember that God refers to his Word as a sword, then this definition makes sense. God's Word in your heart and mouth is the sword that will divide deception from truth, the world's confession of doubt from your confession of faith, and worldly philosophy from the simplicity of your relationship to Him. But greatest of all, God's Word in your heart and mouth is the sword that will conquer the most seemingly

289

unconquerable enemy of them all: religious tradition masquerading as truth.

Remember my former pastor who said what a shame it was to the Israelites that God had to stoop to use a woman? He is the same man who said that your faith never rises above your level of self-esteem. Too bad he never made the obvious connection between the distorted, demeaning way he approached the story of Deborah and the women of his assembly (including me!), whose spiritual growth and self-esteem were roadblocked by his well-meaning but chauvinist preaching. Because, at the heart of all the traditions I've recounted here is the message that God doesn't love as much, or think as highly of women as He does men. *Satan's plan is and always has been to destroy the relationship between God and his creation—YOU.*

> *At the heart of all the traditions I've recounted here is the message that God doesn't love as much or think as highly of women as He does men.*

In this context, his creation is women. When I was a young woman, he nearly succeeded with his evil plan. Satan almost destroyed my faith. For nearly two decades, because of perverted teachings from the mouths of ministers who taught twisted interpretations of Scripture inspired by Satan, I was tempted to believe God loved women less than men, that He had no big plans for women. After years of listening to these lies, I suspected that God's character was not as pure and loving as it truly is. I was like the daughter of

> *I was like the daughter of Abraham, whom Jesus said the enemy had bound, leaving her crippled, unable to stand up straight for 18 years.*

Abraham, whom Jesus said the enemy had bound, leaving her crippled, unable to stand up straight for 18 years. When I look back on those awful days, the mental picture I have of myself is exactly that: bent over in the spirit.

But you don't have to suffer as I did. You don't have to believe his lies now that they've been exposed. God loves you as much as He loves any man, and the only limit upon your life is the size of your faith.

Be careful what you believe. Don't let someone else's darkness become your light. If you don't think God esteems you as highly and as precious as his Word says He does, if you are not convinced of his love and good plans for you, then your faith will be inhibited as mine was. You will never fulfill the individual call of dominion God has placed in your heart. You will still get your prayers answered, but your prayers, like your faith, will be small.

Remember, Jesus said religious tradition makes his Word of "no effect." Satan's goal is to pluck the fruit from your tree before it ripens, to discourage you so that you never come into the fullness of what God plans to do for you and through you. That's why Jesus said to be careful of what and how you hear. Teaching that discourages your spiritual and material dominion solely because you're female; that portrays you as inferior in any way to men and implies God-ordained, second-class Kingdom status; that confines you to the most menial Gospel

> *Satan's goal is to pluck the fruit from your tree before it ripens, to discourage you so that you never come into the fullness of what God plans to do for you and through you.* That's why Jesus said to be careful of what and how you hear.

work; that keeps you from ministering God's Word; that portrays your unique physical needs as unimportant to God—teaching like this is seed that produces a harvest of death. It kills self-esteem, faith, and love because the foundation of this doctrine is a lack of respect for women as creatures made in God's image to partner with men.

And it's all lies.

No wonder feminist philosophy has so much appeal. The bosom of feminism is the only place some women experience genuine acceptance and respect; it's the only supportive group that encourages them to be all they can by using all they have. *Feminism is attractive because unlike religious tradition, feminism first and foremost assumes women have what it takes.* Feminism says, "You're somebody! You're unique! You can do anything! Love yourself!" Its message works because it builds up the feminine psyche that has been torn down by religious tradition and its worldly cousin, sexism. Politically oriented feminism especially gives women a false sense of dominion, one that mimics the true one Christ died to give them.

And the message of religious tradition? It's as harsh as battery acid and as subtle as a baseball bat. "Submit woman! Take your lower place and be quiet!" You can't blame women for choosing one over the other. How tragic that we have lost so many to this pseudo-religion when Jesus loves women so much, has elevated them like no social movement ever can, and would give them the world, literally, if they ask.

Speaking of feminism, if there's such a thing as a

292

Christian feminist, I want to be one like the late Christian missionary Gladys Aylward.

Gladys was born in the United Kingdom in 1902 into a family of modest means. She spent her teen years working as a domestic. In her 20s she felt a strong call of God to travel to China to spread the Gospel. Her parents were flummoxed. No one in her family had ever traveled to Asia! They didn't disapprove, they just didn't understand their daughter's desire to travel so far to a people so different from her own.

Though Gladys was poor and poorly educated, trained to do nothing but wait on women of means, still she managed to get accepted into a China Inland Mission missionary school. But after only three months she was cut from the program when the administration deemed her incapable of achieving fluency in Chinese.

Gladys was undeterred. She ignored the naysayers and listened only to the still, small voice of the Holy Spirit who encouraged her to follow Him to China. She saved her meager wages for months until she had enough for train fare to Asia. With no financial backing and no husband, carrying only one suitcase, a teapot, and enough food stuffed into a satchel for the trip, she set off for Yangcheng, Shanxi Province.

For 45 years Gladys Aylward served the spiritual needs of the Chinese people. Her work was overshadowed by poverty, war, illness (she nearly died of typhus and pneumonia, which she suffered simultaneously), loneliness, isolation, and much loss. She established an orphanage and traveled all over China, preaching the Gospel. She led untold numbers to Christ. She died in Taiwan at the age of 67.

She became fluent in Chinese within a year of arriving in Yangcheng.

You may know Gladys' story under another name, the 1958 movie, "The Inn of the Sixth Happiness," with

Ingrid Bergman.

* * *

I leave you with a revelation that, strangely, came to me long after I finished this book.

I spent 18 years intensely searching, straining to find the truth about women, God, and the Church. It wasn't a pastime; I needed this to live. I needed a foundation for my life: I *had* to know who I am in God and what He wants me to do. I read everything and listened to anyone: books, magazines, sermons, and friends, always hoping I'd find something that satisfied my keen longing for spiritual identity as a woman in the Church.

Why was it so important to find? Because from my earliest awareness I sensed God had an individual plan for my life and I felt responsible to fulfill it. I even prayed about it as a child.

Many people were ready to give me the answers, as if God had shared his plan for *me* with *them* but not me. Now I realize that what I sought was not a deep doctrine or a packaged answer constructed from a handful of Bible verses that deal with women. What I sought was not something another human being could give, because what I sought was myself.

But when I finally learned to seek his voice above all hissing lips, when I sought *Him*, I found what I was looking for.

> "Beware lest any man spoil you through philosophy and vain deceit, after the tradition of men, after the rudiments of the world, and not after Christ." (Col. 2:8).

294

Jesus truly is the answer to your every need.

NOW CONSIDER the amazing healing at the Pool of Bethesda in John 5. Read carefully. I don't want you to miss this great key.

Jesus has just healed a man who has been paralyzed for 38 years, when He says to the man: "Take up thy bed and walk."

Jesus could have just told him to stand up or to try and walk.

Jesus could have extended a hand to help the man stand up.

Jesus could have instructed others standing by to help the man.

But that's not what Jesus did. No, Jesus gave him specific instructions, not just to stand up, but to TAKE UP THY BED. That is, pick up your bed and walk.

This is no light matter for the healed man, a Jew, because the Pharisees—those imposers of burdens impossible to be borne, those perfunctory keepers of every jot and tittle of the law, those hypocrites who intently watched other Jews, waiting to pounce on the innocent for the merest of infractions of man-imposed laws God never intended to lay upon the backs of his people, evil men whom Jesus called vipers and serpents—these same Jews scrupulously persecuted those who carried anything of any weight on the Sabbath as a violation of some extrabiblical divine decree.

(Even today in Jerusalem, hotels have "Jewish" elevators that stop at every floor on the Sabbath so that Jewish guests returning to their rooms won't violate the extrabiblical law by laboring themselves to push a button! When we visited Israel a few years ago, my husband and I were perfectly content to ride the "Gentile" elevators in our multifloor hotel to avoid the long, drawn out ride the Jewish guests had to suffer.

295

But I digress.)

Back to the Pool of Bethesda. The Jews watched this newly healed man pick up his bed and carry it in violation of their tradition. But instead of rejoicing at the miracle they had just witnessed, they castigated the healed man for carrying his bed on the Sabbath.

Jesus knew the healed man would suffer persecution because of this act. Yet he instructed the man to do it anyway.

Why?

I said at the beginning of this book that when it comes to spurious Christian traditions, I have learned over many years to ignore them.

But I was late to the party. I must have read John 5 one hundred times before it dawned on me that here Jesus gives us a concrete example of how to deal with traditionalists. *Ignore them.*

Jesus ignored them. And by commanding the man to pick up his bed, He challenged him to choose who he would listen to and who he would ignore: God's Word or the word of the naysayers, the traditionalists.

Jesus' challenge to the healed man is my challenge to you.

Seek God. Focus on his Word. Listen for his voice. He will show you his plan for your life. He has already given you the ability, authority, and supply to take dominion over your circumstances. Seek Him and let Him show you how to walk in it.

He loves you. He will not fail you.

SOURCES

Achtemeier, Paul J., General Ed. *Harper's Bible Dictionary*. San Francisco: Harper &
Row, 1985.

Agonito, Rosemary. *History of Ideas on Women*. New York: G.P. Putnam's Sons, 1977.

Alexander, David and Patricia, Eds. *Eerdman's Handbook to the Bible*. Grand Rapids: William B. Eerdmans Publishing Co., 1973.

Andelin, Helen. *Fascinating Womanhood*. New York: Bantam Press, 1992.

Archer, Gleason L., Ed. *Encyclopedia of Bible Difficulties*. Zondervan Publishing
House: Grand Rapids, 1982.

Augustine, Saint. *The City of God*. New York: The Modern Library, 1950.

Baskin, Alex, Ed. *Woman Rebel*. Stony Brook: State University of New York, 1976.

Bartlett A.M., John. *A Complete Concordance of Shakespeare*. New York: St. Martin's
Press, 1984.

Bartlett, John. *Bartlett's Familiar Quotations*. Ed. by June Morison Beck. Boston:
Little, Brown & Co., 1980.

Bartley, Nancy. "Woman's Bad Case of 'Flu' Turns Out to Be Healthy Baby," *Seattle
Times*, March 5, 1994.

Bouwsma, William J. *John Calvin, A Sixteenth Century Portrait*. New York: Oxford University Press, 1988.

Brenton, Sir Lancelot C.L. *The Septuagint with Apocrypha: Greek and English*. Grand
Rapids: Zondervan Publishing House, no date given; originally 1851.

Chesler, Ellen. *Woman of Valor: Margaret Sanger and the Birth Control Movement in America*. New York: Simon & Schuster, 1992.

Cohen, A. *Everyman's Talmud*. New York: Schocken Books, 1975.

Cook, Dr. William A. *Natural Childbirth: Fact and Fallacy*. Chicago: Nelson-Hall, 1982.

Dennett, Mary Ware. *Birth Control Laws: Shall you Keep Them, Change Them, or Abolish Them*. New York: Da Capo Press, 1970.

Dick-Read, Dr. Grantly. *Childbirth Without Fear*. New York: Harper & Row, 1981.

Farmer, David Hugh, 3rd ed. *Oxford Dictionary of the Saints*. Oxford: Oxford University Press, 1992.

Farris, Michael P. *The Home Schooling Father*. Hamilton, VA: Michael P. Farris, 1992.

Friedan, Betty. *The Feminine Mystique*. New York: Mystique, 1983.

Friedman, Richard Elliott. *Who Wrote the Bible?* New York: Summit Books, 1987.

Gaskin, Ina May. *Spiritual Midwifery*. Place of publication not given: Paul Mandelstein, no date given.

Green, Shirley. *The Curious History of Contraception*. New York: St. Martin's Press, 1971.

Greenfield, Dr. Ellen J. *You Can Have an Easier Delivery*. Chicago: Contemporary Books, 1988.

Grudem, Wayne and John Piper, Eds. *Recovering Biblical Manhood and Womanhood*. Wheaton: Crossway Books, 1991.

Halley, H.H. *Halley's Bible Handbook*. Grand Rapids: Zondervan Publishing House,

1959.

Hardy, Thomas. *Far From the Madding Crowd.* New York: Penguin Books, 1978.

Hosier, Helen Kooiman. *Kathryn Kuhlman.* Old Tappan, NJ: Fleming H. Revell Co.,
1971.

Jeffrey, David Lyle, General Ed. *A Dictionary of Biblical Tradition in English Literature.* Grand Rapids: William B. Eerdmans Publishing Co., 1992.

Jones, Carl. *Mind Over Labor.* New York: Viking Penguin, Inc., 1987.

Kane, Joseph Nathan et al. *Facts About the States.* New York: H.W. Wilson Co., 1989.

Kitzinger, Sheila. *Home Birth.* New York: Dorling Kindersley, Inc., 1991.

LaHaye, Beverly and Tim. *The Act of Marriage.* Grand Rapids: The Zondervan Corporation, 1976.

Leavitt, Judith Walzer, Ed. *Women and Health in America.* Madison: University of Wisconsin Press, 1984.

Luther, Martin. *Luther's Commentary on Gen..* Grand Rapids, MI: Zondervan Publishing House, 1958.

Malcolm, Kari Torjesen. *Women at the Crossroads.* Downers Grove: InterVarsity Press, 1992.

Martin, Luther. *Luther's Commentary on Gen..* Grand Rapids: Zondervan Publishing House, 1958.

Martin, Walter, Dr. *The Kingdom of the Cults.* Minneapolis: Bethany House Publishers,
1985.

McDannell, Colleen. *The Christian Home in Victorian America, 1840-1900.* Bloomington: Indiana University Press, 1986.

Milburn, Joyce and Lynnette Smith. *The Natural*

Childbirth Book. Minneapolis:
    Bethany Fellowship, Inc., 1981.
    Milton, John. *Paradise Lost*. New York: New American Library, 1968.
    Mitford, Jessica. *The American Way of Birth*. New York: The Penguin Group, 1992.
    Modu, Emmanuel. *The Lemonade Stand, A Guide to Encouraging the Entrepreneur in*
    Your Child. Holbrook, MA: Bob Adams, Inc., 1991.
    Neusner, Jacob. *Invitation to the Talmud*. San Francisco: Harper & Row, 1984.
    Packer, J.I., Ed. et al. *The Bible Almanac*. Nashville: Thomas Nelson Publishers, 1980.
    Packer, J.I. et al. *Public Life in Bible Times*. Nashville: Thomas Nelson Publishers,
        1985.
    Paul, Shalom M., Ed. et al. *Illustrated Dictionary and Concordance of the Bible*. Jerusalem: G.G. The Jerusalem Publishing House Ltd., 1986.
    Penn-Lewis, Jessie. *The Magna Charta of Woman*. Minneapolis: Bethany Fellowship,
        Inc., 1975.
    Pohle, Ella E. *Dr. C.I. Scofield's Question Box*. Chicago: Moody Press, no date given.
    Rion, Hanna. *The Truth About Twilight Sleep*. New York: McBride, Nast & Co., 1915.
    Rowbotham, Sheila. *Hidden From History*. New York: Pantheon Books, 1973.
    Ryken, Leland. *Worldly Saints: The Puritans as They Really Were*. Grand Rapids: Academie Books, Zondervan Publishing House, 1986.
    Schneir, Miriam, Ed. *Feminism: The Essential Historical Writings*. New York: Vintage Books, 1972.
    Shaheen, Naseeb. *Biblical References in Shakespeare's Tragedies*. Newark: University

of Delaware Press, 1987.

Shakespeare, William. *The Complete Works of Shakespeare*. Lexington: Xerox
Publishing House, 1971.

Stephen, Sir Leslie and Sir Sidney Lee, Eds. *Dictionary of National Biography*. London: Oxford University Press, 1917.

Strong, James H. *Strong's Exhaustive Concordance*. Grand Rapids: Baker Book House, 1989.

Tucker, Ruth A. *Women in the Maze*. Downers Grove: InterVarsity Press, 1992.

Tyndale, William. *The NT*. Cambridge: Cambridge University Press, 1938.

Tyndale, William. *The Pentateuch*. Footwell: Centaur Press, 1967.

Wesley, John. *Explanatory Notes Upon the New Testament, Vol. II*. Grand Rapids:
Baker Book House, 1981.

Wesley, John. *Notes Upon the OT, Vol. I*. Salem: Schmul Publishers, 1975.

Wessel, Helen. *The Joy of Natural Childbirth*. New York: Harper & Row, 1973.

Wilde, Oscar. *The Importance of Being Earnest*. New York: Penguin Books, 1985.

About the Author

Virginia (Ginny) Hull Welch was raised in Santa Clara, Calif., where she earned a Bachelor's in English. She married and moved to northern California where she earned a Master's in communications at California State University, Chico and where she was first paid for her writing: $25 for a two-page magazine article on how to get a permanent job through temporary work. Since those early days she has worked as a newspaper (foods and politics) writer, book editor, proposal writer and editor, and freelancer—moving around the United States as she followed her husband's job transfers. She has four grown children, lives in an RV, and travels the country, writing and quilting. *The Hiss from Hell* is her fourth book.

Www.virginiahullwelch.com

Please leave a review at:

LINK TO REVIEW

Other Books by Virginia Hull Welch

The Lesson, inspirational romantic comedy based
on a true story
Crazy Woman Creek, historical western romance
What to Do When the Blessings Stop, nonfiction

I love hearing from you. You can contact me at:
www.virginiahullwelch.com

www.ingramcontent.com/pod-product-compliance
Lightning Source LLC
Chambersburg PA
CBHW032344280326
41935CB00008B/444